Natural Language Processing for Social Media

Third Edition

Synthesis Lectures on Human Language Technologies

Editor
Grame Hirst, *University of Toronto*

Synthesis Lectures on Human Language Technologies is edited by Graeme Hirst of the University of Toronto. The series consists of 50- to 150-page monographs on topics relating to natural language processing, computational linguistics, information retrieval, and spoken language understanding. Emphasis is on important new techniques, on new applications, and on topics that combine two or more HLT subfields.

Natural Language Processing for Social Media, Third Edition
Anna Atefeh Farzindar and Diana Inkpen

ISBN: 978-3-031-01047-7 paperback
ISBN: 978-3-031-02175-6 ebook
ISBN: 978-1-68173-814-7 epub
ISBN: 978-3-031-00186-4 hardcover

DOI 10.1007/978-3-031-02175-6

A Publication in the Springer series
SYNTHESIS LECTURES ON ADVANCES IN AUTOMOTIVE TECHNOLOGY

Lecture #46
Series Editor: Grame Hirst, *University of Toronto*
Series ISSN
Print 1947-4040   Electronic 1947-4059

Cover art illustration by Anna Atefeh Farzindar.

Natural Language Processing for Social Media

Third Edition

Anna Atefeh Farzindar
University of Southern California

Diana Inkpen
University of Ottawa

SYNTHESIS LECTURES ON HUMAN LANGUAGE TECHNOLOGIES #46

ABSTRACT

In recent years, online social networking has revolutionized interpersonal communication. The newer research on language analysis in social media has been increasingly focusing on the latter's impact on our daily lives, both on a personal and a professional level. Natural language processing (NLP) is one of the most promising avenues for social media data processing. It is a scientific challenge to develop powerful methods and algorithms that extract relevant information from a large volume of data coming from multiple sources and languages in various formats or in free form. This book will discuss the challenges in analyzing social media texts in contrast with traditional documents.

Research methods in information extraction, automatic categorization and clustering, automatic summarization and indexing, and statistical machine translation need to be adapted to a new kind of data. This book reviews the current research on NLP tools and methods for processing the non-traditional information from social media data that is available in large amounts, and it shows how innovative NLP approaches can integrate appropriate linguistic information in various fields such as social media monitoring, health care, and business intelligence. The book further covers the existing evaluation metrics for NLP and social media applications and the new efforts in evaluation campaigns or shared tasks on new datasets collected from social media. Such tasks are organized by the Association for Computational Linguistics (such as SemEval tasks), the National Institute of Standards and Technology via the Text REtrieval Conference (TREC) and the Text Analysis Conference (TAC), or the Conference and Labs of the Evaluation Forum (CLEF).

In this third edition of the book, the authors added information about recent progress in NLP for social media applications, including more about the modern techniques provided by deep neural networks (DNNs) for modeling language and analyzing social media data.

KEYWORDS

social media, social networking, natural language processing, social computing, big data, semantic analysis, artificial intelligence, deep learning

To my husband Massoud, and my daughters, Tina and Amanda,
who are just about the best children a mom could hope for:
happy, loving, and fun to be with.

– Anna Atefeh Farzindar

To my wonderful husband Nicu with whom I can climb any mountain,
and to our sweet daughter Nicoleta.

– Diana Inkpen

Contents

List of Figures

List of Tables

Preface

This book presents the state-of-the-art in research and empirical studies in the field of Natural Language Processing (NLP) for the semantic analysis of social media data. Because the field is continuously growing, this third edition adds information about recently proposed methods and their results for the tasks and applications that we covered in the first and second editions.

Over the past few years, online social networking sites have revolutionized the way we communicate with individuals, groups and communities, and altered everyday practices. The unprecedented volume and variety of user-generated content and the user interaction network constitute new opportunities for understanding social behavior and building socially intelligent systems.

Much research work on social networks and the mining of the social web is based on graph theory. That is apt because a social structure is made up of a set of social actors and a set of the dyadic ties between these actors. We believe that the graph mining methods for structure, information diffusion or influence spread in social networks need to be combined with the content analysis of social media. This provides the opportunity for new applications that use the information publicly available as a result of social interactions. Adapted classic NLP methods can partially solve the problem of social media content analysis focusing on the posted messages. When we receive a text of less than 10 characters, including an emoticon and a heart, we understand it and even respond to it! It is impossible to use NLP methods to process this type of document, but there is a logical message in social media data based on which two people can communicate. The same logic dominates worldwide, and people from all over the world share and communicate with each other. There is a new and challenging language for NLP.

We believe that we need new theories and algorithms for semantic analysis of social media data, as well as a new way of approaching the big data processing. By semantic analysis, in this book, we mean the linguistic processing of the social media messages enhanced with semantics, and possibly also combining this with the structure of the social networks. We actually use the term in a more general sense to refer to applications that do intelligent processing of social media texts and meta-data. Some applications could access very large amounts of data; therefore the algorithms need to be adapted to be able process data (big data) in an online fashion and without necessarily storing all the data.

This motivated us to give three tutorials on **Applications of Social Media Text Analysis** at EMNLP 2015[1], on **Natural Language Processing for Social Media** at the 29th Canadian Con-

---

[1]http://www.emnlp2015.org/tutorials/3/3_OptionalAttachment.pdf
https://www.cs.cmu.edu/~ark/EMNLP-2015/proceedings/EMNLP-Tutorials/pdf/EMNLP-Tutorials06.pdf

ference on Artificial Intelligence (AI 2016)[2], and on ***How Natural Language Processing Helps Uncover Social Media Insights*** at the 33rd International Florida Artificial Intelligence Research Society Conference (FLAIRS 2020). Also on this topic, we organized several workshops (Semantic Analysis in Social Networks (SASM 2012)[3], Language Analysis in Social Media (LASM 2013[4], and LASM 2014[5]) in conjunction with conferences organized by the Association for Computational Linguistics[6] (ACL, EACL, and NAACL-HLT).

Our goal was to reflect a wide range of research and results in the analysis of language with implications for fields such as NLP, computational linguistics, sociolinguistics and psycholinguistics. Our workshops invited original research on all topics related to the analysis of language in social media, including the following topics:

- What do people talk about on social media?
- How do they express themselves?
- Why do they post on social media?
- How do language and social network properties interact?
- Natural language processing techniques for social media analysis.
- Semantic Web / ontologies / domain models to aid in understanding social data.
- Characterizing participants via linguistic analysis.
- Language, social media and human behavior.

There were several other workshops on similar topics, for example, the ***Making Sense of Microposts*** (#Microposts)[7] workshop series in conjunction with the World Wide Web Conference 2012 to 2016. These workshops focused in particular on short informal texts that are published without much effort (such as tweets, Facebook shares, Instagram-like shares, Google+ messages). There has been another series of Workshops on Natural Language Processing for Social Media (SocialNLP) since 2013. For example, SocialNLP 2017 was in conjunction with EACL 2017[8] and IEEE BigData 2017[9], and SocialNLP 2020 had two editions, one in conjunction with TheWebConf 2020 and one in conjunction with ACL 2020[10].

The **intended audience** of this book is researchers that are interested in developing tools and applications for automatic analysis social of media texts. We assume that the readers have basic knowledge in the area of natural language processing and machine learning. We hope that this book will help the readers better understand computational linguistics and social media analysis, in particular text mining techniques and NLP applications (such as summarization,

---

[2]http://aigicrv.org/2016/
[3]https://aclweb.org/anthology/W/W12/#2100
[4]https://aclweb.org/anthology/W/W13/#1100
[5]https://aclweb.org/anthology/W/W14/#1300
[6]http://www.aclweb.org/
[7]http://microposts2016.seas.upenn.edu/
[8]http://eacl2017.org/
[9]http://cci.drexel.edu/bigdata/bigdata2017/
[10]https://sites.google.com/site/socialnlp2020/

localization detection, sentiment and emotion analysis, topic detection and machine translation) designed specifically for social media texts.

Besides updating each section in this third edition, we added a new section on keyphrase generation from social media messages and one on neural machine translation in Chapter 3 and three new applications in Chapter 4: rumor detection, recommender systems for social media, and preventing sexual harassment. We discuss the new methods and their results. The number of research projects and publications that use social media data is constantly increasing. Finally, we added more than 50 new references to the approximately 400 references from the second edition.

Anna Atefeh Farzindar and Diana Inkpen
March 2020

Acknowledgments

This book would not have been possible without the hard work of many people. We would like to thank our colleagues and students at the University of Southern California and our colleagues at the NLP research group at the University of Ottawa. We would like to thank in particular Prof. Stan Szpakowicz from the University of Ottawa for his comments on the early draft of the book, and two anonymous reviewers for their useful suggestions for revisions and additions. We thank Prof. Graeme Hirst of the University of Toronto and Michael Morgan from Morgan & Claypool Publishers for their continuous encouragement.

Anna Atefeh Farzindar and Diana Inkpen
March 2020

C H A P T E R   1

Introduction to Social Media Analysis

1.1   INTRODUCTION

Social media is a phenomenon that has recently expanded throughout the world and quickly attracted billions of users. This form of electronic communication through social networking platforms allows users to generate its content and share it in various forms of information, personal words, pictures, audio, and videos. Therefore, social computing is formed as an emerging area of research and development that includes a wide range of topics such as Web semantics, artificial intelligence, natural language processing, network analysis, and Big Data analytics.

Over the past few years, online social networking sites (Facebook, Twitter, YouTube, Flickr, MySpace, LinkedIn, Metacafe, Vimeo, etc.) have revolutionized the way we communicate with individuals, groups, and communities, and have altered everyday practices [Boyd and Ellison, 2007].

The broad categories of social media platforms are: content-sharing sites, forums, blogs, and microblogs. On content sharing sites (such as Facebook, Instagram, Foursquare, Flickr, YouTube) people exchange information, messages, photos, videos, or other types of content. On Web user forums (such as StackOverflow, CNET forums, Apple Support) people post specialized information, questions, or answers. Blogs (such as Gizmodo, Mashable, Boing Boing, and many more) allow people to post messages and other content and to share information and opinions. Micro-blogs (such as Twitter, Sina Weibo, Tumblr) are limited to short texts for sharing information and opinions. The modalities of sharing content in order: posts; comments to posts; explicit or implicit connections to build social networks (friend connections, followers, etc.); cross-posts and user linking; social tagging; likes/favorites/starring/voting/rating/etc.; author information; and linking to user profile features.[1] In Table 1.1, we list more details about social media platforms and their characteristics and types of content shared [Barbier et al., 2013].

Social media statistics for January 2014 have shown that Facebook has grown to more than 1 billion active users, adding more than 200 million users in a single year. Statista,[2] the world's largest statistics portal, announced the ranking for social networks based on the number of active users. As presented in Figure 1.1, the ranking shows that Qzone took second place

---

[1]http://people.eng.unimelb.edu.au/tbaldwin/pubs/starsem2014.pdf
[2]http://www.statista.com/

Table 1.1: Social media platforms and their characteristics

Type	Characteristics	Examples
Social Networks	A social networking website allows the user to build a web page and connect with a friend or other acquaintance in order to share user-generated content.	MySpace, Facebook, LinkedIn, Meetup, Google Plus+
Blogs and Blog Comments	A blog is an online journal where the blogger can create the content and display it in reverse chronological order. Blogs are generally maintained by a person or a community. Blog comments are posts by users attached to blogs or online newspaper posts.	Huffington Post, Business Insider, Engadget, and online journals
Microblogs	A microblog is similar to a blog but has a limited content.	Twitter, Tumblr, Sina Weibo, Plurk
Forums	An online forum is a place for members to discuss a topic by posting messages.	Online Discussion Communities, phpBB Developer Forum, Raising Children Forum
Social Bookmarks	Services that allow users to save, organize, and search links to various websites, and to share their bookmarks of Web pages.	Delicious, Pinterest, Google Bookmarks
Wikis	These websites allow people to collaborate and add content or edit the information on a community-based database.	Wikipedia, Wikitravel, Wikihow
Social News	Social news encourage their community to submit news stories, or to vote on the content and share it.	Digg, Slashdot, Reddit
Media Sharing	A website that enables users to capture videos and pictures or upload and share with others.	YouTube, Flickr, Snapchat, Instagram, Vine

with more than 600 million users. Google+, LinkedIn, and Twitter completed the top 5 with 300 million, 259 million, and 232 million active users, respectively.

Statista also provided the growth trend for both Facebook and LinkedIn, illustrated in Figure 1.2 and Figure 1.3, respectively. Figure 1.2 shows that Facebook, by reaching 845 million users at the end of 2011, totaled 1,228 million users by the end of 2013. As depicted in Figure 1.3, LinkedIn also reached 277 million users by the end of 2013, whereas it only had 145 million users

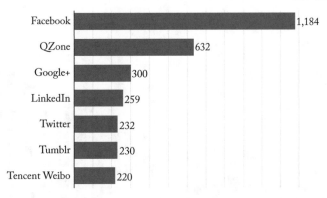

Figure 1.1: Social networks ranked by the number of active users as of January 2014 (in millions) provided by Statista.

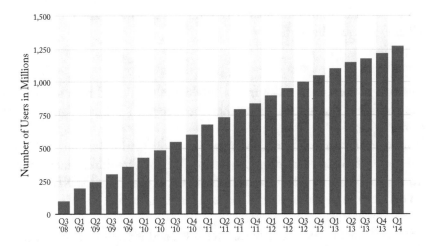

Figure 1.2: Number of monthly active Facebook users from the third quarter of 2008 to the first quarter of 2014 (in millions) provided by Statista.

at the end of 2011. Statista also calculated the annual income for both Facebook and LinkedIn, which in 2013 totalled US$7,872 and US$1,528 million, respectively.

Social computing is an emerging field that focuses on modeling, analysis, and monitoring of social behavior on different media and platforms to produce intelligent applications. Social media is the use of electronic and Internet tools for the purpose of sharing and discussing information and experiences with other human beings in efficient ways [Moturu, 2009]. Various social media platforms such as social networks, forums, blogs, and micro-blogs have recently evolved to ensure the connectivity, collaboration, and formation of virtual communities. While traditional media such as newspapers, television, and radio provide unidirectional communica-

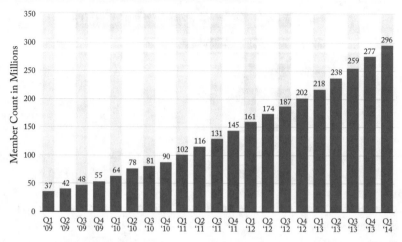

Figure 1.3: Number of LinkedIn members from the first quarter of 2009 to the first quarter of 2014 (in millions) provided by Statista.

tion from business to consumer, social media services have allowed interactions among users across various platforms. Social media have therefore become a primary source of information for business intelligence.

There are several means of interaction in social media platforms. One of the most important is via text posts. The natural language processing (NLP) of traditional media such as written news and articles has been a popular research topic over the past 25 years. NLP typically enables computers to derive meaning from natural language input using the knowledge from computer science, artificial intelligence, and linguistics.

NLP for social media text is a new research area, and it requires adapting the traditional NLP methods to these kinds of texts or developing new methods suitable for information extraction and other tasks in the context of social media.

There are many reasons why the "traditional" NLP are not good enough for social media texts, such as their informal nature, the new type of language, abbreviations, etc. Section 1.3 will discuss these aspects in more detail.

A social network is made up of a set of actors (such as individuals or organizations) and a set of binary relations between these actors (such as relationships, connections, or interactions). From a social network perspective, the goal is to model the structure of a social group to identify how this structure influences other variables and how structures change over time. Semantic analysis in social media (SASM) is the semantic processing of the text messages as well as of the meta-data, in order to build intelligent applications based on social media data.

SASM helps develop automated tools and algorithms to monitor, capture, and analyze the large amounts of data collected from social media in order to predict user behavior or extract other kinds of information. If the amount of data is very large, techniques for "big data" processing need to be used, such as online algorithms that do not need to store all the data in order to update the models based on the incoming data.

In this book, we focus on the analysis of the textual data from social media, via new NLP techniques and applications. Workshops such as the EACL 2014 Workshop on Language Analysis in Social Media [Farzindar et al., 2014], the NAACL/HLT 2013 workshop on Language Analysis in Social Media [Farzindar et al., 2013], and the EACL 2012 Workshop for Semantic Analysis in Social Media [Farzindar and Inkpen, 2012] have been increasingly focusing on NLP techniques and applications that study the effect of social media messages on our daily lives, both personally and professionally.

Social media textual data is the collection of openly available texts that can be obtained publicly via blogs and micro-blogs, Internet forums, user-generated FAQs, chat, podcasts, online games, tags, ratings, and comments. Social media texts have several properties that make them different than traditional texts, because the nature of the social conversations, posted in real time. Detecting groups of topically related conversations is important for applications, as well as detection emotions, rumors, and incentives. As an example, in order to investigate youths' experience of grief and mourning, a study applied NLP techniques to their tweets after the death of friends or family members [Patton et al., 2018]. Determining the locations mentioned in the messages or the locations of the users can also add valuable information. The texts are unstructured and are presented in many formats and written by different people in many languages and styles. Also, the typographic errors and chat slang have become increasingly prevalent on social networking sites like Facebook and Twitter. The authors are not professional writers and their postings are spread in many places on the Web, on various social media platforms.

Monitoring and analyzing this rich and continuous flow of user-generated content can yield unprecedentedly valuable information, which would not have been available from traditional media outlets. Semantic analysis of social media has given rise to the emerging discipline of big data analytics, which draws from social network analysis, machine learning, data mining, information retrieval, and natural language processing [Melville et al., 2009].

Figure 1.4 shows a framework for semantic analysis in social media. The first step is to identify issues and opportunities for collecting data from social networks. The data can be in the form of stored textual information (the big datacould be stored in large and complex databases or text files), it could be dynamic online data collection processed in real time, or it could be retrospective data collection for particular needs. The next step is the SASM pipeline, which consists of specific NLP tools for the social media analysis and data processing. Social media data is made up of large, noisy, and unstructured datasets. SASM transforms social media data to meaningful and understandable messages through social information and knowledge. Then, SASM analyzes the social media information in order to produce social media intelligence. Social media intelligence can be shared with users or presented to decision-makers to improve

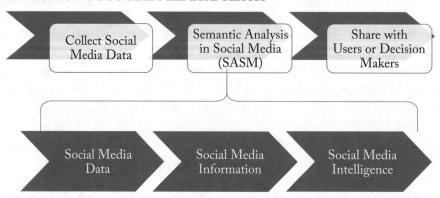

Figure 1.4: A framework for semantic analysis in social media, where NLP tools transform the data into intelligence.

awareness, communication, planning, or problem solving. The presentation of analyzed data by SASM could be completed by data visualization methods.

1.2   SOCIAL MEDIA APPLICATIONS

The automatic processing of social media data needs to design appropriate research methods for applications such as information extraction, automatic categorization, clustering, indexing data for information retrieval, and statistical machine translation. The sheer volume of social media data and the incredible rate at which new content is created makes monitoring, or any other meaningful manual analysis, unfeasible. In many applications, the amount of data is too large for effective real-time human evaluation and analysis of the data for a decision maker.

Social media monitoring is one of the major applications in SASM. Traditionally, **media monitoring** is defined as the activity of monitoring and tracking the output of the hard copy, online, and broadcast media which can be performed for a variety of reasons, including political, commercial, and scientific. The huge volume of information provided via social media networks is an important source for open intelligence. Social media make the direct contact with the target public possible. Unlike traditional news, the opinion and sentiment of authors provide an additional dimension for the social media data. The different sizes of source documents—such as a combination of multiple tweets and blogs—and content variability also render the task of analyzing social media documents difficult.

In social media, the real-time event search or event detection The search queries consider multiple dimensions, including spatial and temporal. In this case, some NLP methods such as information retrieval and summarization of social data in the form of various documents from multiple sources become important in order to support the event search and the detection of relevant information.

The semantic analysis of the meaning of a day's or week's worth of conversations in social networks for a group of topically related discussions or about a specific event presents the challenges of cross-language NLP tasks. Social media—related NLP methods that can extract information of interest to the analyst for preferential inclusion also lead us to domain-based applications in computational linguistics.

1.2.1   CROSS-LANGUAGE DOCUMENT ANALYSIS IN SOCIAL MEDIA DATA

The application of existing NLP techniques to social media from different languages and multiple resources faces several additional challenges; the tools for text analysis are typically designed for specific languages. The main research issue therefore lies in assessing whether language-independence or language-specificity is to be preferred. Users publish content not only in English, but in a multitude of languages [Blodgett et al., 2018] . This means that due to the language barrier, many users cannot access all available content. The use of machine translation technology can help bridge the language gap in such situations. The integration of machine translation and NLP tools opens opportunities for the semantic analysis of text via cross-language processing.

Natural languages constantly evolve and are adapted based on the environment of their use. Diachronic differences measure the semantic drift for these languages [Jaidka et al., 2018].

1.2.2   DEEP LEARNING TECHNIQUES FOR SOCIAL MEDIA DATA

Language-independent NLP tools are very important. They are not only cost- or time-efficient, but can also capture semantic aspects of each language directly. In earlier days, machine learning approaches targeting NLP tasks have mostly relied on shallow models (e.g., Support Vector Machine (SVM) and logistic regression classifiers) that are trained on high-dimensional and sparse features. In the last few years, neural networks based on dense vector representations have produced superior results on various NLP tasks. Deep neural networks [LeCun et al., 2015] enable multi-level automatic feature representation learning. Simple deep learning frameworks were shown to outperform most state-of-the-art approaches in several NLP tasks such as named-entity recognition, semantic role labeling, and part-of-speech tagging [Young et al., 2018]. Then, numerous complex deep learning-based algorithms have been proposed to solve difficult NLP tasks.

Since English is a widely used language, a majority of the research in NLP and deep learning is focused on English. But in multi-lingual countries like India, people generally use words from more than one language in their everyday speech, and on social media sites like Facebook and Twitter. This linguistic behavior is called code-mixing. Deep learning architectures can now be used on such code-mixed tweets, for example for tasks such as humor detection [Sane et al., 2019].

1.2.3   REAL-WORLD APPLICATIONS

The huge volume of publicly available information on social networks and on the Web can benefit different areas such as industry, media, healthcare, politics, public safety, and security. Here, we can name a few innovative integrations for social media monitoring, and some model scenarios of government-user applications in coordination and situational awareness. We will show how NLP tools can help governments interpret data in near real-time and provide enhanced command decision at the strategic and operational levels.

Industry

There is great interest on the part of industry in social media data monitoring. Social media data can dramatically improve business intelligence (BI). Businesses could achieve several goals by integrating social data into their corporate BI systems, such as branding and awareness, customer/prospect engagement, and improving customer service. Online marketing, stock market prediction, product recommendation, and reputation management are some examples of real-world applications for semantic analysis of social media. Recommender systems are a necessity in the modern era of technology. It is the usual tendency of people to get a review from others before going to a restaurant, watching a movie, or buying any product ranging from furniture to electronics or books. A recommender system is built on a similar approach and aims to give a relevant prediction to the target user based on the user's data, the item's data, and other users' feedback for those items. For example, Alharthi et al. [2018] examined the recommender systems in the field of books. These systems analyze the reading behavior of a user and the kind of books he/she likes, as well as their posting on social media, when available.

Media and Journalism

The relationship between journalists and the public became closer thanks to social networking platforms. Statistics published by a 2013 social journalism study show that 25% of major information sources come from social media data.[3] The public relations professionals and journalists use the power of social media to gather the public opinion, perform sentiment analysis, implement crisis monitoring, perform issues- or program-based media analysis, and survey social media.

Healthcare

Over time, social media became part of common healthcare. The healthcare industry uses social media tools for building community engagement and fostering better relationships with their clients. The use of Twitter to discuss recommendations for providers and consumers (patients, families, or caregivers), ailments, treatments, and medication is only one example of social media in healthcare. This was initially referred to as social health. Medical forums appeared due to the needs of the patients to discuss their feelings and experiences.

---

[3]http://www.cision.com/uk/files/2013/10/social-journalism-study-2013.pdf

This book will discuss how NLP methods on social media data can help develop innovative tools and integrate appropriate linguistic information in order to allow better health monitoring (such as disease spread) or availability of information and support for patients.

Politics
Online monitoring can help keep track of mentions made by citizens across the country and of international, national, or local opinion about political parties. For a political party, organizing an election campaign and gaining followers is crucial. Opinion mining, awareness of comments and public posts, and understanding statements made on discussion forums can give political parties a chance to get a better idea of the reality of a specific event, and to take the necessary steps to improve their positions.

Defense and Security
Defense and security organizations are greatly interested in studying these sources of information and summaries to understand situations and perform sentiment analysis of a group of individuals with common interests, and also to be alerted against potential threats to defense and public safety. In this book, we will discuss the issue of information flow from social networks such as MySpace, Facebook, Skyblog, and Twitter. We will present methods for information extraction in Web 2.0 to find links between data entities, and to analyze the characteristics and dynamism of networks through which organizations and discussions evolve. Social data often contain significant information hidden in the texts and network structure. Aggregate social behavior can provide valuable information for the sake of national security.

1.3   CHALLENGES IN SOCIAL MEDIA DATA

The information presented in social media, such as online discussion forums, blogs, and Twitter posts, is highly dynamic and involves interaction among various participants. There is a huge amount of text continuously generated by users in informal environments.

Standard NLP methods applied to social media texts are therefore confronted with difficulties due to non-standard spelling, noise, and limited sets of features for automatic clustering and classification. Social media are important because the use of social networks has made everybody a potential author, so the language is now closer to the user than to any prescribed norms [Beverungen and Kalita, 2011, Zhou and Hovy, 2006]. Blogs, tweets, and status updates are written in an informal, conversational tone—often more of a "stream of consciousness" than the carefully thought out and meticulously edited work that might be expected in traditional print media. This informal nature of social media texts presents new challenges to all levels of automatic language processing.

At the surface level, several issues pose challenges to basic NLP tools developed for traditional data. Inconsistent (or absent) punctuation and capitalization can make detection of sentence boundaries quite difficult—sometimes even for human readers, as in the following tweet:

"#qcpoli enjoyed a hearty laugh today with #plq debate audience for @jflisee #notrehome tune was that the intended reaction?" Emoticons, incorrect or non-standard spelling, and rampant abbreviations complicate tokenization and part-of-speech tagging, among other tasks. Traditional tools must be adapted to consider new variations such as letter repetition ("heyyyyyy"), which are different from common spelling errors. Grammaticality, or frequent lack thereof, is another concern for any syntactic analyses of social media texts, where fragments can be as commonplace as actual full sentences, and the choice between "there," "they are," "they're," and "their" can seem to be made at random.

Social media are also much noisier than traditional print media. Like much else on the Internet, social networks are plagued with spam, ads, and all manner of other unsolicited, irrelevant, or distracting content. Even by ignoring these forms of noise, much of the genuine, legitimate content on social media can be seen as irrelevant with respect to most information needs. André et al. [2012] demonstrate this in a study that assesses user-perceived value of tweets. They collected over 40,000 ratings of tweets from followers, in which only 36% of tweets were rated as "worth reading," while 25% were rated as "not worth reading." The least valued tweets were so-called presence maintenance posts (e.g., "Hullo twitter!"). Pre-processing to filter out spam and other irrelevant content, or models that are better capable of coping with noise are essential in any language-processing effort targeting social media.

Several characteristics of social media text are of particular concern to NLP approaches. The particularities of a given medium and the way in which that medium is used can have a profound effect on what constitutes a successful summarization approach. For example, the 140-character limit imposed on Twitter posts makes for individual tweets that are rather contextually impoverished compared to more traditional documents. However, redundancy can become a problem over multiple tweets, due in part to the practice of retweeting posts. Sharifi et al. [2010] note the redundancy of information as a major issue with microblog summarization in their experiments with data mining techniques to automatically create summary posts of Twitter trending topics.

A major challenge facing detection of events of interest from multiple Twitter streams is therefore to separate the mundane and polluted information from interesting real-world events. In practice, highly scalable and efficient approaches are required for handling and processing the increasingly large amount of Twitter data (especially for real-time event detection). Other challenges are inherent to Twitter design and usage. These are mainly due to the shortness of the messages: the frequent use of (dynamically evolving) informal, irregular, and abbreviated words, the large number of spelling and grammatical errors, and the use of improper sentence structure and mixed languages. Such data sparseness, lack of context, and diversity of vocabulary make the traditional text analysis techniques less suitable for tweets [Metzler et al., 2007]. In addition, different events may enjoy different popularity among users, and can differ significantly in content, number of messages and participants, time periods, inherent structure, and causal relationships [Nallapati et al., 2004].

Across all forms of social media, subjectivity is an ever-present trait. While traditional news texts may strive to present an objective, neutral account of factual information, social media texts are much more subjective and opinion-laden. Whether or not the ultimate information need lies directly in opinion mining and sentiment analysis, subjective information plays a much greater role in semantic analysis of social texts.

Topic drift is much more prominent in social media than in other texts, both because of the conversational tone of social texts and the continuously streaming nature of social media. There are also entirely new dimensions to be explored, where new sources of information and types of features need to be assessed and exploited. While traditional texts can be seen as largely static and self-contained, the information presented in social media, such as online discussion forums, blogs, and Twitter posts, is highly dynamic and involves interaction among various participants. This can be seen as an additional source of complexity that may hamper traditional summariza- tion approaches, but it is also an opportunity, making available additional context that can aid in summarization or making possible entirely new forms of summarization. For instance, Hu et al. [2007a] suggest summarizing a blog post by extracting representative sentences using in- formation from user comments. Chua and Asur [2012] exploit temporal correlation in a stream of tweets to extract relevant tweets for event summarization. Lin et al. [2009] address summa- rization not of the content of posts or messages, but of the social network itself by extracting temporally representative users, actions, and concepts in Flickr data.

As we mentioned, standard NLP approaches applied to social media data are therefore confronted with difficulties due to non-standard spelling, noise, limited sets of features, and errors. Therefore some NLP techniques, including normalization, term expansion, improved feature selection, and noise reduction, have been proposed to improve clustering performance in Twitter news [Beverungen and Kalita, 2011]. Identifying proper names and language switch in a sentence would require rapid and accurate name entity recognition and language detection techniques. Recent research efforts focus on the analysis of language in social media for under- standing social behavior and building socially aware systems. The goal is the analysis of language with implications for fields such as computational linguistics, sociolinguistics, and psycholin- guistics. For example, Eisenstein [2013a] studied the phonological variation and factors when transcribed into social media text.

Several workshops organized by the Association for Computational Linguistics (ACL)[4] and special issues in scientific journals dedicated to semantic analysis in social media show how active this research field is.

In this book, we will cite many papers from conferences such as ACL, AAAI, WWW, etc.; many workshop papers; several books; and many journal papers from various relevant journals.

---

[4]All publications could be found at ACL Anthology https://www.aclweb.org/anthology/

1.4   SEMANTIC ANALYSIS OF SOCIAL MEDIA

Our goal is to focus on innovative NLP applications (such as opinion mining, information extraction, summarization, and machine translation), tools, and methods that integrate appropriate linguistic information in various fields such as social media monitoring for healthcare, security and defense, business intelligence, and politics. The book contains four major chapters.

- **Chapter 1:** This chapter highlights the need for applications that use social media messages and meta-data. We also discuss the difficulty of processing social media data vs. traditional texts such as news articles and scientific papers.

- **Chapter 2:** This chapter discusses existing linguistic pre-processing tools such as tokenizers, part-of-speech taggers, parsers, and named entity recognizers, with a focus on their adaptation to social media data. We briefly discuss evaluation measures for these tools.

- **Chapter 3:** This chapter is the heart of the book. It presents the methods used in applications for semantic analysis of social network texts, in conjunction with social media analytics as well as methods for information extraction and text classification. We focus on tasks such as: geo-location detection, entity linking, opinion mining and sentiment analysis, emotion and mood analysis, event and topic detection, summarization, machine translation, and other tasks. They tend to pre-process the messages with some of the tools mentioned in Chapter 2 in order to extract the knowledge needed in the next processing levels. For each task, we discuss the evaluation metrics and any existing test datasets.

- **Chapter 4:** This chapter presents higher-level applications that use some of the methods from Chapter 3. We look at: healthcare applications, financial applications, predicting voting intentions, media monitoring, security and defense applications, NLP-based information visualization for social media, disaster response applications, NLP-based user modeling, applications for entertainment, rumor detection, and recommender systems.

- **Chapter 5:** This chapter discusses chapter complementary aspects such as data collection and annotation in social media, privacy issues in social media, spam detection in order to avoid spam in the collected datasets, and we describe some of the existing evaluation benchmarks that make available data collected and annotated for various tasks.

- **Chapter 6:** The last chapter summarizes the methods and applications described in the preceding chapters. We conclude with a discussion of the high potential for research, given the social media analysis needs of end-users.

As mentioned in the Preface, the **intended audience** of this book is researchers that are interested in developing tools and applications for automatic analysis of social media texts. We assume that the readers have basic knowledge in the area of natural language processing and machine learning. Nonetheless, we will try to define as many notions as we can, in order to facilitate the understanding for beginners in these two areas. We also assume basic knowledge of computer science in general.

1.5   SUMMARY

In this chapter, we reviewed the structure of social network and social media data as the collection of textual information on the Web. We presented semantic analysis in social media as a new opportunity for big data analytics and for intelligent applications. Social media monitoring and analyzing of the continuous flow of user-generated content can be used as an additional dimension which contains valuable information that would not have been available from traditional media and newspapers. In addition, we mentioned the challenges with social media data, which are due to their large size, and to their noisy, dynamic, and unstructured nature.

CHAPTER 2

Linguistic Pre-processing of Social Media Texts

2.1 INTRODUCTION

In this chapter, we discuss current Natural Language Processing (NLP) linguistic pre-processing methods and tools that were adapted for social media texts. We survey the methods used for adaptation to this kind of texts. We briefly define the evaluation measures used for each type of tool in order to be able to mention the state-of-the-art results.

In general, evaluation in NLP can be done in several ways:

- manually, by having humans judge the output of each tool;

- automatically, on test data that humans have annotated with the expected solution ahead of time; and

- task-based, by using the tools in a task and evaluating how much they contribute to the success in the task.

We primarily focus on the second approach here. It is the most convenient since it allows the automatic evaluation of the tools repeatedly after changing/improving their methods, and it allows comparing different tools on the same test data. Care should be taken when human judges annotate data. There should be at least two annotators that are given proper instructions on what and how to annotate (in an annotation manual). There needs to be a reasonable agreement rate between the two or more annotators, to ensure the quality of the obtained data. When there are disagreements, the expected solution will be obtained by resolving the disagreements by taking a vote (if there are three annotators or more, an odd number), or by having the annotators discuss until they reach an agreement (if there are only two annotators, or an even number). When reporting the inter-annotator agreement for a dataset, the kappa statistic also needs to be reported, in order to compensate the obtained agreement for possible agreements due to chance [Artstein and Poesio, 2008, Carletta, 1996].

NLP tools often use supervised machine learning, and the training data are usually anno-tated by human judges. In such cases, it is convenient to keep aside some of the annotated data for testing and to use the remaining data to train the models. Many of the methods discussed in this book use machine learning algorithms for automatic text classification. That is why we give a very brief introduction here. See, e.g., [Witten and Frank, 2005] for details of the classical algorithms and [Sebastiani, 2002] for how they can be applied to text data. Also see [Eisenstein, 2019] for more details about deep learning classification techniques for text data.

A supervised text classification model predicts the label c of an input x, where x is a vector of feature values extracted from document d. The class c can take two or more possible values from a specified set (or even continuous numeric values, in which case the classifier is called a regression model). The training data contain document vectors for which the classes are provided. The classifier uses the training data to learn associations between features or combinations of features that are strongly associated with one of the classes but not with the other classes. In this way, the trained model can make predictions for unseen test data in the future. There are many classification algorithms. We name here only a few of the classifiers popular in NLP tasks.

Decision trees take one feature at a time, compute its power of discriminating between the classes and build a tree with the most discriminative features in the upper part of the tree; decision trees are useful because the models can be easily understood by humans. Naïve Bayes is a classifier that learns the probabilities of association between features and classes; these models are used because they are known to work well with text data (see a more detailed description in Section 2.8.1). SVMs compute a hyper plane that separates two classes and they can efficiently perform nonlinear classification using what is called a kernel to map the data into a high-dimensional feature space where it become linearly separable [Cortes and Vapnik, 1995]; SVMs are probably the most often used classifiers due to their high performance on many tasks that have small amounts of training data.

Lately, most linguistic tools and applications employ deep neural network classifiers, which were shown to lead to better performance when large amounts of training data are available. These classifiers include Recurrent Neural Networks (RNN) or Convolutional Neural Networks (CNN) [LeCun et al., 2015]. A special type of RNN is Long Short-Term Memory (LSTM) networks, which add some forget gates to allow modeling long-distance context [Hochreiter and Schmidhuber, 1997].

There are many machine learning libraries that can be used. We mention here only a few: Weka[1] and scikit-learn[2] for classical algorithms and PyTorch[3] and TensorFlow[4] for deep learning algorithms. The first one is in Java, while the last three are in Python.

A sequence-tagging model can be seen as a classification model, but fundamentally differs from a conventional one, in the sense that instead of dealing with a single input x and a single label c each time, it predicts a sequence of labels $\mathbf{c} = (c_1, c_2, \ldots, c_n)$ based on a sequence of inputs $\mathbf{x} = (x_1, x_2, \ldots, x_n)$ and the predictions from the previous steps. It was applied with success in natural language processing (for sequential data such as sequences of part-of-speech tags, discussed in the previous chapter) and in bioinformatics (for DNA sequences). There exist a number of sequence-tagging models, including Hidden Markov Model (HMM) [Baum and

---

[1]urlhttps://www.cs.waikato.ac.nz/ml/weka/
[2]urlhttps://scikit-learn.org/stable/
[3]urlhttps://pytorch.org/
[4]urlhttps://www.tensorflow.org/

Petrie, 1966], Conditional Random Field (CRF) [Lafferty et al., 2001], and Maximum Entropy Markov Model (MEMM) [Berger et al., 1996].

Sequence-to-sequence models based on deep learning can also be used to transform sequences into other sequences, for example a sequence of words into a sequence of part-of-speech tags. They are also being used for the latest machine translation system, to transform a sequence of words in one language into a sequence of words in another language [Gehring et al., 2017].

Before the input texts can be fed into classifiers, each text needs to be transformed into a set of features. For some linguistic tools, extracting the words is sufficient while for semantic tasks and applications the texts need to be transformed into vectors of numeric or discrete values. The simplest way to represent texts is using the Bag-of-Words model (BOW) (a word is present or not, possibility with with frequency information), or more advanced and less sparse vectors called word embeddings [Mikolov et al., 2013]. Linguistic features can be used in addition or instead of the word-based features. These representations are important especially for the semantic tasks and applications discussed in the next two chapters.

The remainder of this chapter is structured as follows. Section 2.2 discusses generic methods of adapting NLP tools to social media texts. The next five sections discuss NLP tools of interest: tokenizers, part-of-speech taggers, chunkers, parsers, and named entity recognizers, as well as adaptation techniques for each. Section 2.7 enumerates some of the existing toolkits that were adapted to social media texts in English. Section 2.8 discusses multi-lingual aspects and language identification issues in social media. Section 2.9 summarizes this chapter.

2.2   GENERIC ADAPTATION TECHNIQUES FOR NLP TOOLS

NLP tools are important because they need to be used before we can build any applications that aim to understand texts or extract useful information from texts. Many NLP tools are now available, with acceptable levels of accuracy on texts that are similar to the types of texts used for training the models embedded in these tools. Most of the tools are trained on carefully edited texts, usually newspaper texts, due to the wide availability of these kinds of texts. For example, the Penn TreeBank corpus, consisting of 4.5 million words of American English [Marcus et al., 1993], was manually annotated with part-of-speech tags and parse trees, and it is often the main resource used to train part-of-speech taggers and parsers.

Current NLP tools tend to work poorly on social media texts, because these texts are informal, not carefully edited, and they contain grammatical errors, misspellings, new types of abbreviations, emoticons, etc. They are very different than the types of texts used for training the NLP tools. Therefore, the tools need to be adapted in order to achieve reasonable levels of performance on social media texts.

Table 2.1 shows three examples of Twitter messages, taken from Ritter et al. [2011], just to illustrate how noisy the texts can be.

Table 2.1: Three examples of Twitter texts

No.	Example
1	The Hobbit has FINALLY started filming! I cannot wait!
2	@c@ Yess! Yess! It's official Nintendo announced today that theyWill release the Nintendo 3DS in north America march 27 for $250
3	Government confirms blast n #nuclear plants n #japan...don't knw wht s gona happen nw...

There are two ways to adapt NLP tools to social media texts. The first one is to perform text normalization so that the informal language becomes closer to the type of texts on which the tools were trained. The second one is to re-train the models inside the tool on annotated social media texts. Depending on the goal of the NLP application, a combination of the two techniques could be used, since both have their own limitations, as discussed below (see Eisenstein [2013b] for a more detailed discussion).

2.2.1   TEXT NORMALIZATION

Text normalization is a possible solution for overcoming or reducing linguistic noise. The task can be approached in two stages: first, the identification of orthographic errors in an input text, and second, the correction of these errors. Normalization approaches typically include a dictionary of known correctly spelled terms, and detects in-vocabulary and out-of-vocabulary (OOV) terms with respect to this dictionary. The normalization can be basic or more advanced. Basic normalization deals with the errors detected at the POS tagging stage, such as unknown words, misspelled words, etc. Advanced normalization is more flexible, taking a lightly supervised automatic approach trained on an external dataset (annotated with short forms vs. their equivalent long or corrected forms).

For social media texts, the normalization that can be done is rather shallow. Because of its informal and conversational nature, social media text cannot become carefully edited English. Similar issues appear in SMS text messages on phones, where short forms and phonetic abbreviations are often used to save the typing time. According to Derczynski et al. [2013b], text normalization in Twitter messages did not help too much in the named entity recognition task.

Twitter text normalization into traditional written English [Han and Baldwin, 2011] is not only difficult, but it can be viewed as a "lossy" translation task. For example, many of Twitter's unique linguistic phenomena are due not only to its informal nature, but also to a set of authors that is heavily skewed toward younger ages and minorities, with heavy usage of dialects that are different than standard English [Eisenstein, 2013a, Eisenstein et al., 2011].

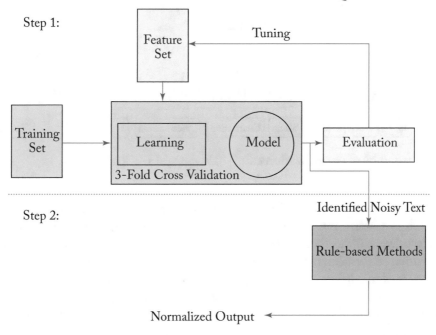

Figure 2.1: Methodology for tweet normalization. The dotted horizontal line separates the two steps (detecting the text to be normalized and applying normalization rules) [Akhtar et al., 2015].

Demir [2016] describes a method of context-tailored text normalization. The method considers contextual and lexical similarities between standard and non-standard words, in order to reduce noise. The non-standard words in the input context in a given sentence are tailored into a direct match, if there are possible shared contexts. A morphological parser is used to analyze all the words in each sentence. Turkish social media texts were used to evaluate the performance of the system. The dataset contains tweets (~11 GB) and clean Turkish texts (~ 6 GB). The system achieved state-of-the-art results on the 715 Turkish tweets.

Akhtar et al. [2015] proposed a hybrid approach for text normalization for tweets. Their methodology proceeds in two phases: the first one detects noisy text, and the second one uses various heuristic-based rules for normalization. The researchers trained a supervised learning model, using 3-fold cross validation to determine the best feature set. Figure 2.1 depicts a schematic diagram of the proposed approach. Their system yielded precision, recall, and F-measure values of 0.90, 0.72, and 0.80, respectively, for their test dataset.

Most practical applications leverage the simpler approach of replacing non-standard words with their standard counterparts as a "one size fits all" task. Baldwin and Li [2015] devised a method that uses a taxonomy of normalization edits. The researchers evaluated this method on

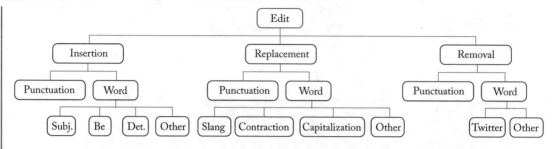

Figure 2.2: Taxonomy of normalization edits [Baldwin and Li, 2015].

three different downstream applications: dependency parsing, named entity recognition, and text-to-speech synthesis. The taxonomy of normalization edits is shown in Figure 2.2. The method categorizes edits at three levels of granularity and its results demonstrate that the targeted application of the taxonomy is an efficient approach to normalization.

The effect of manual vs. automatic lexical normalization for dependency parsing was analyzed by van der Goot [2019]. They showed that for most categories, automatic normalization scores are close to manual normalization but the small differences are important to take into consideration when exploiting normalization in a pipeline setup.

2.2.2 RE-TRAINING NLP TOOLS FOR SOCIAL MEDIA TEXTS

Re-training NLP tools for social media texts is relatively easy if annotated training data are available. In general, adapting a tool to a specific domain or a specific type of text requires producing annotated training data for that kind of text. It is easy to collect text of the required kind, but to annotate it can be a difficult and time-consuming process.

Currently, some annotated social media data have become available, but the volume is not high enough. Several NLP tools have been re-trained on newly annotated data, sometimes by also keeping the original annotated training data for newspaper texts, in order to have a large enough training set. Another approach is to use some unlabeled social media text in an unsupervised manner in addition to the small amounts of annotated social media text.

Another question is what kinds of social media texts to use for training. It seems that Twitter messages are more difficult to process than blog posts or messages from forums. Because of the limitation of Twitter messages to 140 characters, more abbreviations and shortened forms of words are used, and more simplified syntax. Therefore, training data should include several kinds of social media texts (unless somebody is building a tool designed for a particular kind of social media text).

We define the tasks accomplished by each kind of tool and we discuss techniques for adapting them to social media texts.

Table 2.2: Examples of tokenization

	(1)	(2)	(3)
Raw	pdf?"<-Wenn	schriftq.Äquivalent	v.14.4
Tokenized	pdf ? " <- Wenn	schriftq. Äquivalent	v. 14. 4

2.3   TOKENIZERS

The first step in processing a text is to separate the words from punctuation and other symbols. A tool that does this is called a tokenizer. White space is a good indicator of words separation (except in some languages, e.g., Chinese), but even white space is not sufficient. The question of what is a word is not trivial. When doing corpus analysis, there are strings of characters that are clearly words, but there are strings for which this is not clear. Most of the time, punctuation needs to be separated from words, but some abbreviations might contain punctuation characters as part of the word. Take, for example, the sentence: "We bought apples, oranges, etc." The commas clearly need to be separated from the word "apples" and from the word "oranges," but the dot is part of the abbreviation "etc." In this case, the dot also indicates the end of the sentence (two dots were reduced to one). Other examples among the many issues that appear are: how to treat numbers (if they contain commas or dots, these characters should not be separated), or what to do with contractions such as "don't" (perhaps to expand them into two words "do" and "not").

While tokenization usually consists of two subtasks (sentence boundary detection and token boundary detection), the EmpiriST shared task[5] provided sentence boundaries and the participating teams only had to detect token boundaries. Missing whitespace characters presents a major challenge to the task of tokenization. Table 2.2 shows a few examples with their correct tokenization.

Methods for Tokenizers
Horsmann and Zesch [2016] evaluated a method for dealing with token boundaries consisting of three steps. First, the researchers split the text according to the white space characters. Then they employed regular expressions to refine the splitting of alpha-numerical text segments from punctuation characters in special character sequences such as similes. Finally, these sequences of punctuation are reassembled. They merge the most common combinations of characters into a single token using the training data, and use word lists to merge abbreviations with their following dot character. They increase accuracy in the experiment using more in-domain training data.

[5]https://sites.google.com/site/empirist2015/

Evaluation Measures for Tokenizers

Accuracy is a simple measure that calculates how many correct decisions a tool makes. When not all the expected tokens are retrieved, precision and recall are the measure to report. The precision of the tokens recognition measures how many tokens are correct out of how many were found. Recall measures the coverage (from the tokens that should have been retrieved, how many were found). F-measure (or F-score) is often reported when one single number is needed, because F-measure is the harmonic mean of the precision and recall, and it is high only when both the precision and the recall are high.[6] Evaluation measures are rarely reported for tokenizers, one exception being the CleanEval shared task which focused on tokenizing text from web pages [Baroni et al., 2008].

Many NLP projects tend to not mention what kind of tokenization they used, and focus more on higher-level processing. Tokenization, however, can have a large effect on the results obtained at the next levels. For example, Fokkens et al. [2013] replicated two high-level tasks from previous work and obtained very different results, when using the same settings but different tokenization.

Adapting Tokenizers to Social Media Texts

Tokenizers need to deal with the specifics of social media texts. Emoticons need to be detected as tokens. For Twitter messages, user names (starting with @), hashtags (starting with #), and URLs (links to web pages) should be treated as tokens, without separating punctuation or other symbols that are part of the token. Some shallow normalization can be useful at this stage. Derczynski et al. [2013b] tested a tokenizer on Twitter data, and its F-measure was around 80%. By using regular expressions designed specifically for Twitter messages, they were able to increase the F-measure to 96%. More about such regular expressions can be found in [O'Connor et al., 2010].

2.4 PART-OF-SPEECH TAGGERS

Part-of-speech (POS) taggers determine the part of speech of each word in a sentence. They label nouns, verbs, adjectives, adverbs, interjections, conjunctions, etc. Often they use finer-grained tagsets, such as singular nouns, plural nouns, proper nouns, etc. Different tagsets exist, one of the most popular being the Penn TreeBank tagset[7] [Marcus et al., 1993]. See Table 2.3 for one of its more popular lists of the tags. The models embedded in the POS taggers are often complex, based on Hidden Markov Models [Baum and Petrie, 1966], Conditional Random Fields [Lafferty et al., 2001], etc. They need annotated training data in order to learn probabilities and other parameters of the models.

---

[6]The F-score usually gives the same weight to precision and to recall, but it can weight one of them more when needed for an application.

[7]http://www.comp.leeds.ac.uk/ccalas/tagsets/upenn.html

Table 2.3: Penn TreeBank tagset

Number	Tag	Description
1	CC	Coordinating conjunction
2	CD	Cardinal number
3	DT	Determiner
4	EX	Existential there
5	FW	Foreign word
6	IN	Preposition or subordinating conjunction
7	JJ	Adjective
8	JJR	Adjective, comparative
9	JJS	Adjective, superlative
10	LS	List item marker
11	MD	Model
12	NN	Noun, singular or mass
13	NNS	Noun, plural
14	NNP	Proper noun, singular
15	NNPS	Proper noun, plural
16	PDT	Predeterminer
17	POS	Possessive ending
18	PRP	Personal pronoun
19	PRP$	Possessive pronoun
20	RB	Adverb
21	RBR	Adverb, comparative
22	RBS	Adverb, superlative
23	RP	Particle
24	SYM	Symbol
25	TO	To
26	UH	Interjection
27	VB	Verb, base form
28	VBD	Verb, past tense
29	VBG	Verb, gerund or present participle
30	VBN	Verb, past participle
31	VBP	Verb, non-3rd person singular present
32	VBZ	Verb, 3rd person singular present
33	WDT	Wh-determiner
34	WP	Wh-pronoun
35	WP$	Possessive wh-pronoun
36	WRB	Wh-adverb

Methods for Part-of-speech Taggers

Horsmann and Zesch [2016] trained a CRF classifier [Lafferty et al., 2001] using the FlexTag tagger [Zesch and Horsmann, 2016] There are two adaptations involved in this method. The first is a general domain adaptation. The researchers applied a domain adaption strategy, which they proposed as a competitive model to improve the accuracy for tagging social media texts. To train their model, they used the CMC and Web corpora subsets from the EmpiriST shared task and some additional 100,000 tokens of newswire text from the Tiger corpus. The second adaptation is specific to the EmpiriST shared task. Because some POS tags are too rare to be learned from training data, the researchers utilized a post-processing step that leveraged heuristics. This step involved the use of regular expressions and word lists from Wikipedia and Wiktionary to improve named entity recognition and case-insensitive matching. Selecting tags from the larger Tiger corpus introduced bias, so the researchers added extra Boolean features to their model.

Deep learning-based POS taggers became easy to build. They directly tansform sequences of words into sequences of POS taggs. For example, Popov [2016] surveys the techniques that can be applied, starting with word embeddings and enhanced with suffix embeddings.

Evaluation Measures for Part-of-speech Taggers

The accuracy of the tagging is usually measured as the number of tags correctly assigned out of the total number of words/tokens being tagged.

Adapting Part-of-speech Taggers

POS taggers clearly need re-training in order to be usable on social media data. Even the set of POS tags used must be extended in order to adapt to the needs of this kind of text. Ritter et al. [2011] used the Penn TreeBank tagset (Table 2.3) to annotate 800 Twitter messages. They added a few new tags for the Twitter-specific phenomena: retweets, @usernames, #hashtags, and URLs. Words in these categories can be tagged with very high accuracy using simple regular expressions, but they still need to be taken into consideration as features in the re-training of the taggers (for example as tags of the previous word to be tagged). In Ritter et al. [2011], the POS tagging accuracy drops from about 97% on newspaper text to 80% on the 800 tweets. These numbers are reported for the Stanford POS tagger [Toutanova et al., 2003]. Their POS tagger T-POS—based on a Conditional Random Field classifier and on the clustering of out-of-vocabulary (OOV) words—also obtained low performance on Twitter data (81%). By re-training the T-POS tagger on the annotated Twitter data (which is rather small), the accuracy increases to 85%. The best accuracy raises to 88% when the size of the training data is increased by adding to the Twitter data the initial Penn TreeBank training data, plus 40,000 tokens of annotated Internet Relay Chat (IRC) data [Forsyth and Martell, 2007], which is similar in style to Twitter data. Similar numbers are reported by Derczynski et al. [2013b] on a part of the same Twitter dataset.

A key reason for the drop in accuracy on Twitter data is that the data contains far more OOV words than grammatical text. Many of these OOV words come from spelling variation, e.g., the use of the word *n* for *in* in Example 3 from Table 2.1 The tag for proper nouns (NNP) is the most frequent tag for OOV words, while in fact only about one third are proper nouns.

Gimpel et al. [2011] developed a new POS tagset for Twitter (see Table 2.4), that is more coarse-grained, and it pays particular attention to punctuation, emoticons, and Twitter-specific tags (@usernames, #hashtags, URLs). They manually tagged 1,827 tweets with the new tagset; then, they trained a POS tagging model that uses features geared toward Twitter text. The experiments conducted to evaluate the model showed 90% accuracy for the POS tagging task. Owoputi et al. [2013] improved on the model by using word clustering techniques and trained the POS tagger on a better dataset of tweets and chat messages.[8] Some of the expressions used in Twitter messages are formal, and some are informal. Therefore, POS tagging for the formal Twitter contexts can be learned together with the exiting news datasets, while POS tagging for the informal Twitter context should be learned separately. Gui et al. [2018] proposed a hypernetwork-based method to generate different parameters to separately model contexts with different expression styles. Experimental results on three test datasets showed that their approach achieves better performance than state-of-the-art methods in most cases.

2.5   CHUNKERS AND PARSERS

A **chunker** detects noun phrases, verb phrases, adjectival phrases, and adverbial phrases, by determining the start point and the end point of every such phrase. Chunkers are often referred to as shallow parsers because they do not attempt to connect the phrases in order to detect the syntactic structure of the whole sentence.

A **parser** performs the syntactic analysis of a sentence, and usually produces a parse tree. The trees are often used in future processing stages, toward semantic analysis or information extraction.

A **dependency parser** extracts pairs of words that are in a syntactic dependency relation, rather than a parse tree. Relations can be verb-subject, verb-object, noun-modifier, etc.

Methods for Parsers

The methods used to build parsers range from early rule-based approaches, to robust probabilistic models and to new types of deep learning-based parsers. For example, Chen and Manning [2014] present a fast and accurate dependency parser using neural networks, trained on newspaper text. Another example is Parsey McParseface[9], an open-sourced machine learning model-based authored by Google and based on the Tensorflow framework. It contains a globally normalized transition-based neural network model that achieves state-of-the-art part-of-speech tagging, dependency parsing, and sentence compression results.

---

[8]This data set is available at http://code.google.com/p/ark-tweet-nlp/downloads/list.
[9]https://deepai.org/machine-learning-model/parseymcparseface

Table 2.4: **POS** tagset from Gimpel et al. [2011]

Tag	Description
N	Common noun
O	Pronoun (personal/WH, not possessive)
ˆ	Proper noun
S	Nominal + possessive
Z	Proper noun + possessive
V	Verb including copula, auxiliaries
L	Nominal + verbal (e.g., i'm), verbal _ nominal (let's)
M	Proper noun + verbal
A	Adjective
R	Adverb
!	Interjection
D	Determiner
P	Pre- or postposition, or subordinating conjunction
&	Coordinating conjunction
T	Verb particle
X	Existential there, predeterminers
Y	X + verbal
#	Hashtag (indicates topic/category for tweet)
@	At-mention (indicates a user as a recipient of a tweet)
~	Discourse marker, indications of continuation across multiple tweets
U	URL or email address
E	Emoticon
$	Numeral
,	Punctuation
G	Other abbreviations, foreign words, possessive endings, symbols, garbage

Evaluation Measures for Chunking and Parsing

The Parseval evaluation campaign [Harrison et al., 1991] proposed measures that compare the phrase-structure bracketings[10] produced by the parser with bracketings in the annotated corpus (treebank). One computes the number of bracketing matches M with respect to the number

---

[10]A bracketing is a pair of matching opening and closing brackets in a linearized tree structure.

of bracketings P returned by the parser (expressed as precision M/P) and with respect to the number C of bracketings in the corpus (expressed as recall M/C). Their harmonic mean, the F-measure, is most often reported for parsers. In addition, the mean number of crossing brackets per sentence could be reported, to count the number of cases when a bracketed sequence from the parser overlaps with one from the treebank (i.e., neither is properly contained in the other). For chunking, the accuracy can be reported as the tag correctness for each chunk (labeled accuracy), or separately for each token in each chunk (token-level accuracy). The former is stricter because it does not give credit to a chunk that is partially correct but incomplete, for example one or more words too short or too long.

Adapting Parsers

Parsing performance also decreases on social media text. Foster et al. [2011] tested four dependency parsers and showed that their performance decreases from 90% F-score on newspaper text to 70–80% on social media text (70% on Twitter data and 80% on discussion forum texts). After retraining on a small amount of social media training data (1,000 manually corrected parses) plus a large amount of unannotated social media text, the performance increased to 80–83%. Ovrelid and Skjærholt [2012] also show the labeled accuracy of dependency parsers decreasing from newspaper data to Twitter data.

Ritter et al. [2011] also explored shallow parsing and noun phrase chunking for Twitter data. The token-level accuracy for the shallow parsing of tweets was 83% with the OpenNLP chunker and 87% with their shallow parser T-chunk. Both were re-trained on a small amount of annotated Twitter data plus the Conference on Natural Language Learning (CoNLL) 2000 shared task data [Tjong Kim Sang and Buchholz, 2000].

Khan et al. [2013] reported experiments on parser adaptation to social media texts and other kinds of Web texts. They found that text normalization helps increase performance by a few percentage points, and that a tree reviser based on grammar comparison helps to a small degree. A dependency parser named TweeboParser[11] was developed specifically on a recently annotated Twitter treebank for 929 tweets [Kong et al., 2014]. It uses the POS tagset from Gimpel et al. [2011] presented in Table 2.4. Table 2.5 shows an example of output of the parser for the tweet: "They say you are what you eat, but it's Friday and I don't care! #TGIF (@ Ogalo Crows Nest) http://t.co/l3uLuKGk:"

The columns represent, in order: ID is the token counter, starting at 1 for each new sentence; FORM is the word form or punctuation symbol; CPOSTAG is the coarse-grained part-of-speech tag, where the tagset depends on the language; POSTAG is the fine-grained part-of-speech tag, where the tagset depends on the language, or it is identical to the coarse-grained part-of-speech tag, if not available; HEAD is the head of the current token, which is either an ID (−1 indicates that the word is not included in the parse tree; some treebanks also used zero as ID); and finally, DEPREL is the dependency relation to the HEAD. The set of dependency re-

---

[11]http://www.ark.cs.cmu.edu/TweetNLP/#tweeboparser_tweebank

Table 2.5: Example of tweet parsed with the TweeboParser

ID	FORM	CPOSTAG	POSTAG	HEAD	DEPREL
1	They	O	O	2	_
2	say	V	V	9	CONJ
3	you	O	O	4	_
4	are	V	V	2	_
5	what	O	O	7	_
6	you	O	O	7	_
7	eat	V	V	4	_
8	,	,	,	−1	_
9	but	&	&	0	_
10	it's	L	L	9	CONJ
11	Friday	^	^	10	_
12	and	&	&	0	_
13	O	O	O	14	_
14	don't	V	V	12	CONJ
15	care	V	V	14	_
16	!	,	,	−1	_
17	#TGIF	#	#	−1	_
18	{@	P	P	0	_
19	Ogalo	^	^	21	MWE
20	Crows	^	^	21	MWE
21	Nest	^	^	18	_
22	)	,	,	−1	_
23	http://t.co/13uLuKGk	U	U	−1	_

lations depends on the particular language. Depending on the original treebank annotation, the dependency relation may be meaningful or simply "ROOT." So, for this tweet, the dependency relations are MWE (multi-word expression), CONJ (Conjunct), and many other relations between the word IDs, but they are not named (probably due to the limited training data used when the parser was trained). The dependency relations from the Stanford dependency parser are included, if they can be detected in a tweet. If they cannot be named, they are still in the table, but without a label.

2.6   NAMED ENTITY RECOGNIZERS

A named entity recognizer (NER) detects names in the texts, as well as dates, currency amounts, and other kinds of entities. NER tools often focus on three types of names: Person, Organization, and Location, by detecting the boundaries of these phrases. There are a few other types of tools that can be useful in the early stages of NLP applications. One example is a **co-reference resolution** tool that can be used to detect the noun that a pronoun refers to or to detect different noun phrases that refer to the same entity. In fact, NER is a semantic task, not a linguistic pre-processing task, but we introduce it this chapter because it became part of many of the recent NLP tools discussed in this chapter. We will talk more about specific kind of entities in Sections 3.2 and 3.3, in the context of integrating more and more semantic knowledge when solving the respective tasks.

Methods for NER

NER is composed of two sub-tasks: detecting entities (the span of text where a name starts and where it ends) and determining/classifying the type of entity. The methods used in NER are either based on linguistic grammars for each type of entity, either based on statistical methods. Semi-supervised learning techniques were proposed, but supervised learning, especially based on CRFs for sequence learning, are the most prevalent. Hand-crafted grammar-based systems typically obtain good precision, but at the cost of lower recall and months of work by experienced computational linguists. Supervised learning techniques were used more recently due the availability of annotated training datasets, mostly for newspaper texts, such as data from MUC 6, MUC 7, and ACE,[12] and also the CoNLL 2003 English NER dataset [Tjong Kim Sang and De Meulder, 2003].

Tkachenko et al. [2013] described a supervised learning method for named-entity recognition. Feature engineering and learning algorithm selection are critical factors when designing a NER system. Possible features could include word lemmas, part-of-speech tags, and occurrence in some dictionary that encodes characteristic attributes of words relevant for the classification task. Tkachenko et al. [2013] included morphological, dictionary-based, WordNet-based, and global features. For their learning algorithm, the researchers chose CRFs, which have a sequential nature and ability to handle a large number of features. As also mentioned above, CRFs are widely used for the task of NER. For the Estonian dataset, the system produced a gold standard NER corpus, on which their CRF-based model achieved an overall F-score of 0.87.

He and Sun [2017] developed a semi-supervised leaning model based on deep neural networks (B-LSTM). This system combined transition probabilities with deep learning to train the model directly on F-score and label accuracy. The researchers used a modified, labeled corpus which corrected labeling errors in data developed by Peng and Dredze [2016] for NER in Chinese social media. They evaluated their model on NER and nominal mention tasks. The

---

[12]http://www.cs.technion.ac.il/~gabr/resources/data/ne_datasets.html

result for NER on the dataset of Peng and Dredze [2016] is the state-of-the-art NER system in Chinese Social Media. Their Bi-LSTM model achieved an F-score of 0.53.

Approaches based on deep learning were shown to benefit NER systems as well. Aguilar et al. [2017] proposed a multi-task approach by employing the task of Named Entity (NE) segmentation together with the task of fine-grained NE categorization. The multi-task neural network architecture learns higher-order feature representations from word and character sequences along with basic part-of-speech tags and gazetteer information. This neural network acts as a feature extractor to feed a Conditional Random Fields classifier. They obtained the best results in the 3rd Workshop on Noisy User-generated Text (WNUT-2017) with a 0.4186 entity detection F-score. Aguilar et al. [2018] extended the system's architecture and improved the results with 2-3%.

Evaluation Measures for NER

The precision, recall, and F-measure can be calculated at sequence level (whole span of text) or at token level. The former is stricter because each named entity that is longer than one word has to have an exact start and end point. Once entities have been determined, the accuracy of assigning them to tags such as Person, Organization, etc., can be calculated.

Adaptation for Named Entity Recognition

Named entity recognition methods typically have 85–90% accuracy on long and carefully edited texts, but their performance decreases to 30–50% on tweets [Li et al., 2012a, Liu et al., 2012b, Ritter et al., 2011].

Ritter et al. [2011] reported that the Stanford NER obtains 44% accuracy on Twitter data. They also presented new NER methods for social media texts based on labeled Latent Dirichlet Allocation (LDA)[13] [Ramage et al., 2009], that allowed their T-Seg NER system to reach an accuracy of 67%.

Derczynski et al. [2013b] reported that NER performance drops from 77% F-score on newspaper text to 60% on Twitter data, and that after adaptation it increases to 80% (with the ANNIE NER system from GATE) [Cunningham et al., 2002]. The performance on newspaper data was computed on the CoNLL 2003 English NER dataset [Tjong Kim Sang and De Meulder, 2003], while the performance on social media data was computed on part of the Ritter dataset [Ritter et al., 2011], which contains of 2,400 tweets comprising 34,000 tokens.

Particular attention is given to microtext normalization, as a way of removing some of the linguistic noise prior to part-of-speech tagging and entity recognition [Derczynski et al., 2013a, Han and Baldwin, 2011]. Some research has focused on named entity recognition algorithms specifically for Twitter messages, training new CRF model on Twitter data [Ritter et al., 2011].

---

[13]LDA is a method that assumes a number of hidden topics for a corpus, and discovers a cluster of words for each topic, with associated probabilities. Then, for each document, LDA can estimate a probability distribution over the topics. The topics—word clusters—do not have names, but names can be given, for example, by choosing the word with the highest probability in each cluster.

An NER tool can detect various kinds of named entities, or focus only on one kind. For example, Derczynski and Bontcheva [2014] presented methods for detecting person entities. Chapter 3 will discuss methods for detecting other specific kinds of entities. The NER tools can detect entities, disambiguate them (when more than one entity with the same name exists), or solve co-references (when there are several ways to refer to the same entity).

2.7   EXISTING NLP TOOLKITS FOR ENGLISH AND THEIR ADAPTATION

There are many NLP tools developed for generic English and fewer for other languages. We list here several selected tools that have been adapted for social media text. Others may be available, just perhaps not useful in social media texts, although new tools are being developed or adapted. Nonetheless, we will briefly mention several toolkits that offer a collection of tools, also called suites if the tools can be used in a sequence of consecutive steps, from tokenization to named entity recognition or more. Some of them can be re-trained for social media texts.

SpaCy is a suite of NLP tool based on deep learning technology. It inlcued general-purpose pretrained models to predict named entities, part-of-speech tags and syntactic dependencies, and it can be used out-of-the-box and fine-tuned on more specific data.[14]

The Stanford CoreNLP is an integrated suite of NLP tools for English programmed in Java, including tokenization, part-of-speech tagging, named entity recognition, parsing, and co-reference. A text classifier is also available.[15]

Open NLP includes tokenization, sentence segmentation, part-of-speech tagging, named entity extraction, chunking, parsing, and co-reference resolution, implemented in Java. It also includes maximum entropy and perceptron-based machine learning algorithms.[16]

FreeLing includes tools for English and several other languages: text tokenization, sentence splitting, morphological analysis, phonetic encoding, named entity recognition, POS tagging, chart-based shallow parsing, rule-based dependency parsing, nominal co-reference resolution, etc.[17]

NLTK is a suite of text processing libraries in Python for classification, tokenization, stemming, POS tagging, parsing, and semantic reasoning.[18]

GATE includes components for diverse language processing tasks, e.g., parsers, morphology, POS tagging. It also contains information retrieval tools, information extraction components for various languages, and many others. The information extraction system (ANNIE) includes a named entity detector.[19]

---

[14]https://spacy.io/
[15]http://nlp.stanford.edu/downloads/
[16]http://opennlp.apache.org/
[17]http://nlp.lsi.upc.edu/freeling/
[18]http://nltk.org/
[19]http://gate.ac.uk/

NLPTools is a library for NLP written in PHP, geared toward text classification, clustering, tokenizing, stemming, etc.[20]

Some components of these toolkits were re-trained for social media texts, such as the Stanford part-of-speech (POS) tagger by Derczynski et al. [2013b], and the OpenNLP chunker by Ritter et al. [2011], as we noted earlier.

One toolkit that was fully adapted to social media text is GATE. A new module or plugin called TwitIE[21] is available [Derczynski et al., 2013a] for tokenization of Twitter texts, as well as POS tagging, name entities recognition, etc.

Two new toolkits were built especially for social media texts: the TweetNLP tools developed at CMU and the Twitter NLP tools developed at the University of Washington (UW).

TweetNLP is a Java-based tokenizer and part-of-speech tagger for Twitter text [Owoputi et al., 2013]. It includes training data of manually labeled POS annotated tweets (that we noted above), a Web-based annotation tool, and hierarchical word clusters from unlabeled tweets.[22] It also includes the TweeboParser mentioned above.

The UW Twitter NLP Tools [Ritter et al., 2011] contain the POS tagger and the annotated Twitter data (mentioned above—see adaptation of POS taggers).[23]

A few other tools for English are in development, and a few tools for other languages have been adapted or can be adapted to social media text. The development of the latter is slower, due to the difficulty in producing annotated training data for many languages, but there is progress. For example, a treebank for French social media texts was developed by Seddah et al. [2012].

2.8 MULTI-LINGUALITY AND ADAPTATION TO SOCIAL MEDIA TEXTS

Social media messages are available in many languages. Some messages could be mixed, for example part in English and part in another language. This is called "code switching." If tools for multiple languages are available, a language identification tool needs to be run on the texts before using the right language-specific tools for the next processing steps.

2.8.1 LANGUAGE IDENTIFICATION

Language identification can reach very high accuracy for long texts (98–99%), but it needs adaptation to social media texts, especially to short texts such as Twitter messages.

Derczynski et al. [2013b] showed that language identification accuracy decreases to around 90% on Twitter data, and that re-training can lead to 95–97% accuracy levels. This increase is easily achievable for tools that classify into a small number of languages, while tools that classify into a large number of languages (close to 100 languages) cannot be further im-

---

[20]http://php-nlp-tools.com/
[21]https://gate.ac.uk/wiki/twitie.html
[22]http://www.ark.cs.cmu.edu/TweetNLP/
[23]https://github.com/aritter/twitter_nlp

proved on short informal texts. Lui and Baldwin [2014] tested six language identification tools and obtained the best results on Twitter data by majority voting over three of them, up to an F-score of 0.89.

Barman et al. [2014] presented a new dataset containing Facebook posts and comments that exhibit code mixing between Bengali, English, and Hindi. The researchers demonstrated some preliminary word-level language identification experiments using this dataset. The methods surveyed included a simple unsupervised dictionary-based approach, supervised word-level classification with and without contextual clues, and sequence labeling using Conditional Random Fields. The preliminary results demonstrated the superiority of supervised classification and sequence labeling over dictionary-based classification, suggesting that contextual clues are necessary for accurate classifiers. The CRF model achieved the best result with an F-score of 0.95.

There is a lot of work on language identification in social media. Twitter has been a favorite target, and a number of papers deal with language identification of Twitter messages specifically Bergsma et al. [2012], Carter et al. [2013], Goldszmidt et al. [2013], Mayer [2012], Tromp and Pechenizkiy [2011]. Tromp and Pechenizkiy [2011] proposed a graph-based n-gram approach that works well on tweets. Lui and Baldwin [2014] looked specifically at the problem of adapting existing language identification tools to Twitter messages, including challenges in obtaining data for evaluation, as well as the effectiveness of proposed strategies. They tested several tools on Twitter data (including a newly collected corpus for English, Japanese, and Chinese). The tests were done with off-the-shelf tools, before and after a simple cleaning of the Twitter data, such as removing hashtags, mentions, emoticons, etc. The improvement after the cleaning was small. Bergsma et al. [2012] looked at less common languages, in order to collect language-specific corpora. The nine languages they focused on (Arabic, Farsi, Urdu, Hindi, Nepali, Marathi, Russian, Bulgarian, Ukrainian) use three different non-Latin scripts: Arabic, Devanagari, and Cyrillic. Their method for language identification was based on language models.

Most of the methods used only the text of the message, but Carter et al. [2013] also looked at the use of metadata, an approach which is unique to social media. They identified five microblog characteristics that can help in language identification: the language profile of the blogger, the content of an attached hyperlink, the language profile of other users mentioned in the post, the language profile of a tag, and the language of the original post, if the post is a reply. Further, they presented methods that combine the prior language class probabilities in a post-dependent and post-independent way. Their test results on 1,000 posts from 5 languages (Dutch, English, French, German, and Spanish) showed improvements in accuracy by 5% over the baseline, and showed that post-dependent combinations of the priors achieved the best performance.

Taking a broader view of social media, Nguyen and Doğruöz [2013] looked at language identification in a mixed Dutch-Turkish Web forum. Mayer [2012] considered language identification of private messages between eBay users.

Here are some of the available **tools** for language identification.

- langid.py[24] [Lui and Baldwin, 2012] works for 97 languages and uses a feature set selected from multiple sources, combined via a multinomial Naïve Bayes classifier.

- CLD2,[25] the language identifier embedded in the Chrome Web browser,[26] uses a Naïve Bayes classifier and script-specific tokenization strategies.

- LangDetect[27] is a Naïve Bayes classifier, using a representation based on character n-grams without feature selection, with a set of normalization heuristics.

- whatlang [Brown, 2013] uses a vector-space model with per-feature weighting over character n-grams.

- YALI[28] computes a per-language score using the relative frequency of a set of byte n-grams selected by term frequency.

- TextCat[29] is an implementation of the method of Cavnar and Trenkle [1994] and it uses an adhoc rank-order statistic over character n-grams.

Only some of the available **tools** were trained directly on social media data.

- LDIG[30] is an off-the-shelf Java language identification tool targeted specifically at Twitter messages. It has pre-trained models for 47 languages. It uses a document representation based on data structures named tries.[31]

- MSR-LID [Goldszmidt et al., 2013] is based on rank-order statistics over character n-grams, and Spearman's coefficient to measure correlations. Twitter-specific training data was acquired through a bootstrapping approach.

Some **datasets** of social media texts annotated with language labels are available.

- The dataset of Tromp and Pechenizkiy [2011] contains 9,066 Twitter messages labeled with one of the six languages: German, English, Spanish, French, Italian, and Dutch.[32]

- The Twituser language identification dataset[33] of Lui and Baldwin [2014] for English, Japanese, and Chinese.

---

[24]https://github.com/saffsd/langid.py
[25]http://blog.mikemccandless.com/2011/10/accuracy-and-performance-of-googles.html
[26]http://www.google.com/chrome
[27]https://code.google.com/p/language-detection/
[28]https://github.com/martin-majlis/YALI
[29]http://odur.let.rug.nl/~vannoord/TextCat/
[30]https://github.com/shuyo/ldig
[31]http://en.wikipedia.org/wiki/Trie
[32]http://www.win.tue.nl/~mpechen/projects/smm/
[33]http://people.eng.unimelb.edu.au/tbaldwin/data/lasm2014-twituser-v1.tgz

2.8.2   DIALECT IDENTIFICATION

Sometimes it is not enough that a language has been identified correctly. A case in point is Arabic. It is the official language in 22 countries, spoken by more than 350 million people worldwide.[34] Modern Standard Arabic (MSA) is the written form of Arabic used in education; it is also the formal communication language. Arabic dialects or colloquial languages are spoken varieties of Arabic, and spoken daily by Arab people. There are more than 22 dialects; some countries share the same dialect, while many dialects may exist alongside MSA within the same Arab country. Arabic speakers prefer to use their own local dialect. Recently, more attention has been given to the Arabic dialects and the written varieties of Arabic found on social networking sites such as chats, micro-blogs, blogs, and forums which are the target of research on sentiment analysis and opinion extraction.

Huang [2015] shows us an approach to improving Arabic dialect classification with semi-supervised learning. He trained multiple classifiers using a combination of weakly supervised, strongly supervised, and unsupervised classifiers. These combinations yielded significant and consistent improvement on two test sets. The dialect classification accuracy improved by 5% over the strongly supervised classifier and 20% over the weakly supervised classifier. Furthermore, when applying the improved dialect classifier to build a MSA language model (LM), the new model size was reduced by 70%, while the English-Arabic translation quality improved by 0.6 BLEU points.

Arabic Dialects (AD) or daily language differs from MSA especially in social media communication. However, most Arabic social media texts have mixed forms and many variations especially between MSA and AD. Figure 2.3 illustrates the AD distribution.

There is a possible division of regional language within the six regional groups, as follows: Egyptian, Levantine, Gulf, Iraqi, Maghrebi, and others, as shown in Figure 2.4.

Dialect identification is closely related to the language identification problem. The dialect identification task attempts to identify the spoken dialect from within a set of texts that use the same character set in a known language.

Due to the similarity of dialects within a language, dialect identification is more difficult than language identification. Machine learning approaches and language models which are used for language identification need to be adapted for dialect identification as well.

Several projects on NLP for MSA have been carried out, but research on Dialectal Arabic NLP is in early stages [Habash, 2010].

When processing Arabic for the purposes of social media analysis, the first step is to identify the dialect and then map the dialect to MSA, because there is a lack of resources and tools for Dialectal Arabic NLP. We can therefore use MSA tools and resources after mapping the dialect to MSA.

---

[34]http://en.wikipedia.org/wiki/Geographic_distribution_of_Arabic#Population

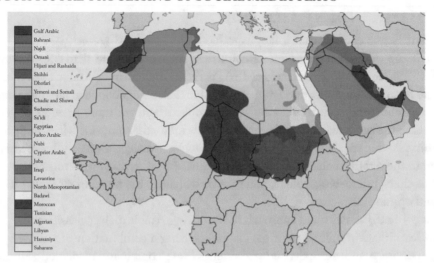

Figure 2.3: Arabic dialects distribution and variation across Asia and Africa [Sadat et al., 2014a].

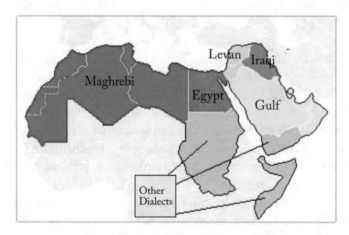

Figure 2.4: Division of Arabic dialects in six groups/divisions [Sadat et al., 2014a].

Diab et al. [2010] have run the COLABA project, a major effort to create resources and processing tools for Dialectal Arabic blogs. They used the BAMA and MAGEAD morphological analyzers. This project focused on four dialects: Egyptian, Iraqi, Levantine, and Moroccan.

Several tools for MSA regarding text processing—BAMA, MAGED, and MADA—will now be described briefly.

BAMA (Buckwalter Arabic Morphological Analyzer) provides morphological annotation for MSA. The BAMA database contains three tables of Arabic stems, complex prefixes, and complex suffixes and three additional tables used for controlling prefix-stem, stem-suffix, and prefix-suffix combinations [Buckwalter, 2004].

MAGEAD is a morphological analyzer and generator for the Arabic languages including MSA and the spoken dialects of Arabic. MAGEAD is modified to analyze the Levantine dialect [Habash and Rambow, 2006].

MADA+TOKEN is a toolkit for morphological analysis and disambiguation for the Arabic language that includes Arabic tokenization, discretization, disambiguation, POS tagging, stemming, and lemmatization. MADA selects the best analysis result within all possible analyses for each word in the current context by using SVM models classifying into 19 weighted morphological features. The selected analyses carry complete diacritic, lexemic, glossary, and morphological information. TOKEN takes the information provided by MADA to generate tokenized output in a wide variety of customizable formats. MADA depends on three resources: BAMA, the SRILM toolkit, and SVMTools [Habash et al., 2009].

Going back to the problem of AD identification, we give here a detailed example, with results. Sadat et al. [2014c] provided a framework for AD classification using probabilistic models across social media datasets. They incorporated the two popular techniques for language identification: the character n-gram Markov language model and Naïve Bayes classifiers.[35]

The Markov model calculates the probability that an input text is derived from a given language model built from training data [Dunning, 1994]. This model enables the computation of the probability $P(S)$ or likelihood, of a sentence S, by using the following chain formula in the following equation:

$$P(w_1, w_2, ..., w_n) = P(w_1) \prod_{i=2}^{n} P(w_i|w_1, ...w_{i-1}). \qquad (2.1)$$

The sequence $(w_1, w_2, ..., w_n)$ represents the sequence of characters in a sentence S. $P(w_i|w_1, ...w_{i-1})$ represents the probability of the character w_i given the sequence $w_1, ...w_{i-1}$.

A Naïve Bayes classifier is a simple probabilistic classifier based on applying Bayes' theorem with strong (naïve) independence assumptions. In text classification, this classifier assigns the most likely category or class to a given document d from a set of pre-defined N classes as $c_1, c_2, ..., c_N$. The classification function f maps a document to a category $(f : D \rightarrow C)$ by maximizing the probability of the following equation [Peng and Schuurmans, 2003]:

$$P(c|d) = \frac{P(c) \times P(d|c)}{P(d)}, \qquad (2.2)$$

where d and c denote the document and the category, respectively. In text classification a document d can be represented by a vector of T attributes $d = (t_1, t_2, ..., t_T)$. Assuming that all

---

[35]We will describe the concept of Naïve Bayes classifiers in detail in this section because they tend to work well on textual data and they are fast in terms of training and testing time.

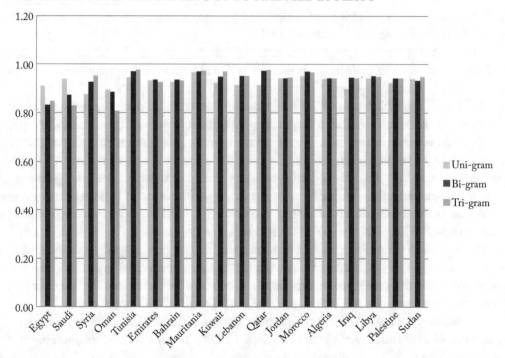

Figure 2.5: Accuracies on the character-based *n*-gram Markov language models for 18 countries [Sadat et al., 2014a].

attributes t_i are independent given the category c, we can calculate $P(d|c)$ with the following equation:

$$\operatorname*{argmax}_{c \in C} P(c|d) = \operatorname*{argmax}_{c \in C} P(c) \times \prod_{i=1}^{T} P(t_i|c). \qquad (2.3)$$

The attribute term t_i can be a vocabulary term, local *n*-gram, word average length, or a global syntactic and semantic property [Peng and Schuurmans, 2003].

Sadat et al. [2014c] presented a set of experiments using these techniques with detailed examination of what models perform best under different conditions in a social media context. Experimental results showed that the Naïve Bayes classifier based on character bigrams can identify the 18 different Arabic dialects considered with an overall accuracy of 98%. The dataset used in the experiments was manually collected from forums and blogs, for each of the 18 dialects.

To look at the problem in more detail, Sadat et al. [2014a] applied both the *n*-gram Markov language model and the Naïve Bayes classifier to classify the eighteen Arabic dialects. The results of this study for the *n*-gram Markov language model is represented in Figure 2.5. This figure shows that the character-based unigram distribution helps the identification of two

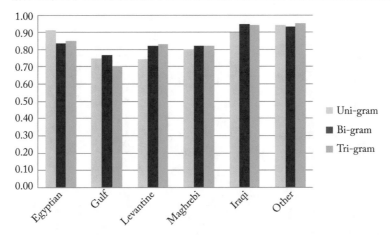

Figure 2.6: Accuracies on the character-based *n*-gram Markov language models for the six divisions/groups [Sadat et al., 2014a].

dialects, the Mauritanian and the Moroccan with an overall F-measure of 60% and an overall accuracy of 96%. Furthermore, the bigram distribution of 2 characters affix helps recognize 4 dialects, the Mauritanian, Moroccan, Tunisian, and Qatari, with an overall F-measure of 70% and overall accuracy of 97%. Lastly, the trigram distribution of three characters affix helps recognize four dialects, the Mauritanian, Tunisian, Qatari, and Kuwaiti, with an overall F-measure of 73% and an overall accuracy of 98%. Overall, for 18 dialects, the bigram model performed better than other models (unigram and trigram models).

Since many dialects are related to a region, and these Arabic dialects are approximately similar, the authors also considered the accuracy of dialects group. Figure 2.6 shows the result on the three different character *n*-gram Markov language models and a classification on the six groups of divisions that were defined in Figure 2.4. Again, the bigram and trigram character Markov language models performed almost the same as in Figure 2.5, although the F-Measure of the bigram model for all dialect groups was higher than for the trigram model, except for the Egyptian dialect. Therefore, on average, for all dialects, the character-based bigram language model performed better than the character-based unigram and trigram models.

Figure 2.7 shows the results on the *n*-gram models using Naïve Bayes classifiers for the different countries, while Figure 2.8 shows the results on the *n*-gram models using Naïve Bayes classifiers for the six divisions according to Figure 2.4. The results show that the Naïve Bayes classifiers based on character unigram, bigram, and trigram have better results than the previous character-based unigram, bigram, and trigram Markov language models, respectively. An overall F-measure of 72% and an accuracy of 97% were noticed for the 18 Arabic dialects. Furthermore, the Naïve Bayes classifier that is based on a bigram model has an overall F-measure of 80% and an accuracy of 98%, except for the Palestinian dialect because of the small size of the data.

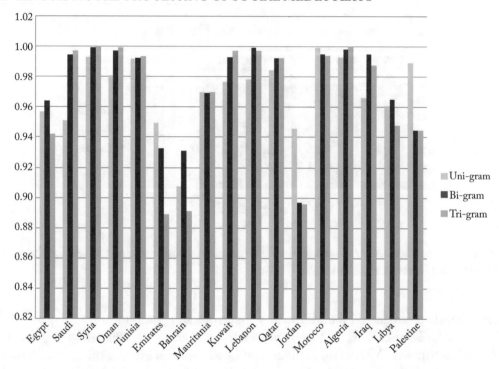

Figure 2.7: Accuracies on the character-based n-gram Naïve Bayes classifiers for 18 countries [Sadat et al., 2014a].

The Naïve Bayes classifier based on the trigram model showed an overall F-measure of 78% and an accuracy of 98% except for the Palestinian and Bahrain dialects. This classifier could not distinguish between the Bahrain and the Emirati dialects because of the similarities on their three affixes. In addition, the Naïve Bayes classifier based on character bigrams performed better than the classifier based on character trigrams, according to Figure 2.7. Also, as shown in Figure 2.8, the accuracy of dialect groups for the Naïve Bayes classifier based on character bigram model yielded better results than the two other models (unigrams and trigrams).

Recently, Zaidan and Callison-Burch [2014] created a large monolingual data set rich in dialectal Arabic content called the Arabic Online Commentary Dataset. They used crowd-sourcing for annotating the texts with the dialect label. They also presented experiments on the automatic classification of the dialects for this dataset, using similar word and character-based language models. The best results were around 85% accuracy for distinguishing MSA from dialectal data and lower accuracies for identifying the correct dialect for the latter case. Then they applied the classifiers to discover new dialectical data from a large Web crawl consisting of 3.5 million pages mined from online Arabic newspapers.

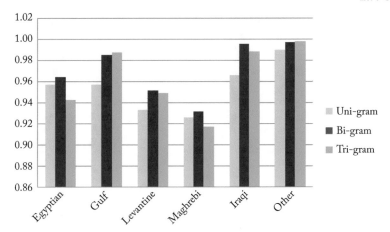

Figure 2.8: Accuracies on the character-based *n*-gram Naïve Bayes classifiers for the six divisions/groups [Sadat et al., 2014a].

Several other projects focused on Arabic dialects: classification [Tillmann et al., 2014], code switching [Elfardy and Diab, 2013], and collecting a Twitter corpus for several dialects [Mubarak and Darwish, 2014].

2.9   SUMMARY

This chapter discussed the issue of adapting NLP tools to social media texts. One way is to use text normalization techniques, in order to make the text closer to standard carefully edited texts on which the NLP tools are usually trained. The normalization that can be achieved in practice is rather shallow and it does not seem to help much in improving the performance of the tools. The second way of adapting the tools is to re-train them on annotated social media data. This significantly improves the performance, although the amount of annotated data available for re-training is still small. Further development of annotated data sets for social media data is needed in order to reach very high levels of performance.

In the next chapter, we will look at advanced methods for various NLP tasks for social media texts. These tasks use as components some of the tools discussed in this chapter.

CHAPTER 3

Semantic Analysis of Social Media Texts

3.1 INTRODUCTION

In this chapter, we discuss current NLP methods for social media applications that aim at extracting useful information from social media data. Examples of such applications are geo-location detection, opinion mining, emotion analysis, event and topic detection, summarization, machine translation, etc. We survey the current techniques, and we briefly define the evaluation measures used for each application, followed by examples of results.

Section 3.2 presents geo-location detection techniques. Section 3.3 discusses entity linking and disambiguation, a task that links detected entities to a database of known entities. Section 3.4 discusses the methods for opinion mining and sentiment analysis, including emotion and mood analysis. Section 3.5 presents event and topic detection. Section 3.6 highlights the various issues in automatic summarization in social media. Section 3.7 presents the adaptation of statistical and neural machine translation for social media text. Section 3.8 summarizes this chapter.

3.2 GEO-LOCATION DETECTION

One of the important topics in semantic analysis in social media is the identification of geo-location information for social content such as blog posts or tweets. By geo-location we mean a real location in the world, such as a region, or a city, or a point described by longitude and latitude. Automatic detection of event location for individuals or group of individuals with common interests is important for marketing purposes, and also for detecting potential threats to public safety.

Geo-location information could be readily available from the user profiles registered on the social network service; however, for several reasons, including privacy, not all users provide correct and precise information about their location. Therefore, other techniques such as inferring the location from the communication network infrastructure or from the text content need to be used in addition to the geo-location information available in some messages. It makes sense to combine multiple sources of evidence when they are available (geo-tags such as longitude, latitude, location names or other measures; the results from geo-location detection based on the content; and information from network infrastructure).

3.2.1   MAPPING SOCIAL MEDIA INFORMATION ON MAPS

Mapping Twitter conversations over time has become a popular way of visualizing conversations around events on the social media platform. A straightforward approach for visualizing tweets on a map is using GPS location information from the geo-tagged tweets. This information, however, is present only in around 1–5% of tweets, which makes for not-so-interesting visualizations of smaller events, or events in smaller countries where there are fewer people to tweet.

Heravi and Salawdeh [2015] presented a method of mapping Twitter conversations on maps to visualize conversations around events on Twitter. The paper presented a tweet location detection system (Twiloc) which uses various features in a tweet for predicting the most likely location for the tweet. The researchers used this as a part of their journalism work for mapping the Twitter conversations around the Ireland-Scotland Euro Qualifiers game. Twiloc resulted in 70% location geo-referenced tweets for this dataset, as opposed to the 4.5% originally geo-tagged tweets (by users). They further used Twiloc for geo-tagging the Dublin Marathon tweets and compared their results with the results they got from using CartoDB Tweet Maps for the same event. Twiloc resulted in slightly more geo-referenced tweets in comparison to CartoDB, 66.5% to 60%, respectively. Overall, Twiloc shows promising results for location detection and geo-tagging tweets on the datasets presented in the paper. However, further testing and evaluation of results for determining the quality of detected locations is required.

3.2.2   READILY AVAILABLE GEO-LOCATION INFORMATION

Information is becoming increasingly geographic as it becomes easier to geo-tag all forms of data, and many devices have embedded GPS [Backstrom et al., 2010]. Hecht et al. [2011] showed that, left to their own devices, the vast majority of users (64% of the geo-located tweets) prefer to provide their locational information at the city level, with state level coming in as second choice. Stefanidis et al. [2013] reported that approximately 16% of the Twitter feeds they have collected had detailed location information (coordinates), while another 45% had locational information at coarser granularity (e.g., city level). Cheng et al. [2010] reported that 5% of users in their study listed locational information at the level of coordinates, with another 21% of users listing locational information at the city level. This has directed the research community to focus on the techniques discussed below as alternatives to improve the identification of event and user locations from social networks.

3.2.3   GEO-LOCATION BASED ON NETWORK INFRASTRUCTURE

The geo-location information can be deduced from the network infrastructure. Poese et al. [2011] and Eriksson et al. [2010] proposed using IP addresses. They use geo-location databases for linking IP addresses to locations. There are several databases that can be used for mapping between IP blocks and a geographic location. They are usually accurate at country level, but they are a lot less accurate at city level. Poese et al. [2011] showed that these databases are not very reliable, for the following reasons. First, the vast majority of entries in the databases refer only to a few popular countries (such as U.S.). This creates an imbalance in the representation of countries across the IP blocks of the databases. Second, the entries do not always reflect the original allocation of IP blocks. Eriksson et al. [2010] used a Naïve Bayes classifier to achieve a better accuracy for location prediction based on IP mappings from several sources.

3.2.4   GEO-LOCATION BASED ON THE SOCIAL NETWORK STRUCTURE

Another approach to geolocating users of online social networks can be based solely on their lists of friends ("you are where your friends are") or follower-followee relations. Users tend to interact more regularly with other users close to themselves and, in many cases, a person's social network is sufficient to reveal their location [Rout et al., 2013]. Backstrom et al. [2010] were the first to create a model for the distribution of the distances between pairs of friends; then they used this distribution to find the most likely location for a given user. The disadvantage of the approach is that it assumes that all users have the same distribution of friends in terms of distance and it does not account for the density of the population in each area. Rout et al. [2013] showed that using the density of the population leads to more accurate user location detection. They also parsed the location field from the users' Twitter profile as an additional source of information. An analysis of how users use the location field was presented by Hecht et al. [2011].

3.2.5   CONTENT-BASED LOCATION DETECTION

Geo-location information can be determined from the content of the tweets, Facebook, and blog postings, although this is challenging because the location names mentioned in these texts are often ambiguous. For example, there might exist several cities with the same name, so a disambiguation module is needed. Another level of ambiguity is to detect locations in the first place, to not confuse them with proper names. For example, *Georgia* can be the name of a person, the name of a state in the U.S., or the name of a country. The challenges are even bigger in social media text where users might not use capital letters for names and locations, giving Named Entity Recognition (NER) tools a harder time.

As mentioned in Chapter 2, some NER tools detect entities such as People, Organizations, and Locations. Therefore, they include locations, but they do not target such more detailed information as: is the location a city, a province, state, or county, in what country is it, etc. Location detection should also go further to disambiguate the location when there is more than one geographic location with the same name. For example, there are many cities named *Ottawa*, in different countries. The largest in terms of population size is *Ottawa, ON, Canada*. There are three cities in different U.S. states: *Ottawa, IL, Ottawa, KS*, and *Ottawa, OH*. There are also several other smaller places named *Ottawa*: a city in *Ivory Coast*, a county in *Quebec*, a small village in *Wisconsin, U.S.*, and *Ottawa, KwaZulu-Natal, South Africa*. It is not trivial to decide which of the locations with the same name is referred to in a context. If there is evidence about the country or the state/province, a decision can be based on this information. A default choice is always to choose the city with the largest population, since there is a higher chance that more people from a larger place post messages about that location.

Finding Location-indicative Words

Han et al. [2012] presented a method of finding and ranking location-indicative words (LIWs) via feature selection. As a first step, to determine the statistical "signature" of LIWs, they use manually pre-identified seed sets of: (1) local words (denoted as 1-local) that are used primarily in a single city, namely "yinz" (used in Pittsburgh to designate locals), "dippy" (used in Pittsburgh to refer to a style of fried egg, or something that can be dipped in coffee, etc.), and "hoagie" (used primarily in Philadelphia, to refer to a kind of sandwich); (2) semi-local words (n-local) that refer to some feature of a relatively limited subset of cities, namely "ferry" (found, *e.g.*, in Seattle, New York, and Sydney), "Chinatown" (common in many of the largest cities in the USA, Canada, and Australia, but much less common in European and Asian cities), and "tram" (found, *e.g.*, in Vienna, Melbourne, and Prague); and (3) common words (common) which are not expected to have substantial regional frequency variation, namely "Twitter," "iPhone," and "today." They use this small set of nine words to empirically motivate this feature selection approach. Their results show that an information-gain ratio-based approach surpasses other methods at LIW selection, outperforming state-of-the-art geolocation prediction methods by 10.6% in accuracy and reducing the mean and median of prediction error distance by 45 km and 209 km, respectively, on the dataset of Roller et al. [2012] (adapted at city level instead of user level).

User Locations

Detecting the physical location of a user is a different task than detecting the locations of the events mentioned in the text content, but similar techniques can disambiguate the location when there exist several locations with the same name. A user who has a Twitter account can write anything in the space for user location, a fully correct name with province/state and country, but could also specify only the city name. Sometimes any string or misspellings are found in that field. Many users do not specify their location at all.

Several methods have been proposed to predict users' locations based on the social media texts data they generate. One of the very first is by Cheng et al. [2010], who first learned the location distribution for each word, then inferred the location of users at the U.S. city level according to the words in their tweets. Specifically, they estimated the posterior probability of a user being from a city c given all his/her tweets t by computing:

$$P(c|t) = \prod_{w \in t} P(c|w) \times P(w), \qquad (3.1)$$

where w is a word contained in this user's tweets. To improve the initial results, they also used several smoothing techniques such as Laplace smoothing, a so-called *data-driven geographic smoothing*, and a *model-based smoothing*. The size of the dataset collected in their work is large, containing 4,124,960 tweets from 130,689 users.

A topic model approach was proposed by Eisenstein et al. [2010]. They treated tweets as documents generated by two latent variables, topic, and region, and trained a system called *geographic topic model*, which could predict authors' locations based on text alone. The classes were U.S. states for the first task, U.S. regions (North-East, North-West, South-East, and South-West) for the second task, and numerical values for longitude and latitude for a third task. Similar to Cheng et al. [2010], their model also relied on learning regional word distributions. The average distance from the model's predictions to the actual locations (as declared by users) was 900 km. By comparison, their dataset is much smaller, containing 380,000 tweets from 9,500 users from the contiguous United States (excluding Hawaii, Alaska, and all off-shore territories), annotated automatically based on the provided user geo-coordinates. This dataset is made available,[1] and it has been used by a number of researchers.

Roller et al. [2012] used a variant of the K-Nearest Neighbors classifier;[2] they divided the geographic surface of the Earth into *grids* and then constructed a pseudo-document for each grid; a location for a test document was chosen based on the most similar pseudo-document. Their dataset is available,[3] and it is very large (the tweets of 429,694 users for training, 10,000 users for validation, and 10,000 users for testing). Another type of model was a variant of Gaussian mixture models (GMMs) proposed by Priedhorsky et al. [2014]. Their approach resembles that of Cheng et al. [2010] in constructing location-sensitive *n*-grams; besides the text of the tweets, they also used information such as users' time zones for prediction. Han et al. [2014] investigated a range of feature selection methods to obtain location-indicative words and evaluated the impact of non-geotagged tweets, language, and user-declared metadata on geolocation prediction. Liu and Inkpen [2015] proposed a deep neural network (DeepNN) architecture for the same task. They built three models (one to predict U.S. states, one for U.S. regions, and one for the numeric values of longitude and latitude). They tested the models on both the Eisenstein dataset and the Roller dataset, with results similar to the state-of-the-art.

On other types of social media data than tweets, we mention the work of Popescu and Grefenstette [2010], who presented methods for analyzing textual metadata associated with Flickr photos that unveil users' home location and gender, and the work of Backstrom et al. [2010], who introduced an algorithm that predicts the location of Facebook users by analyzing their social networks. Wing and Baldridge [2014] used data from Twitter, Wikipedia, and Flickr. They applied logistic regression models to a hierarchy of nodes in the grid (the same grid as that used by Roller et al. [2012]).

---

[1]http://www.ark.cs.cmu.edu/GeoTwitter

[2]A machine learning algorithm that computes the k most similar training data points for a new test document and assigns it the majority class of the *k* neighbors.

[3]https://github.com/utcompling/textgrounder/wiki/RollerEtAl_EMNLP2012

Location Mentions

Detecting all locations mentioned in a message differs from detecting the location of each user. The mentions could refer to locations near the user's homes, or to places they travel to, or to events anywhere in the world. The methods of detecting locations mentioned in messages are similar to those used for NER. The most successful methods use machine learning classifiers such as CRF to detect sequences of words that represent locations. Gazetteers and other dictionaries or geographical resources play an important role. They could contain a list of places: cities, states/provinces/counties, countries, rivers, mountains, etc. Abbreviations for country codes, states or provinces, etc., need to be considered when detecting the locations, as well as alternative spellings for places (e.g., *Los Angeles—L.A. – LA*). One very useful resource for this kind of information is GeoNames,[4] a geographical database that covers all countries and contains over eight million place names, available for download free of charge. It contains information about countries, cities, mountains, lakes, and a lot more. Another available resource is OpenStreetMap.[5] It is open in the sense that people can add new locations and the resources it provides can be used for any purpose (with attribution). The main advantage of using it is that it offers the possibility to display any detected locations on the map.

Sequence classification techniques (such as CRF) are most useful when detecting location expressions mentioned in texts. Inkpen et al. [2015] proposed methods of extracting locations mentioned in texts and disambiguating them when a location can also be a proper name, or a common noun, or when multiple locations with the same name exist. This is a sub-task of named entity recognition, but with deeper focus on location mentions in text in order to classify them as cities, provinces/states, or countries. The authors annotated a dataset of 6,000 Twitter messages.[6] An initial annotation was done using gazetteer lookups in GATE [Cunningham et al., 2002], then two annotators performed manual annotations in order to add, correct, or remove missing locations. The kappa coefficient for the agreement between the annotators was 0.88, as measured on a sample of 1,000 messages. An example of annotated tweet is displayed in Table 3.1. Then CRF classifiers were trained with various sets of features (such as bag of word, gazetteer, part-of-speech, and context-based features) to detect spans of text that denote the locations. In the next stage, the authors applied disambiguation rules in case a detected location mention corresponded to more than one geographic location.

Another dataset of social media data annotated with location expressions was produced by Liu et al. [2014]. It contains a variety of social media data: 500 blogs, 500 YouTube comments, 500 forums, 1,000 Twitter messages, and 500 English Wikipedia articles.[7] The annotated location expressions are generic, without distinguishing the type of location or the exact geographical location.

---

[4]http://www.geonames.org/
[5]http://www.openstreetmap.org
[6]https://github.com/rex911/locdet
[7]The data is available at http://people.eng.unimelb.edu.au/tbaldwin/etc/locexp-locweb2014.tgz.

Table 3.1: An example of annotation with the true location [Inkpen et al., 2015]

Mon Jun 24 23:52:31 +0000 2013
\<location locType='city', trueLoc='22321'\>Seguin \</location\>
\<location locType='SP', trueLoc='12'\>Tx \</location\>
RT himawari0127i: #RETWEET#TEAMFAIRYROSE #TMW #TFBJP #500aday #ANDROID #JP
#FF #Yes #No #RT #ipadgames #TAF #NEW #TRU #TLA #THF 51

3.2.6   EVALUATION MEASURES FOR GEO-LOCATION DETECTION

For user location, the set of classes could be fixed (for example states or regions), in which case the accuracy of the classification is often reported. When longitude and latitude are predicted, the distance from the predicted to the actual location is often reported in kilometers or in miles, as a measure of the prediction error [Eisenstein et al., 2010].

For location mentions in texts, the set of locations is open, the task is information extraction where a place can be denoted by one or more consecutive words. The evaluation measures for location mention detection are often the precision of the extracted locations (among the locations found, how many are correct), recall (how many of the mentioned locations are retrieved), and the F-measure that combines the two. These measures are often reported at text span level (therefore penalizing if a word is missing from an expression or if there are extra words), and at token level, which is more lenient. For matching a location phrase to an actual location, accuracy is often reported [Inkpen et al., 2015].

Results For detecting user locations based on all the tweets written by each user, the best model of Cheng et al. [2010] managed to make acceptable numeric predictions (less than 100 miles away from the actual location) 51% of the time, and the average error distance was 535.564 miles. Eisenstein et al. [2010] reported accuracies of 24% at state level and 58% at region level on their dataset of 380,000 tweets from 9,500 users (20% of the dataset was used as a test set, and the rest was used for training and development). On the same test set, Liu and Inkpen [2015] reported accuracies of 34% at state level and 61% at region level. Similar results were reported in most of the papers cited in the user location detection section above.

For more comparison, we show detailed results for user location detection on two datasets. Results on the dataset of Eisenstein et al. [2010] are shown in Table 3.2. The DeepNN model of Liu and Inkpen [2015] gives the best results, an accuracy of 61.1% and 34.8%, for region classification and state classification, respectively. Among all previous work that uses the same dataset, only Eisenstein et al. [2010] report the classification accuracy of their models. It is surprising to find that the simple models based on SVM and Naïve Bayes performed well. Table 3.3 shows the mean error distance for various models trained on the same dataset. Table 3.4 compares the results of various models on the Roller dataset. The model of Han et al. [2014], which

Table 3.2: Classification accuracies for user location detection on the Eisenstein dataset [Liu and Inkpen, 2015]

Model	Accuracy (%) (4 Regions)	Accuracy (%) (49 States)
Geo topic model [Eisenstein et al., 2010]	58.0	24.0
DeepNN model [Liu and Inkpen, 2015]	**61.1**	**34.8**
Naïve Bayes	54.8	30.1
SVM	56.4	27.5

Table 3.3: Mean error distance of predictions on the Eisenstein dataset [Liu and Inkpen, 2015]

Model	Mean Error Distance (km)
[Liu and Inkpen, 2015]	**855.9**
[Priedhorsky et al., 2014]	870.0
[Roller et al., 2012]	897.0
[Eisenstein et al., 2010]	900.0

Table 3.4: Results for user location prediction on the Roller dataset [Liu and Inkpen, 2015]

Model	Mean Error (km)	Median Error (km)	Accuracy (%)
[Roller et al., 2012]	860	463	34.6
[Han et al., 2014]	-	260	45.0
[Liu and Inkpen, 2015]	733	377	24.2

included extensive feature engineering, outperformed other models. The DeepNN model, despite the computational limitation, achieved better results than that of Roller et al. [2012] using a smaller number of features.

For detecting locations mentioned in each message, the F-measure obtained by Inkpen et al. [2015] was about 0.80 at the text span level for city names, and 0.90 for states/provinces and a similar value for country names, on their dataset of 6,000 tweets (reported for cross-validation). See Table 3.5 for the results at city level, which was the most difficult class due to the variety of names. The table shows precision, recall, and F-measure at token level and at span level, for the CRF classifier with various sets of features (Gazetteer, BoW, parts of speech, and windows features). We can see that adding more specific types of features improves the results. The results

Table 3.5: Performance of the classifiers trained on different features for cities [Inkpen et al., 2015]

Features	Token			Span			Separate Test Set	
	P	R	F	P	R	F	Token F	Span F
Baseline-Gazetteer Matching	0.14	0.71	0.23	0.13	0.68	0.22	–	–
Baseline-BOW	0.91	0.59	0.71	0.87	0.56	0.68	0.70	0.68
BOW+POS	0.87	0.60	0.71	0.84	0.55	0.66	0.71	0.68
BOW+GAZ	0.84	0.77	0.80	0.81	0.75	0.78	0.78	0.75
BOW+WIN	0.87	0.71	0.78	0.85	0.69	0.76	0.77	0.77
BOW+POS+GAZ	0.85	**0.78**	0.71	0.82	**0.75**	0.78	0.79	0.77
BOW+WIN+GAZ	**0.91**	0.76	0.82	**0.89**	0.74	**0.81**	**0.82**	0.81
BOW+POS+WIN	0.82	0.76	0.79	0.80	**0.75**	0.77	0.80	0.79
BOW+POS+WIN+GAZ	0.89	0.77	**0.83**	0.87	**0.75**	**0.81**	0.81	**0.82**

are reported by cross-validation of the dataset of 6,000 tweets, and when training on 70% of the data and testing on the remaining 30%, with similar results. For the exact geographical locations on the map that correspond to the location phrases, the accuracy was up to 98% (as evaluated on a small sample of the test data with disambiguated physical locations). Liu et al. [2014] reported results on extracting generic location expressions. The authors evaluated existing NER tools (for locations only) on this dataset, with rather low results (F-measures in the range of 0.30–0.42).

3.3   ENTITY LINKING AND DISAMBIGUATION

In the previous section, we have discussed extensions of the NER task with a focus on determining different kinds of locations mentioned in social media texts, disambiguating them to real locations, as well as determining the users' locations. One of the first works in recognition and semantic disambiguation of named entities in newspaper stories, based on information extracted from Wikipedia, was proposed by Cucerzan [2007]. Then there were shared tasks at Text Analysis Conference (TAC) on Knowledge Base Population (KBP) (2009–2013) in order to foster the development and evaluation of technologies for building and populating knowledge bases about named entities from unstructured text. A snapshot of the English Wikipedia from October 2008 was used as the knowledge base.[8] Each node in the reference knowledge base corresponds to a Wikipedia page for a person (PER), organization (ORG), or geopolitical entity (GPE) and consists of predefined attributes ("slots") derived from Wikipedia infoboxes. Unstructured text from the Wikipedia page is also available in the reference knowledge base.

---

[8]http://www.nist.gov/tac/2013/KBP/

3.3.1   DETECTING ENTITIES AND LINKED DATA

In this section, we discuss the task of extracting entities from social media texts and disambiguating them to linked data entities. *Linked data* is a term used for data resources that are created using Semantic Web standards. Examples of linked data resources are DBpedia, YAGO, and BabelNet.[9] DBPedia is a crowd-sourced community effort to extract structured information from Wikipedia and make this information available on the Web. It facilitates sophisticated queries against Wikipedia, and linking the different datasets on the Web to Wikipedia data. YAGO[10] is a large semantic knowledge base, derived from Wikipedia, WordNet, and GeoNames. Currently, YAGO has knowledge of more than 10 million entities (persons, organizations, cities, etc.) and contains more than 120 million facts about these entities. BabelNet[11] is both a multilingual encyclopedic dictionary, with lexicographic and encyclopedic coverage of terms, and a semantic network which connects concepts and named entities in a very large network of semantic relations, made up of more than 13 million entries, called Babel synsets. Each Babel synset represents a given meaning and contains all the synonyms which express that meaning in a range of different languages.

One of the main goals of the Linked Data initiative is to allow automatic systems to make use of this structured information. The Linked Data initiative defines the best practices for publishing and connecting structured data on the Web, in order to address the key drawbacks of the classic Web (Web 2.0): lack of content structuring and lack of support for expressive queries and content processing for applications. With the change from linked documents to data linking, the Web could become a global data space. Linked data provide the opportunity of obtaining complete answers with the evolution of new data sources. The key characteristics that underlie linked data are machine readability, clearly defined meaning, and the capability of being linked to and from external data sources [Bizer et al., 2009].

The key criteria for the existence of Linked Data are documents containing data in the RDF (Resource Description Framework) format. The two main technologies that are used in Linked Data are Uniform Resource Identifier (URI) and HyperText Transfer Protocol (HTTP). The capability of representing a more generic overview has made URIs an entity identification mechanism preferred to URLs. In addition, the document representation in the RDF format resembles a graph-based model represented by triples, Subject, Predicate, and Object, which in turn resembles a URI representing a resource, relationship between Subject and Object and similar representation of a resource. HTTP is used as the data access mechanism and RDF as the data model, simplifying data access and clear separation from data presentation and formatting.

The key components for constructing this Web of data are the vocabularies: collections of classes and properties expressed in RDF using RDFS (RDF Schema)[12] and OWL (Web Ontol-

---

[9]http://dbpedia.org/About
[10]http://www.mpi-inf.mpg.de/departments/databases-and-information-systems/research/yago-naga/yago/
[11]http://babelnet.org/about
[12]http://www.w3.org/TR/rdf-schema/

ogy Language).[13] The RDF triples can be used in creating links between classes and properties between vocabularies. OWL is a Semantic Web language used to represent rich and complex knowledge about things, group of things, and relations between things (as defined by the World Wide Web Consortium, W3C,[14] in 2012). RDFS is an extension of the RDF vocabulary which provides a data modeling vocabulary (as defined by W3C in 2014).

Prior to publishing linked data, it is important to determine the key entities, properties, and their relationships. Once identified, the information has to be published using RDF linked with other relevant data sources. In further illustrating the publication process, several key steps can be identified: selecting or creating a vocabulary; partitioning data meaningfully into several pages rather than publishing everything in one page having a URI to identify each page and entity; adding metadata to each page; and creating a semantic site map.

Several online tools try to identify named entities in text and link them to linked data resources. Although one can use these tools via their API and Web interfaces, they use different data resources and different techniques to identify named entities, and not all of them reveal this information. One of the major tasks in NER is disambiguation—identifying the right entity among a number of entities with the same names. For example, *apple* stands for both *Apple, Inc.* the company and for the fruit. Hakimov et al. [2012] developed such a tool called NERSO (Named Entity Recognition Using Semantic Open Data) to automatically extract named entities, disambiguate and link them to DBpedia entities. Their disambiguation method is based on constructing a graph of linked data entities and scoring them using a graph-based centrality algorithm.

There have been attempts to map microblog posts (most often tweets) to encyclopedia articles [Lösch and Müller, 2011] or other linked data. Most of the methods are based on exploring the semantic networks of linked data, by matching the texts of the messages within the semantic networks, and then using graph processing techniques for disambiguation. Ferragina and Scaiella [2010] presented a system that annotates short text fragments with Wikipedia entities. Hakimov et al. [2012] also detected entities and disambiguated them using linked data and graph-based centrality scoring. Meij et al. [2012] added semantics to microblog posts by similar linking to encyclopedic resources. Dlugolinský et al. [2014] combined several named entity recognition methods for concept extraction in microposts. Bellaachia and Al-Dhelaan [2014] extracted key phrases from messages using graph-based methods. Prapula et al. [2014] automatically detected significant events related to each entity, by detecting episodes among the streaming tweets related to the given entity over a period of time (from the entity's birth) and providing visual information like sentiment scoring and frequency of tweets over time for each episode.

Moro et al. [2014] presented a unified graph-based approach to entity linking for the named entities and word sense disambiguation of the common nouns, based on a loose iden-

---

[13]http://www.w3.org/2001/sw/wiki/OWL
[14]http://www.w3.org/

tification of candidate meanings coupled with a densest subgraph heuristic which selects high-coherence semantic interpretations. Their method had three steps: (1) the automatic creation of semantic signatures, i.e., related concepts and named entities, for each node in the reference semantic network; (2) the unconstrained identification of candidate meanings for all possible textual fragments; and (3) the linking based on a high-coherence densest subgraph algorithm. Their system, called Babelfy,[15] uses BabelNet as the linked data resource. Gella et al. [2014] looks at word-sense disambiguation specifically for Twitter messages.

Derczynski et al. [2014] compared several named entity linking (NEL) systems, including YODIE, DBpedia Spotlight, Zemanta, and TextRazor. The researchers generated a corpus of 177 entity mentions across 182 microblog texts. Among the reviewed NEL systems, YODIE performed the best with an F-score of 0.45. The researchers note that the main challenges in microblog texts stem from their short length, noisy content, lack of context, and multilingualism. However, they concluded that effective preprocessing is the key to improve the performance of NEL tasks involving microblogs.

Dredze et al. [2016] endeavoured to construct a social media corpus for cross-document coreference resolution—a problem closely related to disambiguation, but without a knowledge base to link entities. Using the Twitter Streaming API, the researchers pulled tweets from the day of the Grammy Awards Show, or the "Grammies." From these tweets, they distilled a corpus that included hashtags related to the Grammies and included mentions of particular people. This final set included 15,736 tweets. They randomly selected five thousand tweets for annotation. With this corpus, they then experimented with the Green and Phylo cross-document coreference resolution models. In the Green model, entities with dissimilar mention strings were flagged as unable to be linked. With that constraint, entities were then disambiguated using hierarchical clustering. The Phylo model learned groups of name variants via transducers, then attempted to link terms it predicted to be variants of each other. In this experiment, the Green model outperformed the Phylo model.

Moon et al. [2018] introduced a new task called Multimodal Named Entity Recognition for noisy user-generated data such as tweets or Snapchat captions, which comprise short text with accompanying images. These social media posts often come in inconsistent or incomplete syntax and lexical notations with very limited surrounding textual contexts, bringing significant challenges for NER. They created a new dataset called SnapCaptions (Snapchat image-caption pairs submitted to public and crowd-sourced stories with fully annotated named entities). Then, they built a state-of-the-art Bi-LSTM word/character-based NER models with a deep image network which incorporates relevant visual context to augment textual information, and a generic modality-attention module which learns to attenuate irrelevant modalities while amplifying the most informative ones to extract contexts from, adaptive to each sample and token. The proposed model with modality attention significantly outperforms the state-of-the-art text-only NER models by successfully leveraging provided visual contexts.

---

[15]http://babelfy.org

3.3.2   EVALUATION MEASURES FOR ENTITY LINKING

The evaluation measure most often used in the task of entity linking are precision, recall, F-measure, and accuracy, since this is an information extraction task.

Results For this task, Moro et al. [2014] report the results on two datasets. KORE50 [Hoffart et al., 2012] consists of 50 short English sentences (mean length of 14 words) with a total number of 144 mentions manually annotated using YAGO2, for which a Wikipedia mapping is available. This dataset was built with the idea of testing against a high level of ambiguity for the entity linking task. AIDA-CoNLL6 [Hoffart et al., 2011] consists of 1,392 English articles, for a total of roughly 35,000 named entity mentions annotated with YAGO concepts separated in development, training, and test sets. The reported accuracy for their system and several other state-of-the art systems was up to 71% on the first dataset and up to 82% on the second dataset, but those were not social media texts. The shared tasks at the Making Sense of Microposts series of workshops made available Twitter data annotated with entities for the participants in the task to test their entity linking methods. The results reported for the shared tasks are lower, because the task is more difficult.

3.4   OPINION MINING AND EMOTION ANALYSIS

3.4.1   SENTIMENT ANALYSIS

What people think is always an important piece of information. Asking a friend to recommend a dentist or writing a reference letter for a job application are examples of this importance in our daily life [Liu, 2012, Pang and Lee, 2008]. On social media platforms such as weblogs, social blogs, microblogging, wikis, and discussion forums, people can easily express and share their opinions. These opinions can be accessed by people who need more information in order to make decisions. The complexity of these decisions varies from simple things, such as choosing a restaurant for lunch or buying a smartphone, to such grave matters as approving laws in the parliament and even critical decisions such as monitoring public safety by security officers.

Due to the mass of information exchanged daily on social media, the traditional monitoring techniques are not useful. Therefore, a number of research directions aim to establish automated tools which should be intelligent enough to extract the opinion of a writer from a given text. Processing a text in order to identify and extract its subjective information is known as sentiment analysis, also referred to as opinion mining.[16] The basic goal of sentiment analysis is to identify the overall polarity of a document: positive, negative, or neutral [Pang and Lee, 2008]. The polarity magnitude is also taken into account, for example on a scale of 1–5 stars for movie reviews. Sentiment analysis is not an easy job even for humans, because sometimes two people disagree on the sentiment expressed in a given text. Therefore, such analysis is a difficult

---

[16]The terms sentiment analysis and opinion mining tend to be used inter-changeably, but there are subtle differences between them. An opinion is a belief, while a sentiment is a feeling.

task for the algorithms and it gets harder when the texts get shorter. Another challenge is to connect the opinion to the entity that is the target of the opinion, and it is often the case that there are multiple aspects of the entities. Users could express positive opinions toward some aspects and negative toward other aspects (for example, a user could like a hotel for its location but not for its quality). Popescu and Etzioni [2005], among others, developed methods for extracting aspects and opinions on them from product reviews.

There is a huge demand from major companies, so most research has focused on product reviews, aiming to predict whether a review has a positive or a negative opinion. There also is, however, some research on investigating the sentiment of informal social interactions. From the perspective of social sciences, the informal social interactions provide more clues about the public opinion about various topics. For instance, a study was conducted to measure the levels of happiness based on the sentiment analysis of the songs, blogs, and presidential speeches [Dodds and Danforth, 2010]. In this study, the age and geographic differences in the levels of happiness were analyzed as well.

One of the social concerns is the dramatic changes in social interactions when an important event occurs. These changes can be detected by a sharp increase in the frequency of terms related to the event. Identifiable changes are useful in detecting new events and determining their importance for the public [Thelwall et al., 2011].

Although the analysis of social interaction is similar to product review analysis, there are many differences between these two domains: the length of the context (a product review is longer than a typical social interaction); the topic of the context which could be anything in social interaction but is known in a product review; and the informality of the spelling and the frequent use of abbreviations in social media texts. Furthermore, in informal social interactions, no clear standard exists, while metadata (such as star rating and thumbing up/down) often accompany product reviews [Paltoglou and Thelwall, 2012].

There are many challenges when one applies typical opinion mining and sentiment analysis techniques to social media [Maynard et al., 2012]. Microposts such as tweets are challenging because they do not contain much contextual information and assume much implicit knowledge. Ambiguity is a particular problem since we cannot easily make use of coreference information. Unlike in blog posts and comments, tweets do not typically follow a conversation thread, and appear more in isolation from other tweets. They also exhibit more language variation, tend to be less grammatical than longer posts, contain non-standard capitalization, and make frequent use of emoticons, abbreviations, and hashtags, which can form an important part of the meaning. Typically, they also contain extensive use of irony and sarcasm, which are particularly difficult for a machine to detect. On the other hand, they tend to focus on the topics more explicitly and most often a tweet is about a single topic.

Twitter was often targeted by sentiment analysis projects in order to investigate how the public mood is affected by the social, political, cultural, and economic events. Guerra et al. [2014] showed that Twitter users tend to report more positive opinions than negative ones, and more extreme opinions rather than average ones. This has an effect on the training data that can be collected, because imbalanced data are more difficult for classification tasks.

A benchmark dataset was created for a shared task at SemEval 2013 (sentiment analysis in Twitter).[17] The dataset consists of approximately 8,000 tweets annotated with the labels: positive, negative, neutral, and objective (no opinion). There were two sub-tasks. Given a message that contains a marked instance of a word or phrase, the goal of Task A was to determine whether that instance is positive, negative, or neutral in that context. The goal of Task B was to classify whether the message expresses a positive, negative, or neutral sentiment. For messages conveying both a positive and negative sentiment, the stronger sentiment needed to be chosen. There were also messages annotated as objective, expressing facts not opinions. Here is an example of one of the annotated messages. It includes the message ID, the user ID, the topic, the label, and the text of the message:

100032373000896513 15486118 lady gaga "positive" Wow!! Lady Gaga is actually at the Britney Spears Femme Fatale Concert tonight!!! She still listens to her music!!!! WOW!!!

More editions have been held at SemEval 2014,[18] 2015,[19] and 2016[20] and more datasets were released, for various sub-tasks (an expression-level task, a message-level task, a topic-related task, a trend task, and a task on prior polarity of terms).

The methods used in sentiment analysis are based on learning from annotated data, or on counting the number of positive and negative terms. Hybrid systems were also proposed. Many lists of positive and negative terms were developed, all of them with limited coverage. Also, some words have different polarity depending on the sense of the word in the context or in the domain. Here are several lists of positive/negative words, called polarity lexicons: the General Inquirer [Stone et al., 1962], the MPQA polarity lexicon [Wiebe et al., 2005], Senti-WordNet [Baccianella et al., 2010], Bing Liu's polarity lexicon [Hu and Liu, 2004], and LIWC (Linguistic Inquiry and Word Count) [Pennebaker et al., 2007]. Intensity levels for these words could also be available in some of the resources. The lexicons can be used directly in methods that count polarity-bearing words (then choose as the text polarity the one that corresponds to the largest value according to some formula, possibly normalized by the length of the text), or these counts (values) can be used as features in machine learning techniques. The task is difficult because of the polarity of the words changes with the domain and even in the same domain it changes in different contexts [Wilson et al., 2009]. Another drawback of using lexicons is their limited coverage, but they can still be useful as a basis to which domain specific words and their polarities can be added.

An early work that focused on sentiment classification in Twitter messages was done by Go et al. [2009]. They classified messages as either positive or negative with respect to a query term.

---

[17]http://www.cs.york.ac.uk/semeval-2013/task2/

[18]http://alt.qcri.org/semeval2014/task9/

[19]http://alt.qcri.org/semeval2015/task10/

[20]http://alt.qcri.org/semeval2016/task4/

This is useful for consumers who want to research the sentiment of products before purchase, or companies that want to monitor the public sentiment of their brands. They used machine learning algorithms (Naïve Bayes, Maximum Entropy, and SVM) for classifying the sentiment of Twitter messages using distant supervision. Distant supervision means that the training data was automatically collected by using positive and negative emoticons as noisy labels. This type of training data is easy to collect, but is not very reliable. Pak and Paroubek [2010b] also collected automatically a corpus for sentiment analysis and opinion mining purposes from Twitter and built a classifier to determine positive, negative, and neutral sentiments.

Adjectives were considered the most important features in sentiment analysis, starting from the early work on customer reviews [Hatzivassiloglou and McKeown, 1997]. Moghaddam and Popowich [2010] determined the polarity of reviews by identifying the polarity of the adjectives that appear in them. Pak and Paroubek [2010a] studied ambiguous sentiment adjectives and presented experiments on the SemEval 2010 data, for the task of disambiguating sentiment ambiguous adjectives for Chinese.

Many of the methods from the sentiment analysis in the Twitter SemEval task are based on machine learning methods that use a large variety of features, from simple (words) to complex linguistic and sentiment-related features. Mohammad et al. [2013] used SVM classifiers with features such as: n-grams, character n-grams, emoticons, hashtags, capitalization information, parts of speech, negation features, word clusters, and multiple lexicons. In the 2015 sub-tasks, similarly to the previous two years, almost all systems used supervised learning. Popular machine learning approaches included SVM, Maximum Entropy, CRFs, and linear regression. In several of the subtasks, the top system used deep neural networks and word embeddings, and some systems benefited from special weighting of the positive and negative examples. The most important features were those derived from sentiment lexicons. Other important features included bag-of-word features, hashtags, handling of negation, word shape and punctuation features, elongated words, etc. Moreover, tweet pre-processing and normalization were an important part of the processing pipeline [Rosenthal et al., 2015].

3.4.2   EMOTION ANALYSIS

Emotion analysis emerged as a task somewhat more specific than opinion analysis, since it looks at fine-grained types of emotion. Research on emotion detection started with Holzman and Pottenger [2003] and Rubin et al. [2004] who investigated emotion detection on very small datasets. More recently, work was done on classifying blog sentences [Aman and Szpakowicz, 2007] and newspaper headlines [Strapparava and Mihalcea, 2007] into the six classes of emotions proposed by Ekman [1992]. Classification of sentences by emotions was also done into the nine classes of emotions proposed by Izard [1971], for types of sentences [Neviarouskaya et al., 2009] and on sentences from fairy tales [Alm et al., 2005].

There is no consensus on how many emotion classes should be used. Plutchik's wheel of emotions proposes many emotions and arranges them in a wheel where each emotion type has a corresponding emotion with inverse polarity [Plutchik and Kellerman, 1980]. Ekman's six emotions classes (*happiness, anger, sadness, fear, disgust*, and *surprise*) are the ones used more often because they have associated facial expressions [Ekman, 1992].

Most of the methods used in emotion classification are based on machine learning. SVM classifiers tend to achieve the best results on this task. Rule-based approaches were also proposed [Neviarouskaya et al., 2009]. Lists of emotion words were developed in order to add term counting features to the classification. Examples of such emotion lexicons are WordNetAffect [Strapparava and Valitutti, 2004] and ANEW (Affective Norms for English Words) [Bradley and Lang, 1999]. LIWC also has labeled emotions words in addition to the labels for positivity/negativity mentioned above. Mohammad and Turney [2013] collected a larger emotion lexicon by crowdsourcing.

In Bollen et al. [2011], other types of emotions were extracted, including tension, depression, anger, vigor, fatigue, and confusion. The results of this analysis showed that the events that cause these emotions have a significant, immediate, and highly specific effect on the public mood in various dimensions. Jung et al. [2006] used some common-sense knowledge from ConceptNet [Liu and Singh, 2004], and a list of affective words [Bradley and Lang, 1999] to treat four emotions classes (a subset of Ekman's six emotions).

Among the work on emotion analysis, that on social media data was focused on blogs and on tweets. Aman and Szpakowicz [2007] applied SVM classifiers to the dataset of annotated blog sentences mentioned above, and used emotion words from Roget's thesaurus as features for classification. Ghazi et al. [2010] applied hierarchical classification to the same dataset, by classifying the blog sentences into neutral or expressing emotions, then the latter ones into positive and negative emotions. The positive ones were mostly in the class of *happiness*, while the rest were negative. Surprise could be positive or negative (but it was mostly negative in that dataset). Syntactic dependency features were also explored for the same task [Ghazi et al., 2014].

On Twitter data, Mohammad and Kiritchenko [2014] used hashtags to capture fine-grained emotion categories. The hashtags were used to label the data, with the risk of obtaining noisy training data. The experiments showed that classification is still possible in this setting called distant supervision. Similarly, Abdul-Mageed and Ungar [2017] built a very large dataset for fine-grained emotion detection using carefully chosen hashtags for automatic labeling of the data. Because the training data was large enough, they were able to train deep learning models that achieved high accuracies.

Nakov et al. [2016] discuss the fourth year of the SemEval task called "Sentiment Analysis in Twitter" task. This latest iteration included five subtasks. Subtasks A, C, and D predict tweets as having positive, negative, or neutral sentiment. The remaining subtasks challenged researchers to map the sentiment of tweets on given topics to a five-point scale. A total of 43 teams participated in this SemEval-2016 Task 4, representing 25 countries. Many top-ranked teams showcased the efficacy of deep learning, including convolutional neural networks, recurrent neural networks, and word embeddings in such analysis. The following are examples of teams that achieved high ranks in these tasks.

One such team was Deriu et al. [2016]. Their sentiment classification model used an ensemble of convolutional neural networks with distant supervision (tweets labeled by hashtags rather then human annotators). This combination achieved a winning F-score 0.63 on the Twitter-2016 test set. Palogiannidi et al. [2016] prsesented a method of sentiment analysis using semantic-affective model adaptation. They used a large generic corpus which included 116M sentences. Balikas and Amini [2016] proposed a two-step approach. In the first step, they generated and validated diverse feature sets for Twitter sentiment evaluation. In the second step, they focused on the optimization of the evaluation measure of the different subtasks. This method included feature extraction, feature representation, and feature transformation, and ranked among the top ten teams in four out of five subtasks. Stojanovski et al. [2016] used a deep learning architecture for sentiment analysis that employed convolutional and gated recurrent neural networks. Their system leveraged preprocessing, pre-trained word embeddings, convolutional neural networks, gated recurrent neural networks, and network fusion (sharing layers across networks) and achieved the second-best average rank on the binary and 5-point classification and quantification subtasks.

A few researchers focused on mood classification in social media data. Moods are similar to emotions, but they express more transient states. LiveJournal is a website that allows users to write how they feel and to label their blog posts with one of the 132 existing moods, or even to created new labels. Mishne [2005] collected a corpus of posts from LiveJournal annotated with mood labels, and implemented an SVM classifier to automatically classify blogs into the 40 most frequent moods. He used features such as frequency counts, lengths, sentiment orientations, emphasized words, and special symbols. Keshtkar and Inkpen [2012] further investigated this dataset by adding more sentiment orientation features. Moreover, they proposed a hierarchical classifier based on the hierarchy of moods (using SVM in each branch of the hierarchy). They experimented with all 132 moods. Since 132 classes are easily confused (for humans and for the automatic system), the hierarchical approach was essential in order to obtain good classification results (see Table 3.7). The features used in the classification started with Bag-of-Word features and added semantic orientation features calculated by using multiple polarity lexicons.

3.4.3 SARCASM DETECTION

One of the problems in opinion mining systems is that sarcastic or ironic statements could easily fool these systems. The difference between irony and sarcasm is subtle; it lies in the idea that irony can be involuntary, while sarcasm is deliberate.

Irony, generally speaking, can naturally occur in both language and circumstance; one experiences irony when the opposite of an expected situation or idea occurs. In essence, an individual does not need to go out of their way to experience an ironic situation or idea: they can occur naturally. Sarcasm, for its part, can make use of irony to make an observation or remark about an idea, person, or situation. Sarcasm is generally intended to express ridicule or reservation about an expression or idea, and that is why it tends to find broader usage than irony. For an automatic system, the difference between them is difficult to catch, and perhaps not necessary. From applications' point of view, it is important to detect sarcastic/ironic statements in order to distinguish them from genuine opinions.

Several researchers attempted to detect sarcastic statements, mainly by using classification approaches. SVM and other classifiers were used, and many sets of features were tested. The features include specific punctuation (exclamation marks, etc.), Twitter-specific symbols, syntactic information, world knowledge, etc. González-Ibáñez et al. [2011] explored lexical and pragmatic features and found that smileys, frowns, and ToUser features were among the most discriminating for the classification task. They also found that human judges have a hard time performing the sarcasm detection task. Barbieri et al. [2014] proposed lexical features that aim to detect sarcasm by its structure, by computing unexpectedness, intensity of terms, and imbalance between styles. Riloff et al. [2013] identified only sarcastic messages created by a contrast between a positive sentiment and a negative situation. Their bootstrapping method acquired a list of positive sentiment phrases and a list of negative activities and states.

Training data for detecting sarcasm can be manually annotated as sarcastic or not, or can be obtained automatically. Many researchers worked on Twitter data, and collected messages with the #sarcasm hashtag to use as training examples for the sarcasm class. For the negative class they collected other messages not including this hashtags; but there is no guarantee that some sarcastic messages were included as examples of the non-sarcastic class. Ideally, the latter examples should be manually checked, but this is time consuming, so it is not usually done. Davidov et al. [2010] proposed a semi-supervised approach in order to reduce the need for annotated training data. Lukin and Walker [2013] also used bootstrapping, but they worked on online dialog texts, unlike the previously cited work focused on Twitter messages.

3.4.4 EVALUATION MEASURES FOR OPINION AND EMOTION CLASSIFICATION

The evaluation measures used for opinion and emotion analysis are usually the classification accuracy (when the task is framed as classification) and the precision, recall, and F-measure for each opinion or emotion class. This allows the analysis to point out which classes are difficult for the classifier, either because of lack of training data, or poor quality of the data, or simply because some classes are easy to confuse even for humans. When measuring the intensity of the emotions, the classes could be on a scale (such as −10 to +10), in which case mean absolute error (MAE) or root-mean-squared error (RMSE) are used to capture the magnitude of the errors. The MAE measures the average magnitude of the errors in a set of predictions, without considering their direction; it measures accuracy for continuous variables. The RMSE is a quadratic score which measures the average magnitude of the error.

Results For sentiment analysis, the best result on the test set from the SemEval task of Twitter messages classification was an F-measure of 69% in the message-level task and an F-measure of 88.9% in the term-level task [Mohammad et al., 2013]. Go et al. [2009] report results of up to 80% accuracy for their experiments on Twitter data collected via distant supervision.

For emotion classification on blog data, Aman and Szpakowicz [2007] reported results for each of the six classes of emotions. The F-measures varies from 50% for *sadness* to 75% for *happiness*. Ghazi et al. [2010] report similar on the same dataset. Moreover, when moving from the standard flat classification to hierarchical classification, the total accuracy over all classes increases from 61% to 68%. On Twitter data, Mohammad and Kiritchenko [2014] reported F-measures from 18–49% on the 6 emotion classes, on the noisy dataset that they collected via distant supervision. Table 3.6 shows detailed results per class for a subset of the Aman dataset (for the sentences that contain at least one explicit emotion word), obtained by Ghazi et al. [2014] using SVM, with various features, starting with Bag-of-Words (BoW), and followed by emotion lexicon features plus syntactic dependency features.

Thelwall et al. [2011] tested their SentiStrength system on a dataset of MySpace comments. SentiStrength predicts the strength of positive emotions on a scale 1–5, and the strengths of negative emotions separately, also on a scale 1–5. Their system uses a lookup table of term sentiment strengths optimized by machine learning, and it can predict positive emotions with 60.6% accuracy and negative emotions with 72.8% accuracy.

For mood classification, the accuracy reported by Mishne [2005] was 67% for the 40 most frequent moods, while Keshtkar and Inkpen [2012] reported 85% on the same set of classes. The latter work also reports very high accuracy levels when classifying into subclasses of the mood hierarchy. When combining over all levels, in a pipeline, the accuracy increases to 55% as compared to a flat classification accuracy into all the 132 moods, which got a low accuracy of 25%. The results are presented in Table 3.7; the classifiers from all the levels are applied successively (the errors from all the levels are multiplied) to build the hierarchical classifier; its results are compared to the results of the flat classification, for both BoW features and BoW+Semantic Orientation features and with a trivial baseline of always choosing the most frequent class.

3.5 EVENT AND TOPIC DETECTION

Event detection in social media texts is important because people tend to post many messages about current events, and many users read those comments in order to find the information that they need. Event detection techniques can be classified according to the event type (specified or unspecified), the detection task (retrospective or new event detection), and the detection method (supervised or unsupervised), as described in the survey paper by Farzindar and Khreich [2013].

3.5.1 SPECIFIED VS. UNSPECIFIED EVENT DETECTION

Depending on the information available on the event of interest, event detection can be classified into techniques for specified and for unspecified events. When no prior information is available

Table 3.6: Classification results for emotion classes and non-emotion by Ghazi et al. [2014]

		Precision	Recall	F-measure
SVM + BoW	Happiness	0.59	0.67	0.63
	Sadness	0.38	0.45	0.41
	Anger	0.40	0.31	0.35
Accuracy 50.72%	Surprise	0.41	**0.33**	0.37
	Disgust	0.51	0.43	0.47
	Fear	0.55	0.50	0.52
	Non-emotion	0.49	0.48	0.48
SVM + extra features	Happiness	**0.68**	**0.78**	**0.73**
	Sadness	**0.49**	**0.58**	**0.53**
	Anger	**0.66**	**0.48**	**0.56**
Accuracy **58.88%**	Surprise	**0.61**	0.31	**0.41**
	Disgust	**0.43**	**0.38**	**0.40**
	Fear	**0.67**	**0.63**	**0.65**
	Non-emotion	**0.51**	**0.53**	**0.52**

Table 3.7: Accuracy of the mood classification by Keshtkar and Inkpen [2012]

Method	Accuracy (%)
Baseline	7.00
Flat Classification BoW	18.29
Flat Classification BoW + SO	24.73
Hierarchical Classification BoW	23.65
Hierarchical Classification BoW + SO	55.24

about the event, the unspecified event detection techniques rely on the temporal signal of social media streams to detect the occurrence of a real-world event. These techniques typically require monitoring for bursts or trends in social media streams, grouping the features with identical trends into events, and ultimately classifying the events into different categories. On the other hand, the specified event detection relies on specific information and features that are known about the event, such as a venue, time, type, and description, which are provided by the user or from the event's context. These features can be exploited by adapting traditional information retrieval and extraction techniques (such as filtering, query generation and expansion, clustering, and information aggregation) to the unique characteristics of social media data.

Unspecified Event Detection

The nature of Twitter posts reflects events as they unfold, so tweets can be particularly useful for detecting unknown events. Unknown events of interest are typically driven by emerging events, breaking news, and general topics that attract the attention of a large number of Twitter users. Since no event information is available, unknown events are typically detected by exploiting the temporal patterns or signals of Twitter streams. New events of general interest exhibit a burst of features in the Twitter streams, yielding, for instance, a sudden increased use of specific keywords. Bursty features that occur frequently together in tweets can then be grouped into trends [Mathioudakis and Koudas, 2010]. In addition to trending events, endogenous or non-event trends are also abundant on Twitter [Naaman et al., 2011]. Techniques for unspecified event detection in Twitter must therefore distinguish trending events of general interest from the trivial or non-event trends (exhibiting similar temporal pattern) using scalable and efficient algorithms. The techniques described below attempted to meet these challenges. Most of them are based on detection topic words that might signal a new event, and then using similarity calculation or classification to detect more messages about the same event.

Sankaranarayanan et al. [2009] presented a system called TwitterStand that captures tweets that correspond to late breaking news. They employed a Naïve Bayes classifier to separate news from irrelevant information, and an online clustering algorithm based on weighted term vectors of TF-IDF[21] values and on cosine similarity[22] to form clusters of news. In addition, hashtags are used to reduce clustering errors. Clusters were also associated with time information. Other issues addressed included removing the noise and determining the relevant locations associated with the tweets. Similarly, Phuvipadawat and Murata [2010] collected, grouped, ranked, and tracked breaking news from Twitter. They collected sample tweets from Twitter API using predefined search queries (e.g., #breakingnews) and index their content with Apache Lucene. Similar messages were then grouped to form a news story based on TF-IDF with an increased weight for proper noun terms, hashtags, and usernames. The authors used a weighted combination of reliability, and popularity of tweets with a time adjustment for the freshness of the messages to rank each cluster. New messages were included in a cluster if they were similar to the first message and to the top k terms in that cluster. The authors stressed the importance of proper noun identification in enhancing the similarity comparison between tweets, and hence improving the overall system accuracy. An application based on the proposed method called Hot-stream has been developed.

Petrovic et al. [2010] adapted the approach proposed for news media by Allan et al. [2000]. Cosine similarity between documents was used to detect new events that have never appeared in previous tweets. Replies, retweets, and hashtags were not considered in their experiments, nor the significance of newly detected events (e.g., trivial or not). Results have shown that ranking

---

[21]Term frequency/inverse document frequency, computed as the frequency of a term in the current document multiplied by the logarithm of N/df, where N is the total number of documents, and df is the number of documents that contain the term. The idea is that terms that appear in few documents are considered more discriminative.

[22]The cosine between two vectors indicates how similar they are in a vector space. Small angle means high similarity.

according to the number of users is better than ranking according to the number of tweets, and considering entropy of the message reduces the amount of spam messages in the output.

Becker et al. [2011b] focused on online identification of real-world event content and its associated Twitter messages using an online clustering technique, which continuously clusters similar tweets, and then classifies the cluster's content into real-world events or non-events. These non-events involve Twitter-centric topics, which are trending activities in Twitter that do not reflect any real-world occurrences [Naaman et al., 2011]. Twitter-centric activities are difficult to detect, because they often share similar temporal distribution characteristics with real-world events. Each message is represented as a TF-IDF weight vector of its textual content, and cosine similarity is used to compute the distance from a message to cluster centroids. In addition to traditional pre-processing steps such as stop-word elimination and stemming, the weights of hashtag terms were doubled since they are considered strongly indicative of the message content. The authors combined temporal, social, topical, and Twitter-centric features. Since the clusters constantly evolve over time, the features were periodically updated for old clusters and computed for newly formed ones. Finally, an SVM classifier was trained on a labeled set of cluster features, and used to decide whether the cluster (and its associated messages) contains real-world event information.

Long et al. [2011] adapted a traditional clustering approach by integrating some specific features into the characteristics of microblog data. These features are based on "topical words," which are more popular than others with respect to an event. Topical words are extracted from daily messages based on word frequency, word occurrence in hashtag, and word entropy. A (top-down) hierarchical divisive clustering[23] is applied to a co-occurrence graph (connecting messages in which topical words co-occur) to divide topical words into event clusters. To track changes among events at different times, a maximum weighted bipartite graph matching is employed to create event chains, with a variation of Jaccard coefficient[24] as similarity measures between clusters. Finally, cosine similarity augmented with a time interval between messages is used to find top k most relevant posts that summarize an event. These event summaries were then linked to event chain clusters and plotted on a time line. For event detection, the authors found that top-down divisive clustering outperforms both k-means and traditional hierarchical clustering algorithms.

A bursty topic or event in Twitter is one that triggers many related tweets in a short period of time. Ex post facto analysis of such events has long been a topic of social media research; however, real-time detection of bursty events is relatively novel. Xie et al. devised a sketch-based topic model called "TopicSketch" to solve this challenge. This approach involved a soft moving window over a Twitter stream to efficiently detect surges in rare words and rare tuples of words. These frequencies were then stored in a matrix, and decomposed into smaller matrices

---

[23]Divisive clustering starts with all the documents in one cluster. The cluster is split using a flat clustering algorithm. This procedure is applied recursively until each document is in its own singleton cluster.

[24]The Jaccard similarity coefficient measure the similarity between two finite sets, and is defined as the size of the intersection divided by the size of the union of the sets.

that approximated topics by using Singular Value Decomposition (SVD). Evaluated over 30 million tweets in real-time, this approach proved to be both more efficient and effective than previous models.

Weng and Lee [2011] proposed event detection based on clustering of discrete wavelet signals built from individual words generated by Twitter. In contrast with Fourier transforms, which have been proposed for event detection from more traditional media, wavelet transformations were used in both time and frequency domain, in order to identify the time and the duration of a bursty event within the signal. A sliding window was then applied to capture the change over time. Trivial words were filtered out based on (a threshold set on) signal cross-correlation, which measures similarity between two signals as function of a time-lag. The remaining words were then clustered to form events with a modularity-based graph partitioning technique, which splits the graph into subgraphs each corresponding to an event. Finally, significant events were detected from the number of words and the cross-correlation among the words related to an event.

Similarly, Cordeiro [2012] proposed a continuous wavelet transformation based on hashtag occurrences combined with a topic model inference using Latent Dirichlet Allocation (LDA) [Blei et al., 2003]. Instead of individual words, hashtags are used for building wavelet signals. An abrupt increase in the number of occurrences of a given hashtag is considered a good indicator of an event that is happening at a given time. Therefore, all hashtags were retrieved from tweets and then grouped in intervals of five minutes. Hashtag signals were constructed over time by counting the hashtag mentions in each interval, grouping them into separated time series (one for each hashtag), and concatenating all tweets that mention the hashtag during each time series. Adaptive filters were then used to remove noisy hashtag signals, before applying the continuous wavelet transformation and getting a time-frequency representation of the signal. Next, wavelet peak and local maxima detection techniques were used to detect peaks and changes in the hashtag signal. Finally, when an event was detected within a given time interval, LDA was applied to all the tweets related to the hashtag in each corresponding time series in order to extract a set of latent topics, in order to build an event description.

Specified Event Detection

Specified event detection includes known or planned social events. These events could be partially or fully specified with the related content or metadata information such as location, time, venue, and performers. The techniques described below attempt to exploit Twitter textual content or metadata information or both, using a wide range of machine learning, data mining, and text analysis techniques.

Popescu and Pennacchiotti [2010] focused on identifying controversial events that provoke public discussions with opposing opinions in Twitter. Their detection framework is based on the notion of a Twitter snapshot. Given a set of Twitter snapshots, an event detection module first distinguishes between event and non-event snapshots using a supervised Gradient Boosted Decision Trees (GBDT) [Friedman, 2001], trained on a manually labeled dataset. To rank these event snapshots, a controversy model assigns higher scores to controversial event snapshots, based on a regression algorithm applied to a large number of features. Feature analysis of the single-stage system revealed that the event's core is the most relevant feature since it discriminates event from non-event snapshots. Hashtags are found to be important semantic features for tweets, since they help identify the topic of a tweet and estimate the topical cohesiveness of a set of tweets. In addition, the linguistic, structural, and sentiment features also provide considerable effects. The authors concluded that a rich, varied set of features is crucial for controversy detection.

In a follow-up, Popescu et al. [2011] employed the framework described above, but with additional features to extract events and their descriptions from Twitter. The key idea is based on the importance and the number of the entities to capture common-sense intuitions about event and non-event snapshots. As the authors observe: "Most event snapshots have a small set of important entities and additional minor entities while non-event snapshots may have a larger set of equally unimportant entities." These new features are inspired by the document aboutness system [Paranjpe, 2009], and aim at ranking the entities in a snapshot with respect to their relative importance to the snapshot. This includes relative positional information (e.g., offset of a term in snapshot), term-level information (term frequency, Twitter corpus IDF), and snapshot-level information (length of snapshot, category, language). Part-of-speech tagging and regular expressions have also been applied for improved event and main entity extraction. The number of snapshots containing action verbs, the buzziness of an entity in the news on a given day and the number of reply tweets are among the most useful new features found by the authors.

Benson et al. [2011] presented a novel way of identifying Twitter messages for concert events using a factor graph model, which simultaneously analyzes individual messages, clusters them according to event type, and induces a canonical value for each event property. The motivation is to infer a comprehensive list of musical events from Twitter (based on artist-venue pairs) to complete an existing list (e.g., city event calendar table) by discovering new musical events mentioned by Twitter users that are difficult to find in other media sources. At the message level, this approach relies on a CRF model to extract the name of the artist and the location of the event. The input features to CRF model included word shape; a set of regular expressions for common emoticons, time references, and venue types; a bag of words for artist names extracted from external source (e.g., Wikipedia); and a bag of words for city venue names. Clustering was guided by term popularity, which is an alignment score among the message term labels (artist, venue, none) and some candidate value (e.g., specific artist or venue name). To capture the large text variation in Twitter messages, this score was based on a weighted combination of term similarity measures, including complete string matching, and adjacency and equality indicators scaled by the inverse document frequency. In addition, a uniqueness factor (favoring single messages) was employed during clustering to uncover rare event messages that are dominated by the popular ones, and to discourage various messages from the same events to cluster into multiple events. On the other hand, a consistency indicator was employed to discourage messages from multiple events to form a single cluster. A factor graph model was then employed to capture the interaction between all components and provide the final decision. The output of the model was a clustering of messages based on a musical event, where each cluster was represented by an artist-venue pair.

Lee and Sumiya [2010] presented a geo-social local event detection system based on modeling and monitoring crowd behavior via Twitter, to identify local festivals. They relied on geographical regularities deduced from the usual behavior patterns of crowds using geotags. The authors found that an increased user activity combined with an increased number of tweets provide strong indicator of local festivals. Sakaki et al. [2010] exploited tweets to detect specific types of events like earthquakes and typhoons. They formulated event detection as a classification problem, and trained an SVM classifier on a manually labeled Twitter dataset comprising negative events (earthquakes and typhoons) and positive events (or other events or non-events). Three types of features have been employed; the number of words (statistical), the keywords in a tweet message, and the words surrounding users query (contextual). Experiments have shown that the statistical feature by itself provided the best results, while a small improvement in performance was achieved by the combination of the three features. The authors have also applied Kalman filtering and particle filtering [Fox et al., 2003] for the estimation of earthquake center and typhoon trajectory from Twitter temporal and spatial information. They found that particle filters outperformed Kalman filters in both cases, due to the inappropriate Gaussian assumption of the latter for this type of problem.

Becker et al. [2011a] presented a system for augmenting information about planned events with Twitter messages, using a combination of simple rules and query building strategies. To identify Twitter messages for an event, they begin with simple and precise query strategies derived from the event description and its associated aspects (e.g., combining time and venue). In addition, they build queries using URL and hashtag statistics from the high-precision tweets for an event. Finally, they build a rule-based classifier to select among this new set of queries, and then use the selected queries to retrieve additional event messages. In a related work, Becker et al. [2011c] proposed centrality-based approaches to extract high-quality, relevant, and useful Twitter messages related to an event. These approaches are based on the observation that the most topically central messages in a cluster are more likely to reflect key aspects of the event than other, less central cluster messages. The techniques from both works have recently been extended and incorporated into a more general approach that aims at identifying social media contents for known events across different social media sites [Becker et al., 2012].

Massoudi et al. [2011] employed a generative language modeling approach based on query expansion and microblog "quality indicators" to retrieve individual microblog messages. However, the authors only considered the existence of a query term within a specific post and discarded its local frequency. The quality indicators include part of the blog "credibility indicators" proposed by Weerkamp and De Rijke [2008] extended with specific microblog characteristics such as a recency factor, and the number of reposts and followers. The recency factor is based on the difference between the query time and the post time. The query expansion technique selects top k terms that occur in a user-specified number of posts close to the query date. The final query is therefore a weighted mixture of the original and the expanded query. The combination of the quality indicator terms and the microblog characteristics has been shown to outperform each method alone. In addition, tokens with numeric or non-alphabetic characters have turned out beneficial for query expansion.

Rather than retrieving individual microblog messages in response to an event query, Metzler et al. [2012] proposed retrieving a ranked list (or timeline) of historical event summaries. The search task involves temporal query expansion, timespan retrieval, and summarization. In response to a user query, this approach retrieves a ranked set of timespans based on the occurrence of the query keywords. The idea is to capture terms that are heavily discussed and trending during a retrieved timespan because they are more likely to be related to the query. To produce a short summary for each retrieved time interval, a small set of query-relevant messages posted during the timespan are then selected. These relevant messages are retrieved as top-ranked messages according to a weighted variant of the query likelihood scoring function, which is based on the burstiness score for expansion terms and a Dirichlet smoothed language modeling estimate for each term in the message. The authors showed that their approach is more robust and effective than the traditional relevance-based language models [Lavrenko and Croft, 2001] applied to the collected Twitter corpus and to English Gigaword corpus.[25]

Gu et al. [2011] proposed an event modeling approach called ETree for event modeling from Twitter streams. ETree employs n-gram-based content analysis techniques to group a large number of event-related messages into semantically coherent information blocks, an incremental modeling process to construct hierarchical theme structures, and a life cycle based temporal analysis technique to identify potential causal relationships between information blocks. ETree is more efficient than its non-incremental version and to TSCAN—a widely used algorithm that derives major themes of events from the eigenvectors of a temporal block association matrix [Chen and Chen, 2008].

3.5.2 NEW VS. RETROSPECTIVE EVENTS

Similar to event detection from conventional media [Allan, 2002, Yang et al., 1998, 2002], event detection in Twitter can also be classified into retrospective and new event detection depending on the task and application requirements, and on the type of event. Since new event detection (NED) techniques involve continuous monitoring of the Twitter signal for discovering new events in near real-time, they are naturally suited for detecting unknown real-world events or breaking news. In general, trending events on Twitter could be aligned with real-world breaking news. However, sometimes a comment, person, or photo related to real-world breaking news may become more trending on Twitter than the original event. One such example is Bobak Fer-

---

[25] https://catalog.ldc.upenn.edu/LDC2003T05

dowsi's hair style on social media during NASA's operation in 2012, when the media reported: "Mohawk guy Bobak Ferdowsi's hair goes viral as Curiosity lands on Mars."

Although NED approaches do not impose any assumption on the event, they are not restricted to detecting unspecified event. When the monitoring task involves specific events (natural disasters, celebrities, etc.) or a specific information about the event (e.g., geographical location), this information could be integrated into the NED system by, for instance, using filtering techniques [Sakaki et al., 2010] or exploiting additional features such as the controversy [Popescu and Pennacchiotti, 2010] or the geo-tagged information [Lee and Sumiya, 2010], to better focus on the event of interest. Most NED approaches could also be applied to historical data in order to detect and analyze past events.

While most research focuses on new event detection to exploit the timely information provided by Twitter streams, recent studies show an interest in retrospective event detection from Twitter's historical data. Existing microblog search services, such as those offered by Twitter and Google, only provide limited search capabilities that allow individual microblog posts to be retrieved in response to a query [Metzler et al., 2012]. The challenges in finding Twitter messages relevant to a given user query are mainly due to the sparseness of the tweets and the large number of vocabulary mismatches (because the vocabulary dynamically evolves). For example, relevant messages may not contain any query term, or new abbreviations or hashtags may emerge with the event. Traditional query expansion techniques rely on terms that co-occur with query terms in relevant documents. In contrast, event retrieval from Twitter data focuses on temporal and dynamic query expansion techniques. Recent research effort has begun to focus on providing more structured and comprehensive summaries of Twitter events.

3.5.3   EMERGENCY SITUATION AWARENESS

Event detection in Twitter and other social media can be used for emergency situation awareness. New events can be detected and classified as an emergency, and then updates on the situation can be processed in order to keep people informed and to help resolve or alleviate the situation. We present two examples of systems that focus on this kind of monitoring. Both are based on machine learning techniques in order to classify the Twitter messages as being of interest or not.

Yin et al. [2012] implemented a system that extracts situation awareness information from Twitter messages generated during various disasters and crises. They collected tweets for specific areas of interest in Australia and New Zealand since March 2010. The data contained 66 million tweets from approximately 2.51 million distinct Twitter profiles that cover a range of natural disasters and security incidents, including: the tropical cyclone Ului (March 2010), the Brisbane storms (June 2010), the gunman in Melbourne (June 2010), the Christchurch earthquake (September 2010), the Qantas A380 incident (November 2010), the Brisbane floods (January 2011), the tropical cyclone Yasi (February 2011), and the Christchurch earthquake (February 2011). The method started with burst detection for unexpected incidents, followed by a classification for impact assessment. The classifiers (Naïve Bayes and SVM) used lexical features and Twitter-specific features for classification. These features included unigrams, bigrams, word length, the number of hashtags contained in a tweet; the number of user mentions, whether a tweet is retweeted; and whether a tweet is replied to by other users. In a next step, online clustering was applied to topic discovery (using cosine similarity and Jaccard similarity to group messages in the same clusters).

Cobb et al. [2014] described automatic identification of Twitter messages that contribute to situational awareness. They collected tweets broadcasted during each of the emergency events, based on selected keywords. The four datasets were: the 2009 Oklahoma wildfire (527 tweets), the Red River flooding 2009 (453 tweets), the 2010 Red River flooding (499 tweets), and the 2010 Haiti earthquake (486 tweets). Their method was based on Naïve Bayes and Maximum Entropy (MaxEnt) classifiers, in order to differentiate the tweets across several dimensions: subjectivity, personal or impersonal style, and linguistic register (formal or informal style). The features used for classification included: unigrams, bigrams, part-of-speech tags, the subjectivity of the message (objective/subjective), its style (formal/informal), and its tone (personal/impersonal). The last three features were calculated automatically by classifiers designed specifically for this. In an alternative experiment, they were manually annotated.

3.5.4   EVALUATION MEASURES FOR EVENT DETECTION

The evaluation measures for event detection include the accuracy of the extracted information, as well as precision, recall, and F-measure for each type of event. The results vary by task and method and type of events targeted. We noted above which kinds of linguistics information were most useful for each kind of event detection. It is not easy to evaluate the performance of event detection systems due to the need to manually annotate a test set, or to have a human check a representative sample of the system's output. We mention only a few of the results from the many papers cited in this section. Becker et al. [2011b] report precisions scores for event detection around 70–80%, highest for when the number of clusters used by their method to group events is small. They used a very large amount of tweets, so recall levels were not estimated. Benson et al. [2011] report similar levels of precision, and they were able to estimate recall at around 60%, by comparing to the list of events reported each week in the news during the tweet collection.

3.6   AUTOMATIC SUMMARIZATION

Automatic summarization from multiple social media sources is a highly active research topic that aims at reducing and aggregating the amount of information presented to users. This section describes a variety of advanced approaches, and presents their advantages and limitations. In addition, summarization can be very useful for other tasks such as classification and clustering of data from social media. However, the tools for text analysis and summarization are typically designed for specific sources and languages. It is an open question whether to pursue language-independent approaches, or develop and combine specific approaches for each language.

As mentioned earlier, the scale of social media is enormous. Combined with the high level of noise present in social media, this guarantees that most texts are certain to be irrelevant for any particular information need. Accordingly, any summarization task—and indeed most other NLP tasks—must be framed slightly differently than in more traditional domains. In particular, there is an inherent need to narrow in on relevant content, so some forms of information retrieval and/or detection of specific phenomena are generally a prerequisite to summarization. Also, there is less of a focus on what individual "documents" are about, but rather how they can contribute to a summary of some real-world phenomenon. Multi-document summarization, in order to summarize multiple Twitter messages on the same topic, was attempted by several researchers, for example by adapting tools used in multi-document summarization for newspaper articles or other kinds of texts [Inouye and Kalita, 2011, Sharifi et al., 2010]. Solutions may involve clustering the important sentences picked out from the various messages and using only a few representative sentences from each cluster. Machine learning techniques can be used to learn how to rank the selected tweets [Duan et al., 2010].

There are many works summarizing social media messages in terms of the topics and subtopics discussed. Zhao et al. [2011] extracted topical key phrases as a way to summarize a set of Twitter messages. They used a context-sensitive topical PageRank algorithm for keyword ranking and a probabilistic scoring function to estimate the relevance of the key phrases. Judd and Kalita [2013] built extractive summaries for sets of tweets, and because the summaries were very noisy, they parsed them with a dependency parser. The dependencies were then used to eliminate some of the excess text and build better-formed summaries. Hu et al. [2007b] summarized comments to blogs to see if processing the comments can change the understanding of the blog posts. Khabiri et al. [2011] also studied the comment summarization problem: for a set of n user-contributed comments associated with an online resource, they selected the best comments for summarization. They used a clustering algorithm to identify correlated groups of comments, and a precedence-based ranking framework to automatically select informative comments.

In an effort to help companies understand how to transform social media data into actionable business insight, He et al. described an in-depth case study, an application of text mining to analyze unstructured text content on Facebook and Twitter. Specifically, the study focused on the accounts of three major pizza companies: Pizza Hut, Domino's Pizza, and Papa John's Pizza. The researchers used topic modeling and sentiment analysis to determine the nature and efficacy of competitors' social media strategies. These results demonstrated the possible advantages of competitive analysis and the power of text mining as an effective technique to extract business value from the vast amount of available social media data.

As the volume of social media and microblogging data has grown, so has the need for summarization techniques such as identifying emergent keywords. Avudaiappan et al. [2016] presented a system for monitoring keywords and summarizing a document stream with dynamic semantic graphs. The researchers introduced the notion of dynamic eigenvector centrality for ranking emergent keywords, and presented an algorithm for summarizing emergent events from the minimum weight set cover. Specifically, this research featured summarization and detection of events concerning public security.

In this section, we further distinguish between using social media data in automated summarization and using summarization for social media retrieval and event detection. We focus on four types of summarization. We also mention recent work on automatic generation of keyphrases that can enrich social media postings.

3.6.1   UPDATE SUMMARIZATION

Update summarization is a fairly recent area linking news summarization to online and dynamic settings. Update summarization uses Web documents, such as blogs, reviews, and news articles, to identify new information on a topic. As defined at TAC 2008[26] the update summarization task consists in building a short (100-word) summary of a set of newswire articles, under the assumption that the user has already read a given set of earlier articles.

Delort and Alfonseca [2011] proposed a news multi-document summarization system called DUALSUM, using an unsupervised probabilistic approach based on a topic model to identify novelty in a document collection, and applying it to generate summary updates.

Li et al. [2012b] presented a method for update summarization which uses a Multi-level Hierarchical Dirichlet Process (HDP) Model. The paper proposes clustering as a three-level HDP model, which reveals the diversity and commonality between aspects discovered from two different periods of time as history and update.

In 2013, TREC defined Temporal Summarization. Unexpected news events such as natural disasters represent a unique information access problem where the performance of traditional approaches deteriorates. For example, immediately after an event, the corpus may be sparsely populated with relevant content. Even when, after a few hours, relevant content is available, it is often inaccurate or highly redundant. At the same time, crisis events demonstrate a scenario where users urgently need information, especially if they are directly affected by the event. The goal of this evaluation track is to develop systems which allow users to efficiently monitor the information associated with an event over time—specifically those which can broadcast useful, new, and timely sentence-length updates about a developing event, and can track the value of important event-related attributes (e.g., the number of fatalities, financial impact).

3.6.2   NETWORK ACTIVITY SUMMARIZATION

Social media text is by definition social in nature. Individual posts are not static, isolated pieces of text, but are inherently linked to other posts and users according to the parameters of the specific social network. Information about the relations between textual (or other media) entries and interactions between users—information about the structure and activity of the network

---

[26]http://www.nist.gov/tac/2008/summarization/update.summ.08.guidelines.html

itself—can be useful for summarization, both as additional sources of information to aid in summarization of the content of the network, and as a target of summarization in and of itself.

Liu et al. [2012a] leveraged social network features to adapt a graph-based summarization approach to the task of summarizing tweets. They overcome the issue of the brevity of tweets, and the corresponding difficulty of determining salience based solely on terms within a tweet, by incorporating "social signals" of salience from the network. Specifically, they make use of the notion of re-tweets and the number of followers as indicators of salience: tweets are considered more salient if they are re-tweeted more often and/or are posted by users with a higher number of followers. The authors also incorporate a tweets-per-user threshold to ensure summaries maintain some degree of user diversity.

Yan et al. [2012] proposed a graph-based model for tweet recommendation that presents users with items they may have an interest in. The model ranks tweets and their authors simultaneously using the social network connecting the users, the network connecting the tweets, and a third network that ties the two together. Tweet and author entities are ranked following a co-ranking algorithm based on the intuition that there is a mutually reinforcing relationship between tweets and their authors that could be reflected in the rankings. The framework can be parametrized to take into account user preferences, the popularity of tweets and their authors, and diversity.

3.6.3   EVENT SUMMARIZATION

Event summarization seeks to extract social media text representative of some real-world event. Here, an event can be broadly defined as any occurrence unfolding over some spatial and temporal scope [Farzindar and Khreich, 2013]. In practice, the aim is not to summarize any and all events, but events of interest. Unlike in news reports, where events mentioned are, by definition, newsworthy, events of interest must first be identified in social media before they can be summarized. Also, summarization tasks can improve social media retrieval.

For this purpose, Twitter is a popular social media tool because the users can communicate short pieces of information, which are easier to consume and faster to spread. In addition, the Twitter streams can contain a link with points to a blog or a web page with detailed information. Harabagiu and Hickl [2011] summarized the content of multiple tweets on the same topic into a description of fixed length. They used a generative model to induces event structures from text and a user behavior model which captures how users convey relevant content. Another interesting approach to summarizing multiple types of social media is to detect an event of interest from Twitter and summarize the blogs related to the event.

Zubiaga et al. [2012] explored the real-time summarization of scheduled events such as soccer games from Twitter streams. They detected sub-events for each event. They compared the summaries generated in three languages for all the soccer games in Copa America 2011 to reference live reports offered by Yahoo! Sports journalists. We show that simple text analysis methods which do not involve external knowledge lead to summaries that cover 84% of the sub-events on average, and 100% of key types of sub-events (such as goals in soccer). Their approach can be applied to other kinds of scheduled events such as other sports, award ceremonies, keynote talks, TV shows, etc.

3.6.4   OPINION SUMMARIZATION

Summarization can help better understand opinion mining and sentiment analysis in social networks. As mentioned previously, social texts tend to be much more subjective and opinion-laden than other texts. They can thus be a great resource for businesses and other organizations to stay apprised of the public opinion regarding their products and services. Automated opinion summarization techniques are essential to leverage this immense source of opinion data. Such techniques may target a general assessment of sentiment polarity regarding a particular product or service, which can be invaluable for marketing or reputation management (e.g., "Do customers feel positive or negative regarding a particular brand or product?"). Opinion summarization may also target more specific query-based information, such as "Which particular features do customers like best about a given product?"

However, the summarization task is framed, sentiment analysis is necessarily an integral part of any opinion summarization task, and constitutes a challenging area of inquiry in its own right, as we have seen in Section 3.2.

Mithun [2012] presents extractive, query-based opinion summarization of blogs. Extraction and ranking of sentences is performed based on query and topic similarity in a traditional fashion using TF-IDF, but also based on a "subjectivity score." The latter is calculated based on the polarity and sentiment degree of words within the sentence, as determined from MPQA subjectivity lexicon. Extracted sentences must match the polarity of the query. The degree of sentiment of the sentence, determined both from the number of subjective words therein and how strongly weighted each word is, also affects the ranking of the sentences for extraction.

There was work that focused on summarizing contrastive opinions and points of view, although that was on customer reviews for products [Kim and Zhai, 2009, Paul et al., 2010]. Opinions from online reviews were also summarized based on aspects of the products [Titov and McDonald, 2008].

To return to generic text summarization, we would like to mention a mobile app for text summarization that was featured extensively in the news. It was developed by a UK high school student, Nick D'Aloisio, in 2011, when he was just 15 years old. In 2013 he became one of the youngest millionaires when the app, Summly, was acquired by Yahoo for 30 million dollars. Summly uses a summarization algorithm that extracts text from a web page using HTML processing. The app analyzes the text and selects condensed portions of the article as bullet points. The Summly algorithm accomplishes this by using machine learning techniques, including genetic algorithms.[27] In the training phase, it looks at human-authored summaries of articles of various types and from various publications. It then uses these summaries as models for what

---

[27]http://www.wired.com/2011/12/summly-app-summarization/

Summly should be producing, and how it should change its own metrics to better emulate the human summaries.

3.6.5 KEYPHRASE GENERATION

Natural language generation (NLG) aims at generating sentences or longer texts based on some semantic content that needs to be expressed. Alternatively, the input can be a text from which another text needs to be generated. The latter is called text-to-text generation, and it is used to denote the generation of a summary for a given input text, or even for machine translation where the input is text in the source language and the output is text in the target language.

Generating sentences or longer texts is an active area of research for formal texts, but it is not needed for social media texts, where the users themselves produce content.

One type of generation that was studied recently in the context of social media is keyphrase generation. The input to such a system is a social media text and the output is a set of keyphrases. The keyphrases can be extractive (selected from existing words or phases in the current text) or generated based on the whole training data. In this way, a short social media message can be enriched with more content.

Traditionally, generating keyphrases for scientific articles was of interest, especially that training/test data was easily available since the authors provided manual keyphrases with the articles. For social posts, Wang et al. [2019] proposed a sequence-to-sequence-based neural keyphrase generation framework, enabling absent keyphrases to be created. Their model is topic-aware and allows joint modeling of corpus-level latent topic representations, which helps alleviate data sparsity widely exhibited in social media language. Experiments on three datasets collected from English social media (Twitter and StackExchange) and from Chinese social media (Weibo) showed that the model outperforms the extraction and generation models that do not exploit the latent topics. Zhang et al. [2018] presented a neural keyphrase extraction framework for microblog posts that takes their conversation context into account, where four types of neural encoders, namely, averaged embedding, RNN, attention, and memory networks, were proposed to represent the conversation context. Experimental results on Twitter and Weibo datasets showed that these encoders outperformed other state-of-the-art approaches.

3.6.6 EVALUATION MEASURES FOR SUMMARIZATION

The evaluation measures for text summarization can be automatic or manual. An example of automatic measure is ROUGE[28] [Lin and Hovy, 2003] that compares the summary generated by the system with several manually written summaries. It calculates n-gram overlap between the automatic summary and the multiple references, while penalizing for missed n-grams (an n-gram can be a word, a sequence of two words, three words, etc.)

Different versions of ROUGE use skipped n-grams, where the words that match are not necessarily consecutive. The manual evaluation involves humans reading the generated summary

---

[28]Recall-Oriented Understudy of Gisting Evaluation.

and assessing its quality on several criteria. Responsiveness measures the information content on a scale of 1–5. Readability can also be on a scale of 1–5 (as an overall score, or for particular aspects such as grammaticality, non-redundancy, referential clarity, focus, structure, and coherence). These measures and a few others are used by the U.S. National Institute of Standards and Technology (NIST) in Document Understanding Conferences/Text Analysis Conferences (DUC/TAC) evaluation campaigns, discussed later in Section 5.5. Specifically for microblog summarization, Mackie et al. [2014] showed that a new metric, the fraction of topic words found in the summary, better agrees with what users perceive about the quality and effectiveness of microblog summaries than the ROUGE measure that is most commonly reported in the literature.

3.7   MACHINE TRANSLATION

People are communicating in thousands of spoken languages around the world. Facebook and Twitter support hundreds of languages on their platforms. Developing powerful and flexible machine translation systems has long been a research focus for researchers in academia and social media corporations. According to Twitter's blog in January 2015, the number of tweets published each day grew to 500 millions[29] in many languages (with English losing the first place, down to 40% or less).[30] The multilingual aspects hinders the spread of information, a situation witnessed for instance during the Arab Spring.[31]

Solutions for disseminating tweets in different languages have been designed. One solution consists of manually translating tweets, which of course is only viable for a very specific subset of the material appearing on Twitter. For instance, the non-profit organization Meedan[32] was founded in order to organize volunteers willing to translate tweets written in Arabic on Middle East issues. Another solution consists of using machine translation. Several portals facilitate this, mainly by using Google's machine translation API. Ling et al. [2013] were able to extract over 1 million Chinese-English parallel segments from Sina Weibo (the Chinese counterpart of Twitter), based on many re-tweets of English or Chinese messages that users translated into other languages before re-tweeting.

Curiously enough, few studies have focused on the automatic translation of text produced within social networks, even though a growing number of studies concentrate on the automated processing of messages exchanged on social networks. Gimpel et al. [2011] published a review of some of them. Some effort has been invested in translating short text messages (SMSs). Notably, Munro [2010] described the service deployed by a consortium of volunteer organizations named *Mission 4636* during the earthquake which struck Haiti in January 2010. This service routed SMSs alerts reporting trapped people and other emergencies to a set of volunteers who translated

---

[29]http://www.internetlivestats.com/twitter-statistics/
[30]http://www.statista.com/statistics/348508/most-tweeted-language-world-leaders/
[31]http://en.wikipedia.org/wiki/Arab_Spring
[32]http://en.wikipedia.org/wiki/Meedan

Haitian Creole SMSs into English, so that primary emergency responders could understand them. Lewis [2010] describes how the same tragedy has spurred the Microsoft translation team to develop a statistical translation engine (Haitian Creole into English) in as few as five days.

Jehl [2010] addressed the task of translating English tweets into German. She concluded that the proper treatment of unknown words is of the utmost importance, and highlighted the problem of producing translations of up to 140 characters, the upper limit of tweet length. Jehl et al. [2012] described their effort to collect bilingual tweets from a stream of tweets acquired programmatically, and showed the effect of such a collection by developing an Arabic-to-English translation system.

Wang and Ng [2013] proposed a beam-search approach to enhancing a machine translation system. To further improve other downstream NLP applications, the researchers argued for the necessity of other normalization operations, e.g., missing word recovery and punctuation correction. A beam-search decoder was used to integrate various normalization operations. The decoder achieved statistically significant improvements over two strong baselines: an improvement of 9.98% in BLEU score[33] for normalization of Chinese/English social media text, and an improvement of 1.35% in BLEU scores for translation of Chinese/English social media text. Future research is needed to investigate how to integrate more tightly their beam-search decoder for text normalization with a standard MT decoder, e.g., by using a lattice or an N-best list.

3.7.1   NEURAL MACHINE TRANSLATION

In recent years, huge increases in multilingual data, the exponential growth of computer power, and advancement in deep neural networks gave birth to a new generation of machine translation systems [Bahdanau et al., 2015], [Gehring et al., 2017], [Vaswani et al., 2017]. Neural machine translation (NMT) models typically require large amounts of parallel texts. The parallel corpus or bilingual texts consist of the sentences (in the source language) for which there are reference translations (in the target language) and can automatically apply alignment techniques. However, high-quality bilingual data is limited; therefore, the methods need to use monolingual data for which no translations are available. One successful method in NMT is back-translation, whereby an NMT system is trained in the reverse translation direction (target-to-source), and is then used to translate target-side monolingual data back into the source language. For example, in order to train an English-to-German translation model, the first model is trained on German-to-English data and then it is used to translate the monolingual German data. Hoang et al. [2018] used an iterative back-translation method for generating increasingly better synthetic parallel data from monolingual data to train NMT. However, NMT and sequence-to-sequence learning models still require several days to reach state-of-the-art performance on large benchmark datasets using a single machine. Ott et al. [2018] explored how to train state-of-the-art NMT models on large-scale parallel hardware and showed that reduced precision and large-batch training can speed up training by nearly five times on a single 8-GPU machine

---

[33]BLEU is one of the evaluation measures used in MT.

with careful tuning and implementation. NMT approaches are applied very little to social media texts. For example, Tebbifakhr et al. [2019] presented experiments in sentiment classification of Twitter data in German and Italian after translating them into English with an NMT system and then feeding them into an English classifier.

3.7.2   ADAPTING PHRASE-BASED MACHINE TRANSLATION TO NORMALIZE MEDICAL TERMS

Health reports in social media, such as DailyStrength and Twitter, have potential for monitoring health conditions (e.g., adverse drug reactions or infectious diseases) in particular communities. However, for a machine to understand and make inferences on these health conditions, it must possess the ability to recognize when laymen's terms refer to a particular medical concept (which is a type of text normalization). Limsopatham and Collier [2015] adapted an existing phrase-based machine translation (MT) technique by using word vectors to map social media phrases to medical concepts. To evaluate their approach, the researchers used a collection of 25 million tweets related to adverse drug reactions (ADRs). They conducted experiments using 10-fold cross validation, where the Twitter phrases were randomly divided into 10 separated folds. They used three different techniques, including one-hot, CBOW, and GloVe, to generate the word vectors. Their results showed that the combination of a phrase-based MT technique and the similarity between word vector representations outperforms the baselines that apply only one of them by up to 55%.

3.7.3   TRANSLATING GOVERNMENT AGENCIES' TWEET FEEDS

Timely warnings and emergency notifications to the public are some of the most important tasks of governments in matters of public safety. Social media platforms such as Twitter are a convenient way to communicate and push warnings, as mentioned earlier in this chapter.

In June 2013, Environment Canada announced that weather warnings cannot be tweeted because official bilingualism in Canada has proved a barrier to weather warning tweets.[34] In keeping with the Official Languages Act of Canada, most official publications made by the Canadian government must be issued simultaneously in English and French. This includes the material published on Twitter by more than 100 government agencies and bodies[35] and by some politicians, including the Prime Minister. According to the result of our inquiries to a few of these agencies, tweet translation is handled by certified translators hired by the government, and is typically conducted from English to French. A qualitative analysis of the original tweets and their translation shows them to be of very high quality. Most of these institutions have actually set up two Twitter accounts, one for each language, contrary to some users who prefer

---

[34]http://www.cbc.ca/news/canada/saskatchewan/environment-canada-tornado-tweets-stalled-by-language-laws-1.2688958
[35]http://gov.politwitter.ca/directory/network/twitter

to alternate French and English tweets on the same account,[36] or to write single posts in two languages.

The study by Gotti et al. [2013] looked at messages exchanged over Twitter in different languages, with a focus on translating tweets written by government institutions. What sets these messages apart is that, generally speaking, they are written in a proper language (without which their credibility would presumably suffer), while still having to be extremely brief to abide by the ever-present limit of 140 characters. This contrasts with typical social media texts in which a large variability in quality is observed [Agichtein et al., 2008].

Tweets from government institutions can also differ somewhat from some other, more informal social media texts in their intended audience and objectives. Specifically, such tweet feeds often attempt to serve as a credible source of timely information presented in a way that engages members of the lay public. That is why translations should present a similar degree of credibility, ease of understanding, and ability to engage the audience as in the source tweet—all the while conforming to the 140-character limit.

Gotti et al. [2013] attempted to take these matters into account for the task of translating Twitter feeds emitted by Canadian governmental institutions. This could prove very useful, since more than 150 Canadian agencies have official feeds. Moreover, while its population is only 34 million, Canada ranks fifth in the number of Twitter users (3% of all users)[37] after the U.S., the UK, Australia, and Brazil. This certainly explains why the Canadian government, politicians, and institutions increasingly use this social network service. Canadian governmental institutions must disseminate information in both official languages, French and English. A great potential value in targeted computer-aided translation tools has been identified, which could offer a significant reduction over the current time and effort required to translate tweets manually. The authors showed that a state-of-the-art Statistical Machine Translation (SMT) toolkit, used off-the-shelf, and trained on out-of-domain data is, unsurprisingly, not up to the task. They mined bilingual tweets from the Internet and showed that this resource significantly improves the performance of the translation when added to the initial parallel corpus. They tested several simple adaptation scenarios, including the mining of the URLs mentioned in the parallel tweets. Other domain adaptation methods in machine translation [Daumé and Jagarlamudi, 2011, Foster et al., 2010, Razmara et al., 2012, Sankaran et al., 2012, Zhao et al., 2004] could be useful for social media data.

Gotti et al. [2013] showed that unknown words are a concern, and should be dealt with appropriately. The serialization of URLs helped extract words and translate them. This could be extended to user names. The latter do not need to be translated, but reducing the vocabulary size is always desirable when working with a SMT engine. One interesting subcategory of out-of-vocabulary tokens is the hashtags. In 20% of the cases, they require segmentation into words before being translated. Even if they are transformed into regular words (#radon → radon or

---

[36]See, for instance, the account of the Canadian politician Justin Trudeau https://twitter.com/JustinTrudeau.
[37]http://www.techvibes.com/blog/how-canada-stacks-up-against-the-world-on-twitter-2012-10-17

did you know it's best to test for #radon in the fall / winter ? <url> #health #safety
l' automne / l' hiver est le meilleur moment pour tester le taux de radon. <url> #santé #sécurité

Figure 3.1: Example of a pair of tweets extracted from the bilingual feed pair Health Canada/Santé Canada, after tokenization.

#gender equality → gender equality), however, it is not clear at this point how to detect whether they are used like normally occurring words in a sentence, as in (#radon is harmful) or if they are simply tags added to the tweet to categorize it. Gotti et al. [2013] also showed that translating under size constraints can be handled easily by mining the n-best list produced by the decoder, but only up to a point. The remaining 6% of the tweets that were analyzed in detail did not have a shorter version. Numerous ideas are possible to alleviate the problem. One could, for instance, modify the logic of the decoder to penalize hypotheses that promise to yield overlong translations. Another idea would be to inspect manually the strategies of governmental agencies on Twitter when attempting to shorten their messages, and to select those that seem acceptable and implementable, like the suppression of articles or the use of authorized abbreviations.

3.7.4   HASHTAG OCCURRENCE, LAYOUT, AND TRANSLATION

Translating hashtags from one language to another remains one of the challenges in machine translation of tweets. Authors use hashtags liberally within tweets to mark them as belonging to a particular topic, and hashtags can serve to group messages belonging to the topic. They are a very interesting form of metadata and mining and translating them automatically can be very useful. Gotti et al. [2014] addressed this problem in a corpus-driven approach applied to tweets published by the Canadian government. They collected an aligned bilingual corpus of 8,758 tweet pairs in French and English, derived from 12 Canadian government agencies. Figure 3.1 illustrates one pair from the aligned bilingual corpus.

Hashtag Frequencies of Occurrence

In this corpus, hashtags account for 6–8% of all tokens, and exhibit a Zipfian distribution.[38] The specific statistical analysis on the hashtags in this corpus is provided in Table 3.8. The table shows that these tweet pairs consist of 142,136 and 155,153 tokens in English and French, respectively.

Hashtags Layout

The hashtags appear in either a tweet's prologue, announcing its topic, or in the tweet's text instead of traditional words, or in an epilogue. A sample tweet is illustrated in Figure 3.2 which includes hashtags in different parts, as follows:

---

[38]There are a few very frequent hashtags, and many that appear only once.

Table 3.8: Statistics on hashtag use in the aligned bilingual corpus [Gotti et al., 2014]

	English	French
Number of Tweets	8,758	8,758
Number of Togens (words + hashtags)	142,136	155, 153
Number of Hashtags	11,481	10,254
Number of Hashtag types	1,922	1,781
Avg. hashtags/tweet	1.31	1.17
% Hashtags w.r.t. tokens	8.1	6.6
Number of Tweets with at least one hashtag	5,460	5,137

Figure 3.2: An original tweet with hashtags in its three possible regions.

Table 3.9: Distribution of hashtags in epilogues and prologues [Gotti et al., 2014]

	English	French
Number of tweets	8,758	8,758
% of tweets with a prologue	10.7	10.1
% of tweets with an epilogue	87.3	86.5
% of tweets with a prologue and epilogue	10.4	9.8
Number of hashtags	11,481	10,254
% of hashtags in prologues	8.2	8.7
% of hashtags in epilogues	30.9	28.9
Total % of hashtags in prologues and epilogues	39.1	37.5

• Hashtag in prologue: #Canada

• Inline hashtags: #health #mothers #children

• Hashtags in epilogue: #MNC #globalhealth

Table 3.9 represents the distribution of hashtags in epilogues and prologues.

Table 3.10: Percentage of unknown hashtags to English and French vocabularies of the Hansard corpus [Gotti et al., 2014]

	English	French
Number of hashtags	11,481	10,254
Number of hashtag types	1,922	1,781
% OOV hashtags stripped of the # sign	23.2	20.6
% OOV hashtag types stripped of #	16.7	17.4

Table 3.11: Percentage of unknown hashtags to "standard" English and French vocabularies, after automatic segmentation of multiword hashtags into simple words [Gotti et al., 2014]

	English	French
Number of hashtag types	1,922	1,781
% OOV hashtags types (from Table 3.10)	16.7	17.4
% OOV hashtag types after segmentation	3.7	4.7

Hashtags and Out-of-vocabulary (OOV)

Hashtags are words prefixed with a pound sign in 80% of the cases. The rest is mostly multiword hashtags, for which a simple segmentation algorithm can be used. They also can be unknown (out-of-vocabulary, OOV) in a language. Table 3.10 represents statistics on the hashtags and OOV words.

Although there are no specific figures about the distribution of the remaining OOV hashtags, it clearly appears that the majority of them are multiword hashtags (for instance #RaiseAReaderDay or #NouveauBrunswick). A simple hashtag-segmenting procedure backed by the corresponding language's vocabulary is provided by Gotti et al. [2014] in order to approximate the proportion of the OOV hashtags that can be split into English (or French) words. The algorithm simply attempts to find out if an unknown hashtag can be split in substrings that are all known to the underlying vocabulary (including numbers). Table 3.11 represents statistics on the Hashtags and OOVs after segmentation.

A manual analysis of the bilingual alignment of 5,000 hashtags shows that 5% (French) to 18% (English) of them do not have a counterpart in their containing tweet's translation. This analysis further shows that 80% of multiword hashtags are correctly translated by humans, and that the mistranslation of the rest may be due to incomplete translation directives regarding social media. Work on language identification and translation of hashtags was also done by Carter et al. [2011].

Gotti et al. [2014] also designed a baseline system incorporating various evaluation metrics. Using this baseline system, they presented a number of SMT systems incorporating pre-processing and post-processing steps. They showed how these resources and their analysis can guide the design of a SMT pipeline, and its evaluation. A baseline system implementing a tweet-specific tokenizer yielded promising results. The system was improved by translating epilogues, prologues, and text separately.

3.7.5   MACHINE TRANSLATION FOR ARABIC SOCIAL MEDIA

People prefer to interact on social media in their native language. For example, many posts on social media were written in Arabic dialects and English for the same event during the Arab Spring. To facilitate interaction among people with different languages that have common interests, machine translation plays an important role and improves multilingual interactions. However, machine-translating social media messages faces many challenges, because there is a lack of resources for social media.

As discussed earlier, adapting a trained machine translation system to available bilingual resources is difficult. It is even more so when translating dialectal, non-standard, or noisy messages. Nonetheless, when processing Arabic for the purposes of social media analysis and machine translation, despite a lack of resources for Arabic dialects, a machine translation system can be developed, by first mapping dialectal Arabic to Modern Standard Arabic (MSA), which is the formal language in most Arabic countries.

Researchers have used crowdsourcing to build dialectal Arabic to English parallel corpora [Zbib et al., 2012] as a source for machine translation systems, whereas little research has been done to transfer dialectal Arabic into MSA [Bakr et al., 2008, Sawaf, 2010, Shaalan et al., 2007] and then develop a machine translation system by using available NLP tools for MSA.

As discussed in Chapter 2, language processing of dialectal Arabic on social media is a challenging task. Arabic script can be written in various forms: in romanization (using the Latin alphabet), with diacritics, and without diacritics. Some Arabic dialect speakers are unable to understand other Arabic dialects [Shaalan et al., 2007]. In addition, Arabic dialects often deviate from MSA and there are no determined grammar rules for them.

Shaalan et al. [2007] presented a rule-based lexical mapping from Egyptian Arabic to MSA. The mapping from the Egyptian dialect to MSA was done by matching words either one-to-one or one-to-many. The Buckwalter morphological analyzer (BAMA) [Buckwalter, 2004] was used and Buckwalter's tables are enhanced with metadata of Arabic dialect. An Egyptian corpus was created by collecting and extracting Arabic text from the Web and then an Egyptian lexicon was built over an existing Buckwalter MSA lexicon.

Following this research, Bakr et al. [2008] showed that it is better to convert an Arabic dialect to diacritized MSA in order to disambiguate the words. Therefore, the Egyptian corpus was tokenized and POS-tagged in a semi-automatic way. Then, MSA words were tokenized and tagged automatically and the annotation of dialect words was verified manually. Additional tags were used for Arabic dialects. A rule-based approach was applied to convert dialectal Arabic to MSA using POS tags. First, a lookup procedure was applied to each dialect lexicon to get the corresponding discretized MSA word and its correct position in the target sentence. Since there may be different alternatives for each word, these alternatives were then compared with the results obtained from the POS learning and the correct diacritized word was chosen according to its POS.

Similar work was done by Boujelbane et al. [2013] and Al-Gaphari and Al-Yadoumi [2010] for the Tunisian dialect and Sana'ani accent, respectively. Boujelbane et al. [2013] provided a Tunisian corpus as Tunisian Arabic Treebank by transforming MSA Treebank (Penn Arabic Treebank). The mapping from MSA to Tunisian was done by using a rule-based approach to create a bilingual lexicon and dialect corpus. Al-Gaphari and Al-Yadoumi [2010] used a rule-based approach to translate dialects to MSA. Their experiment showed that there is little distortion of MSA in the Sana'ani dialect.

As a part of the social monitoring system TRANSLI (see Appendix A), the core of which is based on statistical machine translation, the first preprocessing step is to identify and classify Twitter feeds in Arabic according to their location. NLP Technologies developed the Arabic Social Media Analysis Tools (ASMAT) project in collaboration with Université du Québec à Montréal (UQAM) [Sadat et al., 2014a,b,c], which aims at creating tools for analyzing social media in Arabic. This project paves the way for applications such as machine translation and sentiment analysis, through pre-processing and normalization.

In general, we can say that little effort has been made regarding the mapping of Arabic dialects to MSA. Language processing of dialectal Arabic suffers from lack of resources and standard grammars as well as lack of language processing tools. Hence, machine translation for Arabic dialects is not a trivial task when there are no resources such as a parallel text or a transfer lexicon.

3.7.6   EVALUATION MEASURES FOR MACHINE TRANSLATION

The **evaluation measures** for machine translation systems can be automatic or manual. One of the automatic measures is BLEU [Papineni et al., 2002]. It calculates n-gram overlap between the automatically translated text and multiple reference translations produced by humans (with the emphasis on precision, unlike ROUGE which emphasizes recall). Manual measures need human judges to rate the generated translated text by different criteria, such as adequacy (whether the translation conveys the correct meaning) and fluency (whether the translation is fluent regardless of the correctness of the meaning).

We show an example of tweet translation and the effect of the hashtag translation. Table 3.12 represents the performance obtained by considering the tweet layout including epilogues and prologues, as well as considering lattice input for hashtag translation. The performance of the system is evaluated using BLEU score and word-error rate (WER). Recall, precision, and F-measure for the hashtags produced by the translation system are also considered for evalua-

Table 3.12: Translation performance obtained by Gotti et al. [2014]

Metric	English→French	French→English
WER	9	48
BLEU	35.22	32.42
BLEUnohash	38.23	36.22
Hash-R	23	19
Hash-P	74	87
Hash-F	35	31

tion, and are referred by hash-R, hash-P, and hash-F, respectively. The hashtags that are left not translated can cause loss of recall.

3.8   SUMMARY

In this chapter, we presented the methods used in NLP applications for social media texts. We looked at methods for the very popular applications of sentiment and emotion analysis in social media messages. We highlighted the new role of computational linguistic tools in information extraction from social media content, since techniques were developed for the extraction of various kinds of information. Event detection is of high interest, and so is the detection of the location of the events or of the users who write about the events. The adaptation of summarization methods to social media texts and the translation of these informal texts into other languages were discussed.

In this chapter, we saw that semantic analysis applications to social media texts have come a long way, but there is still room for improvement. In the future, improved availability of meta-information related to non-textual social media and better semantic analysis of social media texts can accelerate progress in this area by combining the information from the two sources. In the next chapter, we present several applications that make use of the methods and tasks discussed thus far.

CHAPTER 4

Applications of Social Media Text Analysis

4.1 INTRODUCTION

The growing use of social media platforms in everyday life and the place of digital marketing in the corporation or small business have been mentioned previously. This chapter discusses the value of user-generated contents and it highlights the benefits of social media text applications that use natural language processing techniques. These applications of semantic analysis of social media could widely affect individuals, industry, small businesses and restaurants, arts and culture organizations, financial institutions, insurance companies, and educational institutions. Social media analytics could improve or change the strategic plan before execution and further investment of the involved parities by predicting market behaviors or consumer preferences.

Several large companies such as Google, Amazon, and Bloomberg investigate on big data analysis using topic classification and social media mining on what people are saying, and select relevant data by clustering or other machine learning methods. Once clusters of interest are identified, then the application of NLP techniques is one of the most promising avenues for social media data processing.

The rest of this chapter describes the following applications. Section 4.2 presents healthcare applications. Section 4.3 looks into financial applications. Section 4.4 describes current research on predicting voting intentions based on social media postings. Section 4.5 discusses techniques for social media monitoring. Section 4.5 presents digital marketing applications. Section 4.6 presents security and defense applications. Section 4.7 looks at disaster monitoring and response applications. Section 4.8 explains how social media can be used to compute user profiles, in particular NLP-based user modeling. Section 4.9 discusses applications for entertainment. Section 4.10 focuses on NLP-based information visualization for social media. There are also sections for social media applications for government communication, rumor detection, recommender systems, and preventing sexual harassment.

4.2 HEALTHCARE APPLICATIONS

There are many online platforms where people discuss their health. For example EHealth forum[1] is a community site for medical Q&As that offers several subtopics such as mental health, men's

---

[1]http://ehealthforum.com/

and women's health, cancer, relationships, and nutrition. Some of these sites focus on various topics. For example, Spine Health[2] provides information on back pain and neck pain relief where members can discuss pain, conditions, and treatment. The language is often informal, and users may sometimes use medical terms, but most of the time lay language terms are used. Various information can be extracted automatically from such postings and discussions. For example the automatic Q&A can run through the various forums to find the appropriate treatment for disc herniation and verify if a lumbar micro-discectomy surgery may be the right solution. Also, through various discussion forums, the NLP-based system can find advice on how the mind, body, and soul can help improve back pain with methods such as quitting smoking, exercising, and rehabilitation.

Opinion mining in medical forums is similar to opinion mining in blogs, but the interest is focused on a specific health problem. For example, Ali et al. [2013] collected texts from medical forums about hearing devices and classified them into negative (talking about the stigma associated with the wearing of hearing aids), neutral, or positive. A preliminary step can be an automatic filtering of the posts to keep only those relevant to the topic (and include opinions). For the opinion classification task, the techniques are based on machine learning and/or counting of polarity terms similar to those discussed in Section 3.4.

An important aspect specific to the health-related applications is the need for privacy protection. De-identification is the process of removing personal data from documents with sensitive content in order to protect an individual's privacy from a third party [Uzuner et al., 2007, Yeniterzi et al., 2010]. De-identification is very important in health informatics, especially when dealing with patient records. It can be viewed as the detection of personal health information (PHI), such as names, dates of birth, addresses, health insurance numbers, etc. On social media forum such as Patients like me,[3] there is a need for detecting PHI and warning the users to revise their postings to not reveal too much confidential personal information. Detection of PHI on various kinds of text was investigated by Sokolova et al. [2009]. Opinion analysis that takes into account the detection of sensitive information in Tweeter messages about health issues was investigated by Bobicev et al. [2012], among others. A somewhat inverse problem to the de-identification is to link mentions of the same person across multiple documents or databases [Liu and Ruths, 2013], which could be necessary when the same person has multiple medical records at different clinics or hospitals.

Following clinical trials, pharmaceutical researchers rely on patients self-reporting side-effects of prescription medicine. The monitoring of adverse pharmaceutical side-effects, known as "pharmacovigilance," has become more accessible to researchers due to the vast amounts of information patients now self-report on social media. Nikfarjam et al. [2015] conducted research into the use of NLP techniques on Adverse Drug Reaction (ADR) extraction from social media. The result was a concept extraction system called ADRMine.

---

[2]http://www.spine-health.com/
[3]http://www.patientslikeme.com/

a) **#Schizophrenia**_indication_ *#Seroquel did not suit me at all. Had severe* **tremors**_ADR_ *and* **weight gain**_ADR._

b) *I felt awful, it made my* **stomach hurt**_ADR_*with bad* **heartburn**_ADR_ *too,* **horrid taste in my mouth**_ADR_ *tho it does tend to clear up the* **infection**_Indication._

Figure 4.1: Examples of annotated social media posts discussing ADRs [Nikfarjam et al., 2015].

The training of ARDMine relied on two datasets: an expert-annotated corpus of over 8,000 social media posts from Twitter and DailyStrength (a health-focused social network), and an unlabeled corpus of over 1 million user sentences from social media. The researchers learned word embeddings using the larger, unlabeled corpus, in order to generate token similarity information via k-means clustering. This cluster information served as a feature in the final model. Using existing medical language databases, the researchers compiled a lexicon of over 13,000 ADR-related phrases. The ADRMine system's main predictive component was a CRF classifier, trained on the annotated corpus mentioned above. For features, the researchers used contextual information (the six tokens surrounding the token being classified), a binary feature denoting if the token existed in the ADR phrase lexicon, the token's part-of-speech tag, and a negation tag. Additionally, to improve on baseline performance, the researchers included cluster similarity information, from the k-means clustering mentioned above, on the token being classified and the surrounding context tokens. The final model achieved an F-score of 0.82.

Nikfarjam [2016] extended this research to include DeepHealthMiner, a deep learning approach to classifying ADRs, as shown in Figure 4.2. This model used over 3 million user sentences to generate word embeddings for tokens. These tokens then served as the input into a feedforward neural net, which tried to distinguish ADR tokens in a sentence from other types of tokens. Once a token was flagged as an ADR, it was then compared to a lexicon of ADR phrases in order to predict which ADR the post was discussing. This lexicon-based approach achieved an F-measure of 0.64, lower than that of the ADRMine system.

Stanovsky et al. [2017] also took on the challenging process of extracting ADRs from social media text. Unlike Nikfarjam et al. [2015], these researchers sought to show that quality models could be trained without large amounts of expert-annotated training data. Their approach was to develop an active learning system, whereby only a few seed training examples would be needed before the model could start making predictions. A human arbiter would then quickly accept or reject the model's decisions, allowing it to learn quickly without large amounts of expert-labeled data. The central model in this research was a recursive neural net (RNN), into which word embeddings of posts from a medical social forum were input. To augment the word vectorization, the researchers also leveraged DBpedia knowledge graph embeddings, which can provide more useful vectorizations for domain-specific words. This model achieved an F-score

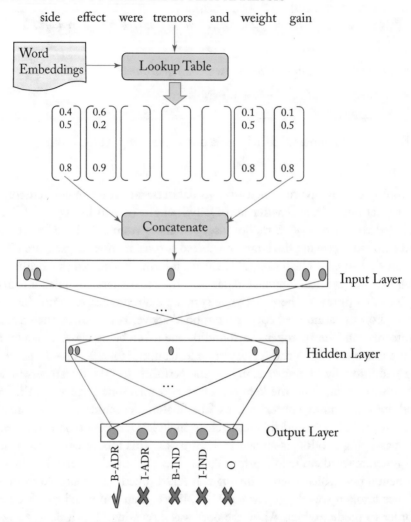

Figure 4.2: The DeepHealthMiner neural net architecture [Nikfarjam, 2016].

of 0.93 when training data was provided and 0.83 when using only active training, thus demonstrating the potential of bootstrapped training when sufficient training data is unavailable.

The tweets use informal language, which is very different from the formal medical language. Manousogiannis et al. [2019] presented a Few-Shot learning method that uses data from the UMLS. They introduced an innovation on the normalization step. They linked ADRs to their related MEDDRA code[4]. They used the pre-trained Google News Word2Vec model to generate the work vectors from their training data. Their new Few-Shot learning method

---

[4]https://www.meddra.org/

reached a better result (relaxed F-score: 0.337 to 0.345) compared with the average (relaxed F-score: 0.2972) in this task.

In general, patients tend to post information about their health, about the effect of treatments and medication, or about their emotional experiences on social media forums (such as PatientsLikeMe). Data about stress or depressive states could also be useful in detecting potential mental health issues. The discussion of people's mental health has recently grown beyond health-specific forums. For example, McClellan et al. used topic modeling to collect 176 million tweets relating to depression or suicide. Using this dataset, the researchers analyzed communication patterns in users discussing these mental health issues. Turcan and McKeown [2019] introduced a stress dataset—Dreaddit. This dataset includes 190,000 posts collected from 5 distinct categories of Reddit communities. Dreaddit can help researchers recognize stress from texts posted by users. Such research could prove useful in improving the logistics and organization of mental health outreach campaigns on social media platforms. In addition to these datasets related to mental disease, there are also datasets about physical health. Pant et al. [2019] provided a dataset named SmokEng with information about tobacco usage. They analyzed Twitter contents and made a fine-grained classification to distinguish the usages of cigarettes, e-cigarettes, and other tobacco productions. This dataset can be used for cigarettes surveillance, helping people live in a healthier life by getting rid of cigarettes.

With the increase in social media usage and the extensive level of self-disclosure [Park et al., 2012], more and more research has been conducted to identify mental disorders at an individual as well as at a society level. Researchers have used features such as behavioral characteristics, depression language, emotion and linguistic style, reduced social activity, increased negative affect, clustered social network, raised interpersonal and medical fears and increased expression in religious involvement, use of negative words, in order to determine the cues of major depressive disorder [De Choudhury et al., 2013a]. Tsugawa et al. [2015] also used syntactical features such as bag of words (BOW) and word frequencies to identify the ratio of tweet topics and concluded that topic modeling also adds a positive contribution to the predictive model compared to the use of the bag-of-words model, which could also result in overfitting.

The successful use of NLP techniques in identifying the progress and level of depression of individuals in online therapy could bring greater insights to clinicians, to apply interventions effectively and efficiently. Howes et al. [2014] used 882 transcripts gathered from an online psychological therapy provider to determined that use of linguistic features can be considered more valuable in predicting the progress of a patient than sentiment and topic-based analysis. Contrary to traditional sentiment analysis approaches that use three main polarity classes (i.e., positive, negative, and neutral), Shickel et al. [2016], divided the neutral class into two classes: neither positive nor negative and both positive and negative. With the use of syntactic, lexical, and also by representing words as vectors in the vector space (word embeddings), the authors managed to achieve an overall accuracy of 78% for the four-class polarity prediction.

Identifying symptoms of schizophrenia (SZ), a chronic and uncommon mental disorder that affects a person's thoughts and behaviors, is difficult. Approximately 1% of the U.S. population suffers from this condition which makes people seldom disagree with having this disorder. Linguistic abnormalities are a major symptom of SZ and several of the other occurring symptoms are manifested through language. Zomick et al. [2019] explore the linguistic indicators of SZ by leveraging the vast amount of data from Reddit discussion forums and use NLP and statistical techniques to study the linguistic characteristics of SZ. They collected and analyzed a large corpus of Reddit posts from users claiming to have received a formal diagnosis of SZ and identified several linguistic features that differentiated these users from a control (CTL) group. This was done by implementing a Logistic Regression model with default parameters. They averaged the LIWC features across all comments per user and trained the model to determine whether the aggregated LIWC features were from the posts of a user from the SZ group or the CTL group. Since the data was balanced across groups, the random baseline was set to 50%. The average performance of the classifier across 5 folds was 81.56% accuracy, and the standard deviation was 2.29. Similarly, Mitchell et al. [2015] utilized the corpus data from Twitter, which is collected in an analogous manner. They afterward applied an Support Vector Machine classifier on these data and obtained an 82.3% classification accuracy.

De Choudhury et al. [2013b] proposed methods to identify the level of depression among social media users including automatic calculations of a social media depression (SMDI: Social Media Depression Index). Schwartz et al. [2014] used a classification model trained with n-grams, linguistic behavior and Latent Dirichlet Allocation (LDA) topics as features for predicting the individuals who are susceptible to having depression. In addition to open-vocabulary analysis and lexicon-based approaches such as LIWC, Coppersmith et al. [2014a] suggested language models, primarily based on unigrams and character 5-grams to determine the existence of mental disorders.

The Computational Linguistics and Clinical Psychology (CLPsych) 2015 shared task [Coppersmith et al., 2015b] used self-reporting data on Twitter about Post Traumatic Stress Disorder (PTSD) and depression, collected according to the procedure introduced by Coppersmith et al. [2014b]. The shared task participants were provided with a dataset of self-reported users on PTSD and depression. For each user in the dataset, nearly 3,200 most recent posts were collected using the Twitter API. Resnik et al. [2015], whose system ranked first in the CLPsych 2015 Shared Task, created 16 systems based on features derived using supervised LDA, supervised anchors (for topic modeling), lexical TF-IDF, and a combination of all. An SVM classifier with a linear kernel obtained an average precision above 0.80 for all the three tasks (i.e., depression vs. control, PTSD vs. control and depression vs. PTSD) and a maximum precision of 0.893 for differentiating PTSD users from the control group. Preotiuc-Pietro et al. [2015] employed user metadata and textual features from the corpus provided by the CLPsych 2015 Shared Task to develop a linear classifier to predict users having either one of the mental illnesses. They used the bag-of-words approach to aggregate word counts, topics derived from clustering methods, and metadata (e.g., followers, followees, age, gender) from the users Twitter profile as the main feature categories. With the use of logistic regression and linear SVM in an ensemble of classifiers, the authors obtained an average precision above 0.800 for all the three tasks and with a maximum score of 0.867 for differentiating users in the control group from the users with depression. Kirinde Gamaarachchige and Inkpen [2019] investigate the impact of using emotional patterns identified by the clinical practitioners and computational linguists to enhance the prediction capabilities of a mental illness detection model built using a deep neural network architecture. Their tests were also on the CLPysch 2015 dataset.

The use of the supervised LDA and the supervised anchor model proved to be highly successful compared to the unsupervised clustering approaches, and even more efficient than using linguistic methods such as the use of n-grams and other lexicon-based approaches. Resnik et al. [2015] proved that such approaches can be successfully used in identifying users with depression, who have self-disclosed their mental illnesses on Twitter. In general, a clear distinction in the lexical and syntactic structure of the language used by individuals with different mental disorders, as well as between individuals within a control group, can be identified throughout the literature mentioned above, as well as from the explorative analysis conducted by Gkotsis et al. [2016].

Coppersmith et al. [2015a] introduced a novel method of leveraging self-diagnoses posted on Twitter to identify users with mental health conditions. They expanded this research to include results for 10 different conditions and to control for gender and age demographics. The data collection process involved scanning through posts on Twitter for statements such as "I have just been diagnosed with X" where X matched one of the 10 conditions being examined. For each diagnosed user, over 100 tweets were collected. To discriminate between conditions, the researchers examined differences in LIWC categories between users with various conditions. Such analysis demonstrated that certain conditions (*e.g.,* eating disorder and seasonal affective disorder) display distinct linguistic patterns, while others (*e.g.,* anxiety and depression) are harder to distinguish. To broaden the vocabulary used in this discrimination, the researchers included use of character-based n-gram models (CLMs). Using CLM scores for each condition achieved high accuracy in discrimination for particular conditions (86% accuracy for anxiety, 76% accuracy for eating disorders). This suggests that using linguistic features for mental health condition discrimination could prove fruitful moving forward.

Benton et al. [2017] leveraged the datasets from Coppersmith et al. [2015a] to design a novel neural architecture for mental health diagnoses through Twitter. Using three datasets identifying Twitter users as belonging to a certain set of mental health disorders, the researchers trained a multi-task learning (MLT) model that shared parameters of three independently trained neural nets. They hypothesized that the patterns expressed in the three datasets would be highly correlated, and thus good candidates for MLT. The results of these experiments varied across disease classification, but demonstrated great improvements in the bipolar disorder and post-traumatic stress disorder (PTSD) tasks, which had the least training data.

Jamil et al. [2017] proposed an automated system that can identify at-risk users from their public social media activity, more specifically, from Twitter. The data was collected from the #BellLetsTalk campaign, which is a wide-reaching, multi-year program designed to break the silence around mental illness and support mental health across Canada. The annotated dataset included 160 users. The researchers trained a user-level classifier for detecting at-risk users. They also trained a tweet-level classifier for predicting whether a tweet indicates depression. This task was much more difficult due to the imbalanced data (on average, there were about 5% depression tweets and 95% non-depression tweets per depressed user) and to the lack of information in a short tweet.. To handle the class imbalance, undersampling methods were used. The resulting classifier at tweet-level had high recall, but low precision. Therefore, this classifier was used only to compute the estimated percentage of depressed tweets and to add this value as a feature for the user-level classifier. The best results for the user-level classification on the #BellLetsTalk dataset were 0.70 precision, 0.85 recall, and 0.77 F-score for an SVM classifer with features such as polarity word counts, depression word counts, and number of pronouns, plus the automatically estimated percentage of depressed tweets for each user.

The task of identifying posts discussing mental health, and also discerning what specific conditions are being discussed, has been a primary focus of social media health research recently. Gkotsis et al. [2016] took such a linguistic approach to analyzing mental health posts on the popular social media forum Reddit. In this study, the task was to determine which linguistic features could be useful in identifying posts related to mental health conditions and other applications such as identifying posts requiring urgent attention. Gkotsis et al. [2016] leveraged data from the popular social media site Reddit, which provides many topic-specific forums (or "subreddits"). The researchers collected posts from 16 subreddits dedicated to discussion of 10 different mental health conditions. The feature set from these texts included measures established from previous psycho-linguistic work, such as LIWC and Coh-Metrix, and different measures of readability and complexity. To examine complexity, the researchers used features such as cohesion (measured in word overlap between sentences), horizontal complexity (measured in sentence count), and vertical complexity (measured in the height of the parse tree for each sentence). The results indicated that there is not much linguistic variance between subreddits, meaning that such features would not be sufficient for classification systems. However, by comparing the differences in vocabularies across mental health discussions, the researchers were able to note significant similarities (60% accuracy in discrimination) between subreddits dedicated to the same condition and differences (90% accuracy in discrimination) between those dedicated to different conditions. By using the Self-reported Mental Health Diagnoses (SMHD) dataset, Sekulic and Strube [2019] applied a Hierarchical Attention Network (HAN) to identify mental diseases. This new method can classify nine different mental disorder (depression, ADHD, anxiety, bipolar, PTSD, autism, OCD, SZ, and eating disorder). For the diseases with thousands of diagnosed users such as depression, ADHD, anxiety, and bipolar, their experiments achieved a better accuracy than the baseline. The classification accuracies were 68.25%, 64.27%, 69.24%, and 67.42%, respectively.

Recently, the shared task at CLPsych 2016[5] and 2017[6] further challenge the research community in the task of developing classifiers to automatically prioritize posts from an online peer-support forum hosted by ReachOut.com. These forums are carefully moderated by a team of trained professionals and volunteers, who ensure they remain safe, positive and healthy. The shared task aims to support these moderators by automatically identifying concerning content, so that it can be addressed as quickly as possible. For this task, ReachOut have annotated a corpus of posts with a red/amber/green semaphore that indicates how urgently they require moderator attention. Systems leveraged the content of the posts, including sentiment, topics, thread context and user history, to classify posts into the three classes: red, amber, or green. A fourth class, named crisis, is also available, with very few training instances. Posts labeled as crisis require the urgent intervention of the moderators. In addition to the 947 training posts, a separate set of 241 test posts were annotated for use in the evaluation of the shared task systems. Some of the best results in the 2016 shared task were obtained by Shickel and Rashidi [2016], who used normalized unigrams in conjunction with a wider range of post features, with some attributes based on the number and content of other posts in the same thread. Their system achieved average precision, recall, and F-measure of 0.84, 0.83, and 0.82, respectively. Brew [2016] demonstrated green precision, recall, and F-measure of 0.93, 0.84, and 0.88, respectively, with better differentiation between amber and red posts. This system used a small feature set and emphasized the use of a SMO classifier with radial kernel. The 2017 shared task used the data from 2016, plus a new test set and the possibility to use additional unlabeled data.

The shared task of 2019's CLPsych workshop[7] focused on predicting a person's degree of suicide risk based on his/her Reddit post. The tasks were based on a four-way scale of no risk, low, moderate, and severe risk. The Reddit website hosts over 130,000 active online forums and communities, where users can post on any topics of their interest. The researchers could participate in one or all of the three tasks. The first two tasks covered a "risk assessment" of suicide based on analyzing suicide-related posts on the SuicideWatch subreddit (Task A) and/or other Reddit forums (Task B), and the third task was about "screening" users based only on their regular (non-SuicideWatch) posts (Task C) [Zirikly et al., 2019].

The researchers were given access to the University of Maryland Reddit Suicidality Dataset [Shing et al., 2018] that was made available with assistance by the American Association of Suicidology. The dataset consisted of 1,200 users annotated with the four-level scale (for supervised learning methods) and another (optional) larger dataset of 10,000 unannotated users.

Ruiz et al. [2019] implemented three machine-learning models: SVM, Naive Bayes, and an ensemble model. Among them, the ensemble model had the best macro-averaged F-score of

---

[5] http://clpsych.org/shared-task-2016/
[6] http://clpsych.org//shared-task-2017/
[7] http://clpsych.org/

0.379, when tested on the holdout test dataset. The Naïve Bayes model had the best performance in two additional binary-classification tasks, i.e., no risk vs. flagged risk (any risk level other than no risk) with F-score 0.836 and no or low risk vs. urgent risk (moderate or severe risk) with F-score 0.736.

Allen et al. [2019] used a CNN architecture to incorporate LIWC (Linguistic Inquiry and Word Count) information of the Reddit posts that resulted in macro-averaged F-score of 0.50 on the test set. Their model was trained for 150 epochs on the entire training dataset available for task A. It also achieved high F-scores (0.90 and 0.82, respectively) for the "flagged" and "urgent" tasks.

Ambalavanan et al. [2019] applied the PyTorch6 implementation of the BERT model. The pre-processed (combined) posts of each user were given as input to the BERT Model with a linear classifier (SoftMax) to predict the output labels. Fine-tuning helped to tune the initial embeddings of BERT to the CLPsych downstream task with the help of error backpropagation. The model used a maximum sentence length of 384 tokens with a batch size of 16 and 75 epochs. It resulted in a 0.477 macro-averaged F-score, along with high F-score for "flagged" (0.882) and "urgent" (0.826) tasks.

With the development of industry, air pollution, which is highly relevant to human health, has become a serious problem in our society. Predicting air pollution levels can help us control and mitigate it. Some past researches only utilize historical air data to predict future air pollution levels, which may ignore the current real-world status. Jiang et al. [2019] combined the historical data and NLP technology to develop an innovative method to predict air pollution. They extracted information from Twitter data and applied CNN to generate feature vectors from the whole corpus in order to improve the prediction accuracy. Compared with their baseline, which is only trained on historical data, their new method improved the marco-average F-score with 0.177%. More discussion of other types of health care applications can be found in Liu et al. [2019a].

4.3   FINANCIAL APPLICATIONS

Behavioral economics studies the correlation between the public mood and economic indicators, and between financial news or rumors and stock exchange fluctuations. The public mood is usually tested via traditional polls (surveys), but they are expensive and time consuming. Recent studies show that using social media data can be useful in financial applications. Twitter data was the most used for studies that try to show the relation between automatic estimations of public mood and socio-economic phenomena. Additionally, there are a few social media platform designed specifically for economic information exchanges among users. We mention below some of these platforms.

Economic indicators are usually computed via traditional socio-economic surveys. Mao and Bollen [2011] investigated whether the results of a variety of such surveys can be replicated using data extracted from large-scale search engines and by using Twitter data. In particular, they examined the results of the Michigan Consumer Confidence Index, Gallup Economic Confidence Index, Unemployment Insurance Weekly Claims reported by U.S. Department of Labor and two investor sentiment surveys. Their results showed statistically significant correlations to these socio-economic indexes. They also found that that investor sentiment automatically obtained from Twitter can be a leading indicator of the financial markets, which existing surveys tend to lag.

The value of the Dow Jones Industrial Average (DJIA) over time is one target of manual and now automatic prediction. Bollen et al. [2010] analyzed the text content of daily Twitter feeds by two mood-tracking tools, one that measured positive vs. negative mood and one that measured mood in terms of six dimensions (*calm, alert, sure, vital, kind,* and *happy*). They cross-validated the resulting mood time series by comparing their ability to detect the public's response to the presidential election and to Thanksgiving 2008. Their results indicated that the accuracy of some DJIA predictions can be significantly improved by the inclusion of specific public mood dimensions, but not necessarily for all the predictions. Their experiments achieved an accuracy of 87.6% in predicting the daily up and down changes in the closing values of the DJIA. Porshnev et al. [2013] also investigated users' moods in Twitter data. They used a lexicon-based approach to evaluate the presence eight basic emotions in more than 755 million tweets. They applied Support Vectors Machine and Neural Networks algorithms to predict DJIA and S&P500 indicators. See Section 3.4 for details about emotion analysis and classification techniques in social media texts.

Ranco et al. formalized public response into the economic principle of an "event study," which relied on peak Twitter volume relating to some company or market indicator. The notion that the stock market and the social media discussion about it are only dependent on each other at certain times prompted the examination of these event studies. To examine the relation of Twitter sentiment to stock market indicators, Ranco et al. used price return data and 1.5 million "money-tagged" tweets from 2013–2014. To predict tweets' sentiment, the researchers used an SVM classifier trained on 100,000 expert-labeled tweets. The training examples used to train the SVM classifier were converted into features using the bag-of-words approach, with tokenization, lemmatization, and TF-IDF weighting.

Sul et al. [2014] also collected data from Twitter posts about firms in the S&P 500 and analyzed their cumulative emotional valence. They compared this to the average daily stock market returns of firms in the S&P 500 and their results showed that the cumulative emotional valence (positive or negative) of tweets about a specific firm was significantly related to that firm's stock returns. The emotional valence of tweets from users with many followers (more than the median) had a stronger impact on same day returns, as emotion was quickly disseminated and incorporated into stock prices. In contrast, the emotional valence of tweets from users with few followers had a stronger impact on future stock returns (10-day returns).

As a fundamental part of capital market, stock investment has great significance in optimizing capital allocation, funding as well as increasing the value of assets. To predict and evaluate the stock price also has important practical significance for investors due to the high income and high-risk characteristics of stock investments. However, the stock prices tend to fluctuate and they are often affected by speculative factors, making it almost impossible to make accurate predictions. Considering conformist mentality is essential for accurately predict stock price. Recently, with expansive development of social networks such as Facebook, Twitter, or Sina weibo, users exchange more and more financial information with other users. Jin et al. [2014] proposed a stock prediction method based on social networks and regression models, and they used a real dataset of NASDAQ market and Twitter data to verify their model. Chen et al. [2014a] also used social media texts for stock market prediction. Chen and Du [2013] predicted the fluctuations of the Shanghai/Shenzhen stock exchange, based on data from the online Chinese stock forum Guba.com.cn. Simsek and Ozdemir [2012] analyzed the relation between Turkish Twitter messages and the Turkish stock market index. Martin [2013] predicted the French stock market fluctuations using social media analysis.

Yang et al. [2014] built models of the financial community network based on Twitter data. Chen et al. [2011] conducted a textual analysis of articles published in the Wall Street Journal and on Seeking Alpha, a social-media platform. They showed that social-media sentiment associates strongly with contemporaneous and subsequent stock returns, even after controlling for traditional-media sentiment. Chen et al. [2014b] also examined Seeking Alpha data. After collecting 97,000 opinion articles and 460,000 comments from the site between 2005 and 2012, they used an unsupervised method to determine the impact of sentiment on cumulative abnormal returns. After controlling for sentiment from other media sources such as Dow-Jones articles, the researchers measured the fraction of negative words across articles and comments. The result was a strong correlation between the negativity of articles and comments for a given period of time and the cumulative abnormal returns for the stocks being discussed. They determined that cumulative abnormal returns were 0.397% lower when the fraction of negative words in articles was 1% higher, and 0.197% lower when the fraction of negative words in comments were 1% higher.

The media effect is stronger for articles more closely followed by market participants and for companies mostly held by retail investors. Bing et al. [2014] used a data mining algorithm to determine if the price of a selection of 30 companies listed in NASDAQ and the New York Stock Exchange can actually be predicted by using 15 million collected tweets. They extracted ambiguous textual tweet data through NLP techniques to define public sentiment, then used of data mining techniques to discover patterns between public sentiment and real stock price movements. They were able to predict the stock closing price of some companies with an average accuracy up to 76.12%.

Schniederjans et al. [2013] conducted research into how individual companies should respond to this overwhelming evidence that user sentiments on social media can predict, and, in some cases, impact their financial performance. This research sought to determine the effectiveness of a brand's own participation in social media as it related to impression management

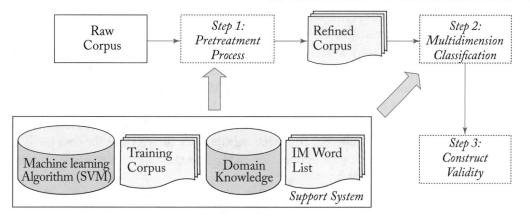

Figure 4.3: SVM-based text mining procedure for impact management [Schniederjans et al., 2013].

(IM). The researchers collected social media data from blogs, forums, and corporate websites for 150 companies. These data were then cleaned of noisy tags and non-informative formatting, split into sentences, and filtered to only include IM-relevant sentences. After preprocessing, the researchers used this data to train an SVM classifier to predict which of 5 IM dimensions each social media post targeted. The SVM classifier (depicted in Figure 4.3) was able to predict which IM dimension a sentence belonged to with an accuracy of 70–75% (the classification procedure was a series of 5 different binary classifiers). The results of the multiple regression confirmed the researchers' hypothesis that social media usage in IM has a positive association with financial performance.

4.4   PREDICTING VOTING INTENTIONS

Research on predicting voting intentions based on social media messages is similar in spirit to the sentiment analysis task described in Section 3.4. Before applying the sentiment analysis techniques, there is a need to detect the topic of the messages, to make sure they are about the desired topic, or about one of the political entities of interest. The simplest way to do this is based on keyword search. Alternatively, text classification methods can be used to classify the messages as relevant or irrelevant to the task [Lampos et al., 2013].

Usually, political intentions are predicted with real polls consisting of a question and a set of predefined answers from which voters can select. The polls can be delivered to the users in person, or by phone or via an online system. Automatic voting intentions prediction based on social media has the advantage that the users do not need to be bothered, therefore the poll is quick and automatic. But its prediction accuracy is probably lower than that of a real poll, because it is difficult to control the sample structure, in order to measure a representative sample of the population under investigation.

An automatic poll that was shown to mimic closely a real political poll automatically determined which of the answers of the poll a voter selected, given a comment she/he wrote after voting, on the SodaHead social polling website. In this study, Persing and Ng [2014] exploited not only the information extracted from the comments but also extra-textual information such as user demographic information and inter-comment constraints. In an evaluation involving nearly one million comments collected from this website, they showed that the vote prediction system that exploited only the textual information can be improved significantly when extended with the extra-textual information.

Tjong Kim Sang and Bos [2012] used Twitter data to predict the 2011 Dutch Senate Election Results. The real election results were used to estimate the accuracy of the automatic prediction. Bermingham and Smeaton [2011] used the 2011 Irish General Election as a case study for investigating the potential to model political sentiment through mining of social media. They combined sentiment analysis using supervised learning and volume-based measures. They evaluated against the conventional election polls and the final election result. They found that the automatic analysis is a good predictor and made some observations related to the task of monitoring public sentiment during election campaigns, including examining a variety of sample sizes and time periods. Pla and Hurtado [2014] predicted the sentiment toward Spanish political parties on the corpus of Twitter messaged developed for the TASS2013 workshop.[8]

In similar studies, Marchetti-Bowick and Chambers [2012] predicted the sentiment toward President Obama expressed in a dataset of tweets. Their results correlated with Gallup's Presidential Job Approval polls. Their study used hashtags as labels of the data and used this automatically labeled data to train supervised classifiers. This way of automatically labeling data is called distant supervision. There is a risk that some labels are not reliable, but the method saves the time and effort to have humans annotated the training data, probably with a small loss in accuracy due to the noisy training data. Mohammad et al. [2014] annotated a set of 2012 U.S. presidential election tweets for a number of attributes pertaining to sentiment, emotion, purpose, and style by crowdsourcing. More than 100,000 crowdsourced responses were obtained for 13 questions on emotions, style, and purpose. They also developed automatic classifiers, using features from state-of-the-art sentiment analysis systems, to predict emotion and purpose labels in new unseen tweets.

On a different application than predicting election results, Burfoot et al. [2011] explored approaches to sentiment classification of U.S. Congressional floor-debate transcripts. Balasubramanyan et al. [2011] looked at the topics discussed in political blog posts and their comments. Arunachalam and Sarkar [2013] suggested that governments could monitor citizens' opinions in social media. Johnson et al. [2017] investigated framing, a political strategy in which politicians carefully word their statements in order to control public perception of issues. They present a

---

[8]http://www.daedalus.es/blog/sentiment-analysis-in-spanish-tass-corpus-released/

collection of weakly supervised models to predict the frames used in political discourse in tweets posted by members of the U.S. Congress, by combining lexical features of tweets and network-based behavioral features of Twitter.

A corpus of tweets mentioning the names of presidents of six G20 countries was analyzed by van den Berg et al. [2019], by studying different naming forms. Then, by annotating these tweets and using entity framing, the authors showed how the varied naming format of the presidents relates to the stance of people toward their solidarity and status.

Internet "trolls" can also influence political voting behavior. Trolls are the people who post provocative words to others. Interestingly, these trolls may express their political stand on the Internet in an aggressive way, which could affect public opinion. To efficiently analyze their political roles, Atanasov et al. [2019] introduced an innovative method based on graph embedding, BERT, and label propagation. By analyzing the posts on Twitter, this model can classify a user's political stand to left-leaning, right-leaning, or news feed.

4.5   MEDIA MONITORING

Media monitoring is an application aimed at watching and tracking broadcast media, online resources, and social media in order to transform unstructured data into meaningful and useful information. This application could be used as a powerful tool for business intelligence (BI) activities. Event detection is a key aspect in social media monitoring, as we described previously in Section 3.5. Some applications involve event detection methods [Farzindar and Khreich, 2013] based on geo-location and time to identify the most popular events in social media platforms such as Instagram, Facebook, and Twitter.

For example, as presented in the news in 2014,[9] the U.S. President published a communication on social media on November 19 announcing that he was going to give a speech about immigration executive action on November 20 from the White House, and he would provide further details the following day in Las Vegas. For this event several places were involved for the same event of interest. Also, this speech had impact locally within the U.S., and globally for the people looking into U.S. immigration policies such as foreign investors from Hong Kong and China.

The Europe Media Monitor (EMM) is a fully automatic system to analyze online news by gathering articles in over 70 languages. Pajzs et al. [2014] added to this system by developing EMM Hungarian text mining tools for named-entity recognition, classification of persons, name lemmatization, etc. They presented several experiments to deal with the high degree of inflection and agglutination of the Hungarian language. These experiments yielded very positive and encouraging results for even shallow learning methods.

Nagarajan et al. [2009] used Twitter to extract crowd-sourced observations on spatio-temporal-thematic analysis to real-world events. The experience integrated a Semantic Web application called Twitris. TwitInfo is another microblog-based event tracking interface on Twitter

---

[9]http://www.cnn.com/2014/11/19/politics/obama-immigration-announcement-thursday/index.html?hpt=hp_t1

with the ability to collect, aggregate, and visualize tweets on user-specified events [Marcus et al., 2011]. The system highlights peaks and labels the high tweet activity for aggregating sentiment visualization.

Shamma et al. [2010.] studied the live visual media events using conversational activity on video footage and Twitter during two events of the first 2008 U.S. Presidential Debate and the Inauguration of Barack Obama.

In Appendix A, we present the architecture and interface of the TRANSLI platform as a case study for social media analytics and monitoring. Monitoring refers to the agglomeration of social media postings relevant to user interests. Analytics refers to the publication of organized information and of the result of analysis, as well as statistics made available through a visual representation on a dashboard. TRANSLI gathers the information for a specific event, such as the launch of a new smartphone based on location, enabling monitoring both locally and globally.[10] The information about such events can be used by journalists to enhance the published news articles. Guo et al. [2013] investigated direct correspondences between news articles and Twitter messages, with the goal of enriching the content of the tweets in order to allow better semantic processing. Diakopoulos et al. [2010] implemented a visualization tool to assist journalists in tracking events in social media.

Public relations agencies rapidly adopted social media. The traditional methods of sending out press releases and waiting for the media to write about their event was replaced by social media. Social sharing press releases and creating social campaigns around customer case studies, publishing short videos on YouTube and choosing the best quotes to share on Twitter or Facebook have dramatically enhanced the world of public relations. However, journalists rely heavily on Twitter, Facebook, and other social media platforms to source and research stories.

Digital Marketing

With more marketing resources being driven toward social media, we can employ NLP techniques to assess brands' marketing strategies.

Chilet et al. [2016] investigated the effects of market pressure on advertising strategies by using Named Entity Recognition (NER). The researchers culled designers' posts from Instagram, fashion reviews, and online product information to create their dataset. To extract fashion symbols from this text, the researchers used NER tagging patterns, along with a manually developed glossary of 3,000 fashion terms. From these extractions, the researchers were able to identify industry leaders, brand similarities, and approximate competition between brands.

Song et al. examined how customer and user posts shape brands' online presences. Using over 300 million blog posts, the researchers leveraged the SOCIALmetrics platform to conduct morphological analysis and parsing. From these insights, they were able to build brand-user mention matrices. The analysis of these mention matrices included measuring similarities of user posting behavior across brands and industries. The study found that user interactions with

---

[10]http://www.nlptechnologies.ca/

products in an online space impacted the rest of the market, due in part to the interconnectedness of user preferences.

Henrich and Lang [2017] took a multi-faceted approach to understanding product audiences on social media, implemented in the Watson Analytics for Social Media product. Using user biographies and "on-topic" posts from thousands of users across social media platforms, the IBM researchers segmented audiences across demographics, product-related behavior, and interests. They combined familiar tools for sentiment analysis, topic-modeling, and spam detection to extract structured data about users, relying heavily on Annotated Query Language for keyword and pattern matching. Due to customer demand for a highly precise model, the IBM researchers sacrificed recall, attaining a precision of 90.0% and a recall of 58.3%.

The fifth task of SemEval 2019[11], HatEval [Basile et al., 2019] was a shared task that aimed at the detection of hate speech against immigrants and women in tweets. It consisted in two datasets—English (EN) and Spanish (ES)—and a total of four sub-tasks (EN-A, EN-B, ES-A, and ES-B). The sub-task A was a binary classification that divided the tweets into hateful and not hateful (HS). The sub-task B was a triple binary classification task. Besides the HS classification, tweets were classified into aggressive and not aggressive (AG) and based on the targets of hate speech such as one person and groups of persons (TR). Most of the submitted implementations by the researchers adopted traditional preprocessing techniques, such as tokenization, lowercase, stop-words, URLs, and punctuation removal. Some researchers also explored Twitter-driven preprocessing procedures such as hashtag segmentation, slang conversion to correct English, and emoji translation into words.

Pérez and Luque [2019] focused on the Spanish sub-tasks and studied multiple models. However, their best performance was achieved from the implementation of a linear-kernel SVM classifier trained on a text representation composed of bag-of-words, bag-of-characters, and tweet embeddings computed from the FastText sentiment-oriented word vectors. For the sub-task A (ES-A), they obtained a macro-averaged F-score of 0.85 and were officially ranked first for this sub-task. The same implementation was used for the ES-B sub-task giving a macro-averaged F-score of 0.758.

Indurthi et al. [2019] participated in the sub-task A for the English language dataset (EN-A) and achieved a macro-averaged F-score of 0.651% on the test dataset, giving the highest results for this sub-task compared to all the other submissions. This team trained an SVM model with RBF kernel only on the provided data, exploiting the sentence embeddings from Google's Universal Sentence Encoder [Cer et al., 2018] as features.

Similarly, OffensEval [Zampieri et al., 2019b] was the sixth task of SemEval 2019 that aimed to identify and categorizing offensive language in social media. It used a new dataset, the Offensive Language Identification Dataset (OLID) [Zampieri et al., 2019a], containing over 14,000 English tweets and also annotated the target and type of the offensive content in each tweet. OffensEval consisted of three sub-tasks. Sub-task A aimed at distinguishing between

---

[11]http://alt.qcri.org/semeval2019/

offensive and non-offensive posts. Sub-task B focused on the type of offensive content in the post. For sub-task C, the systems had to detect the target of the offensive posts.

Most of the best systems used ensembles and state-of-the-art deep learning models, such as BERT [Vaswani et al., 2017]. Liu et al. [2019b] implemented various models, including linear models and LSTMs, but they achieved their highest macro-average F-score of 0.829 (ranking first in sub-task A) by using the BERT-base-uncased model with default-parameters, along with a maximum sentence length of 64 and trained for 2 epochs. They also used multiple pre-processing techniques, like hashtag segmentation and emoji substitution. Using the same implementation, they achieved a macro-average F-score of 0.7159 for sub-task B and 0.5598 for sub-task C, ranking 4th and 18th among all submissions in the respective sub-tasks.

Nikolov and Radivchev [2019] also used BERT after trying many other deep learning methods. They used pre-processing and pre-trained word embeddings based on GloVe. For sub-task A, using the BERT-Large uncased model, they achieved a macro-average F-score of 0.8153 on the test dataset (officially ranking second), while for sub-task C, implementing the BERT-Base uncased model, they achieved a macro-average F-score of approximately 0.66 on the test dataset, ranking first among all submissions for that task. For sub-task B, they used a soft voting classifier resulting in an F-score of 0.6674 (ranking 16th overall).

4.6   SECURITY AND DEFENSE APPLICATIONS

There is a huge amount of user-generated content available over the Internet, in various social media platforms, much of which is textual. Humans can read only a small part of these texts, in order to detect possible threats to security and public safety (such as mentions of terrorist activities or extremizt/radical texts). This is why text mining techniques are important for security and defense applications. Therefore, we need to use automatic methods for extracting information from texts and for detecting messages that should be flagged as possible threats and forwarded to a human for further analysis.

Computer algorithms can be used in various ways in security, defense, and related areas. An example is data mining for intrusion detection [Mohay et al., 2003], called forensic data mining, that aims to find useful patterns in evidence data or to investigate profiles of suspects. In the future work section of their book, Mohay et al. [2003] mentioned potential uses of text categorization for forensic applications, such as authorship attribution for identifying authors (for example the author of a menacing text or posting on the social media) or possible ways to use text mining for evidence extraction, link analysis, and link discovery.

Information extraction from text can target various pieces of information. The task could be a simple key phrase search (with focus on key phrases that could be relevant for detecting terrorist threats) or a sophisticated topic detection task (i.e., to classify a text as being about a terrorism-related topic or not). Topic detection was studied by many researchers, while only a few focused on social media texts [Razavi et al., 2013].

Kaati et al. [2016] used text analysis to analyze Swedish media sites with critical views toward immigration. They focused on detecting narratives containing xenophobic and conspiratorial stereotypes. They used the text analysis tool LIWC and a set of dictionaries to capture xenophobic narratives. The results indicate a statistically significant divergence in language between mainstream media sites and the critical alternative sites.

Location detection from social media texts is another task that could be useful in security applications. This task was discussed in Section 3.2. Extracting locations mentioned in social media messages could be useful in order to detect events or activities located in specific places. For example, potential terrorist plots can target specific geographic areas. Extracting the users' location based on all their social media postings or other social network information can also help, since not all users declare their location in their social media profile. We can use the messages annotated with location information (from the users who declared their locations) as training data for a classifier that can predict the location of any user. The classifier can catch subtle differences in the language (dialect) and the types of entities mentioned. User location can be of interest to defense applications in cases when many disturbing messages are posted by a user, in order to estimate the possible location of this user. Even if such a user declared a location in his/her profile, the classifier could be used to detect fake declarations.

Another task that can help in security applications is emotion detection from social media texts. Anger and sadness detection are of particular interest. Emotion classifiers (including *anger* and *sadness*) were tested on blog data [Ghazi et al., 2010], on LiveJournal data [Keshtkar and Inkpen, 2012], and other kinds of social media postings, as we mentioned in more detail in Section 3.4. Messages that express anger at high intensity levels could be flagged as possible terrorist threats. Combined with topic detection, anger detection could lead to more accurate flagging of the potential threats. Sadness detection in user postings could indicate people who might have suicidal tendencies, or youth that lack a sense of belonging and might be tempted to embark on extremizt or terrorist activities. This analysis could be combined with the analysis of the social network of these users, and a user could be flagged as potentially dangerous when there are links to known suspects.

Sentiment analysis techniques, also discussed in Section 3.4, can be used to detect the opinions regarding social and political events. For example, Colbaugh and Glass [2010] presented a case study involving the estimation of Indonesian public sentiment regarding the July 2009 Jakarta hotel bombings.

In recent years, terrorist organizations such as ISIS have successfully leveraged social media for recruitment and radicalization of citizens of Western countries. This prompted Rowe and Saif [2016] to examine the social media habits of users who have become radicalized. Starting with a seed of Twitter accounts from lists pertaining to the Syria conflict, the researchers then added the followers of these users to produce a list of 154,000 users living in Europe. From this list, they collected 104 million tweets, aiming to examine user behaviors both before and after radicalization. The authors examined both the sharing and linguistic patterns of users to determine if they were pro- or anti-ISIS. For the linguistic analysis, they focused on lexical behaviors such as adopting heavy usage of pro-ISIS terms. The results of this analysis show that the usage of pro-ISIS terms increases dramatically after a user has been "activated."

Situation awareness is an important military concept that involves being aware of what is happening in somebody's vicinity, in order to understand how information, events, and actions can impact goals and objectives, both immediately and in the near future.[12] Somebody who has a good sense of situation awareness has a high degree of knowledge with respect to inputs and outputs of a system, a "feel" for situations, people, and events that play out due to variables the subject can control. Lacking or inadequate situation awareness has been identified as one of the primary factors in accidents attributed to human error. Situation awareness requires a good perception of the environmental elements with respect to time or space, the comprehension of their meaning, and the projection of their status after some variable has changed, such as time, or some other variable, such as a predetermined event. It is also a field of study concerned with perception of the environment critical to decision-makers in complex, dynamic areas from aviation, air traffic control, ship navigation, power plant operations, military command and control, and emergency services such as firefighting and policing. The concept can be extended to more ordinary everyday life activities.

In military and defense applications, the environmental perception information is collected using sensors or other sources (automatic or manual). But in this section, we argue that information automatically extracted from texts could be used to enhance situation awareness (in addition to other data) in the settings where the human operator needs to read a lot of messages or reports. Event detection in social media posting is one way to contribute to situation awareness (see Section 3.5 for techniques for event detection).

Nunes et al. [2016] developed an operational system for detecting cyber threat intelligence from darknet and deepnet social media sites. The system implemented a crawler, a parser, and classification steps. They leveraged an ensemble supervised learning model that included a Naïve-Bayes, Random Forest, SVM, and Logistic Regression classifiers. This approach achieved a recall score of 0.92 on marketplace sites and 0.80 on discussion forums related to hacking.

Another application for enhancing situation awareness is risk extraction from texts. It could extract whole texts that describe risk situations, or it could extract spans of text for particular risk aspects. For example, Razavi et al. [2014] extracted information about maritime situation awareness, from large amounts of textual maritime incident reports. The spans of texts they extract using CRF classifiers are: vessel type, risk type, risk associates, a maritime general location, a maritime absolute location (e.g., latitude/longitude), date and time.

Protecting research and technology from espionage is an application investigated by Thorleuchter and Van Den Poel [2013]. Their system identifies semantic textual patterns representing technologies and their corresponding application fields that are of high relevance for an organization's strategy. These patterns are used to estimate organization's costs of an information

---

[12]http://en.wikipedia.org/wiki/Situation_awareness

leakage for each project. A Web mining approach is proposed to identify worldwide knowledge distribution within the relevant technologies and corresponding application fields. This information is used to estimate the probability that an information leakage occur. A risk assessment methodology calculates the information leakage risk for each project. In a case study, the information leakage risk of defense based research and technology projects is estimated, because these kinds of projects are of particularly interest to espionage agents. Overall, it is shown that the proposed methodology is successful in calculating the espionage information leakage risk of projects. This could help an organization by processing espionage risk management.

Text mining the biomedical literature for identification of potential viruses or bacteria that could be used as bio-terrorism weapons or biomedical hazards is investigated by Hu et al. [2008]. The texts used in the three applications mentioned above are not necessarily social media data, but the approaches can be adapted to social media, if postings are about the respective topics are identified.

Images are a good source of information for military and defense applications. For example, the system described by Brantingham and Hossain [2013] collates imagery of a particular location from a variety of media sources to provide an operator with real-time situational awareness. Zhou et al. [2011] exploited both the image features and their tags (words) in a unified probabilistic framework to recommend additional tags to label images. Images and text captions or tags can be collected from social media, where collaborative image tagging is a popular task.

Conducting real-time examination of a defense or security crisis via social media is also of interest. Simon et al. examined the Twitter usage during the Westgate Mall terror attack in Kenya in 2013. The researchers hypothesized about the social media usage patterns of emergency personnel and the potential security breaches enabled by communication via social media. They collected 67,000 tweets related to the attack at different time intervals. 299 of these tweets were then manually annotated as positive, negative, or neutral. Because Alchemy API[13] sentiment classifier used performed poorly on neutral tweets, they were excluded, producing an accuracy level of 86.2%. From this classification, the researchers examined the relationship between emergency dispatcher sentiment and on-site manager sentiment during the attacks. Contrary to their initial hypothesis, they found the manager sentiment to be more positive.

The NLP applications for disaster and emergency response are discussed more broadly in the following section.

4.7 DISASTER RESPONSE APPLICATIONS

Social media postings can be used for early detection of emergency situations and for crisis management. A sudden change in the topics discussed in social media in a region can indicate a possible emergency situation, for example a natural disaster such as an earthquake, fire, tsunami, or flood. Social media messages can be used for spreading information about the evolution of the situation. Automatic analysis of such information has the potential to aid the general public

---

[13]https://www.alchemyapi.com/

in gathering and digesting information communicated during times of mass emergency. This information can also help in the rescue operations. For example, Imran et al. [2013] classified microblog posts and extracted information about disaster response actions. Most of the reported research work focused on Twitter messages. Some work tried to identify new events (emergencies), while most of the work tried to classify the messages into related to a given emergency situation or not.

Situation awareness is a term also used in military and defense applications (see Section 4.6); but in this section, the term is used in the context of natural disasters, not of social or political events. The work of Yin et al. [2012] is one of the first research endeavours that tried to monitor Twitter streams in order to detect possible emergency situations with the focus on enabling an automatic system to enhance situation awareness. Verma et al. [2011] collected Twitter messages from four different crisis events of varying nature and magnitude and built a classifier to automatically detect messages that may contribute to situational awareness, utilizing a combination of hand-annotated and automatically extracted linguistic features. Their system was able to achieve over 80% accuracy on categorizing tweets that contribute to situational awareness. In addition, the authors showed that the classifier developed for a specific emergency event performed well on similar events. Robinson et al. [2013] developed an earthquake detector for Australia and New Zealand using automatic analysis of Twitter messages. The system was based on their Emergency Situation Awareness platform which provides all-hazard information captured, filtered, and analyzed from Twitter messages. The detector sent email notifications of evidence of earthquakes from Tweets to the Joint Australian Tsunami Warning Center. Power et al. [2013] detected reported fires using Twitter message analysis. They developed a notification system to identify in near-real-time the tweets that describe fire events in Australia. The system identified fire-related alert words published on Twitter which were further processed by a classifier to determine if they correspond to an actual fire event.

Although the high volume of social media activity during natural disasters has spurred advancements in event detection, it has also made it more difficult for response personnel to find relevant information among large amounts of noise. Caragea et al. [2016] sought to develop a means of automatically determining the relevance of Twitter posts to concurrent disasters. Their model consisted of a Convolutional Neural Network (CNN), which was trained on Twitter data from six flood events (about 26,000 tweets). This model outperformed SVM and ANN approaches, achieving an average accuracy of 77.61%. Chowdhury et al. [2020] released a larger dataset of multiple disasters and a dictionary of disaster-related terms. To efficiently detect and extract disaster events from social media, Toujani and Akaichi [2019] introduced a citizen clustering technology. This technology can put events into context and help journalists understand them quickly, allowing for the extraction of useful and accurate information from social media. The authors used fuzzy processing to produce a indicator that represents the degree of danger of each event, which is a good method to determine if a content is reliable.

Social media not only acts as a channel for detecting disaster events, it can also be a useful intra-organization communication tool for the non-governmental organizations (NGOs) and emergency personnel responding to the event. Debnath et al. [2016] examined the possibilities of automatic situation analysis using WhatsApp chat logs for the NGO "Doctors For You" after two natural disasters. These logs contained tens of thousands of lines of text. The researchers extracted four pieces of information to generate a snapshot of the response situation: the places volunteers were visiting, the medical infrastructure of those places, the common grievances the agents were reporting, and the status of relief at certain places. To mine data related to these slots, they used Python's natural language toolkit (NLTK) and the TextBlob sentiment analysis tool.[14] To handle queries about the ongoing situation, the following procedure was devised: determine similar words and phrases to the query using WordNet's network of associated words, retrieve sentences that contain the relevant words and phrases, determine locations using geotagging and common words associated with arrival and departure, and perform sentiment analysis on the related posts in the logs. The results showed great promise for the efficacy of real-time analysis of intra-organization social media communication for situational analysis. The highest precision scores were achieved for automatically determining the locations and the relief status, with more mixed results for determining medical status on-site.

The methods used in these applications were discussed in Section 3.5 which was about new event detection and about detecting which messages talk about specified events, including emergency situations such as the ones mentioned above.

4.8 NLP-BASED USER MODELING

It is possible to learn user profiles based on their social media behavior. In this section, we look in particular at how the totality of the messages posted by a user can be exploited. The ability to detect user attributes, such a gender, age, region of origin, and political orientation solely from messages posted by the user on social media has important applications in advertising, personalization, and recommending systems. These features can also help to improve documentation classification tasks. There are only a few methods taking advantage of them. A Neural User Factor Adaptation (NUFA) model developed by Huang and Paul [2019] successfully improved the accuracy of text classification tasks by employing user factors. This approach achieved an F-score of 0.901 on a Twitter vaccination dataset and 0.852 on an Amazon music review dataset. Some users declare some of these attributes in their profiles, but not all of these attributes have fields for users to complete, and even when the fields are available, not all users provide the information.

---

[14]https://textblob.readthedocs.io/en/dev/

Modeling User Personality

The personality of the user could be modeled based on their social media profiles and based on their posted messages.[15] The style of these texts and the emotions expressed in them can be a source of information.

One of the early work on personality detection from blogs is by Oberlander and Nowson [2006]. They classified authors on four personality traits (neuroticism, extraversion, agreeableness, and conscientiousness) using three class for each trait (high, medium, low), or five classes (highest, relatively high, medium, relatively low, and lowest). They trained binary and multi-class SVM classifiers, using n-gram features. In a similar direction, Celli [2012] present a system for personality recognition that exploits linguistic cues and does not require supervision for evaluation. They run their system on a dataset sampled from the FriendFeed social network. They used the five personality traits from the standard model known in psychology as the Big Five: *extraversion, emotional stability, agreeableness, conscientiousness,* and *openness to experience.* The first four classes are the same as the ones used in the previously mentioned work on blogs [Oberlander and Nowson, 2006]. Making use of the linguistic features associated with those classes, the system of Celli [2012] generated one personality model for each user. The system then evaluated the models by comparing all the posts of one single user (users that have only one post were discarded). As evaluation measures the system provided accuracy (measure of the reliability of the personality model) and validity (measure of the variability of writing style of a user). The analysis of a sample of 748 Italian users of FriendFeed showed that the most frequent personality type is represented by the model of an extravert, insecure, agreeable, organized, and unimaginative person.

Maheshwari et al. [2017] endeavored to divide users by ethical values, using Schwartz's psycholinguistic model of societal sentiment. The Schwartz model includes the following ethical values: Achievement, Benevolence, Conformity, Hedonism, Power, Security, Self-direction, Stimulation, Tradition, and Universalism. Using Amazon Mechanical Turk, the researchers gathered ethical questionnaires from "turkers," who then granted the researchers access to their Twitter feeds. Similarly, the researchers collected questionnaire responses from students and were granted access to their Facebook accounts. This resulted in a social media corpus of 367 Twitter users (averaging 1,608 tweets per user) and 60 Facebook users (averaging 681 messages per user). For linguistic features, the researchers used n-grams, part-of-speech tags, word-level features, a curated lexicon of problem-specific words, and LIWC. The researchers then applied these features to train several classifiers including SVM, Logistic Regression, and Random Forest.

The methods for emotion detection from social media texts were discussed in Section 3.4, but in that section the task was to classify the emotions expressed in each posting, while here we

---

[15]Relevant workshops include: the ACL Joint Workshop on Social Dynamics and Personal Attributes in Social Media http://www.cs.jhu.edu/svitlana/workshop.html and the workshops/shared tasks on Computational Personality Recognition 2014 and 2013 https://sites.google.com/site/wcprst/home/wcpr14.

put together all the postings of a user in order to learn the emotions sequences expressed by the user [Gil et al., 2013].

Modeling User Health Profile

Data analysis of social media postings can provide a wealth of information about the health of individual users, health across groups, and even access to healthy food choices in neighborhoods. It could also provide an opportunity to enhance the data available to mental health clinicians and researchers, enabling a better-informed and better-equipped mental health field. Coppersmith et al. [2014b] presented a system that analyzed mental health phenomena in publicly available Twitter data, demonstrating how the application of simple natural language processing methods can yield insight into specific disorders as well as mental health at large, along with evidence that as-of-yet undiscovered linguistic signals relevant to mental health exist in social media. Their method gathered data for a range of mental illnesses quickly and cheaply, then focused on the analysis of four illnesses: post-traumatic stress disorder (PTSD), depression, bipolar disorder, and seasonal affective disorder (SAD). The privacy of the user needs be carefully protected in such studies, in order to follow ethical principles regarding the balance between the utility of such data and the privacy of mental health-related information.

Social media data can also allow modeling health risk factors. Sadilek and Kautz [2013] explained that research in computational epidemiology has concentrated on estimating summary statistics of populations and simulated scenarios of disease outbreaks, but detailed studies have been limited to small domains, as scaling the methods involved posed considerable challenges. By contrast, automatic methods could model the associations of a large collection of social and environmental factors with the health of particular individuals. Instead of relying on surveys, the authors applied scalable machine learning techniques to noisy data mined from online social media and inferred the health state of a given user in an automated way. They show that the learned patterns can be subsequently leveraged in descriptive as well as predictive fine-grained models of human health. Using a unified statistical model, they quantified the impact of social status, exposure to pollution, interpersonal interactions, and other important lifestyle factors on one's health. The model explained more than 54% of the variance in people's health (as estimated from their online communication), and predicted the future health status of individuals with 91% accuracy. Kashyap and Nahapetian [2014] studied users' health status over time based on their tweets. The purpose of the analysis included individually targeted healthcare personalization, determining health disparities, discovering health access limitations, advertising, and public health monitoring. The approach analyzed over 12,000 tweets spanning as far back as 2010 for 10 classes of users active on Twitter. These automatic methods could complement traditional studies in life sciences, as they enable large-scale and timely measurement, inference, and prediction of previously elusive factors that affect our everyday lives.

Modeling Gender and Ethnicity

Modeling gender is another important user modeling application. One obvious signal of a user's gender is the user's name. The first names can provide strong clues about gender and ethnicity; the last names could carry information about ethnicity. Liu and Ruths [2013] studied the link between gender and first names in English tweets. In this section, we are interested in looking at the messages posted by a user, in addition to user's name. Early classification experiment were done on blog data of users by Schler et al. [2006]. They looked at gender and age of the authors of the blogs and what features to extract from labeled texts in order to train classifiers that can label new blogs. The features included some content words, but mostly stylistic features similar to those used in authorship attribution research. Kokkos and Tzouramanis [2014] trained a Support Vector Machine classifier on Twitter and LinkedIn messages, also using a part-of-speech tagger, in order to infer the gender of a user. They showed that this can be done through the classification of down to one single short message included in a profile, quite independently of whether this message followed a structured and standardized format (as with the attribute summary in LinkedIn) or did not (as with the micro-blogging postings in Twitter). Their experiments on LinkedIn and Twitter data indicated a very high degree of accuracy for the gender identification task, up to 98.4%. Huang and Paul [2019] used the Microsoft Facial Recognition API to help them determine users' gender.

Rao et al. [2010] also looked at gender identification in Twitter data, while Rao et al. [2011] presented minimally supervised models for detecting several latent attributes of social media users, with a focus on ethnicity and gender. Previous work on ethnicity detection used coarse-grained widely separated classes of ethnicity and assumed the existence of large amounts of training data such as the U.S. census data, simplifying the problem. Instead, they examined the content generated by users in addition to name morpho-phonemics to detect ethnicity and gender. They also studied fine grained ethnicity classes, namely those from Nigeria, with very limited amounts of training data.

Modeling nationalities is a related application. Huang et al. [2014] provided a detailed social network analysis for the case of a highly diverse country, Qatar. They looked into user behavior and linking preference (or the lack of) to other nationalities. They did not look at the posted messages, but language identification could be applied on a concatenation of posted messages for a user, as a source of additional information. This could also help in cases of users who have multiple nationalities. As seen in Section 2.8.1, language identification works on short messages, but concatenating messages to produce a longer text increases the accuracy of the predictions (when multiple messages from the same user are available).

Inferring the race of the users based on Twitter data was studied by Mohammady and Culotta [2014]. They built a demographic attribute classifier that uses county information as label, in order to avoid manual labeling of training data. By pairing geolocated social media data with country demographics, they built a regression model to map text to demographics. Then they adopt this model to make predictions at the user level. Their experiments using Twitter data show that the results of this approach is comparable with the results of a fully supervised approach, estimating the race of a user with 80% accuracy. Preoţiuc-Pietro and Ungar [2018] produced a new dataset to improve the prediction accuracy. They made a online survey to ask Twitter users to report their own races. They did predictive experiments on multiple models by using this new labeled dataset and successfully improved the prediction accuracy. Based on this dataset, they developed a model which could classify users in the United States into four races and ethnicities: Non-Hispanic Whites, Hispanic/Latinos, African-Americans and Asians, and it achieved a AUC of 0.884.

Riemer et al. [2015] examined inferring the age of users on Twitter. After manually labeling approximately 2,000 Twitter users as belonging to Generation X, Generation Y, or older, the researchers mined on average 226 tweets from each user. As a comparison with feature-based machine learning models, the researchers trained and tested a Naive Bayes and a Max Entropy classifier, which established a baseline of 0.73, 0.36, and 0.38 F-score for the classes GenY, GenX, and older, respectively. Then they trained unsupervised models using Paragraph Vectors. These served as inputs into a deep learning model. The final model leveraged hidden layer sharing between several other NN classification tasks including gender and ethnicity modeling. The neural network model, along with the hidden layer sharing from the other two classification tasks, produced the best results, with an accuracy of 75.9% and F-scores of 0.89 and 0.59 for GenY and GenX, respectively. The "older" class was best predicted by a neural network that only included hidden layer sharing from the gender classification task.

Modeling User Location

Modeling users' location is a popular application. It can be based on their declared locations, GPS information or time zone (if available), on all the messages written by each user, or by combining several sources of information. The methods used for this were discussed in detail in Section 3.2. We mention here a few more directions of investigation related to user modeling. Predicting user location is needed because many users do not provide real location information, frequently incorporating fake locations or sarcastic comments that can fool traditional geographic information tools. When users did input their location, they almost never specified it at a scale any more detailed than their city. Among others, Hecht et al. [2011] performed machine learning experiments to identify a user's location by only looking at what that user tweeted. They found that a user's country and state can be determined automatically with reasonable accuracy, indicating that users implicitly reveal location information, with or without realizing it. This has implications for location-based services and can raise privacy concerns. Mahmud et al. [2014] used an ensemble of statistical and heuristic classifiers to predict users' locations and a geographic gazetteer dictionary to identify place-name entities. They found that a hierarchical classification approach, where time zone, state, or geographic region is predicted first and city is predicted next, improved the prediction accuracy. They have also analyzed movement variations of Twitter users, built a classifier to predict whether a user was traveling in a certain period of time, and used that information to further improve the location detection accuracy. Kinsella et al. [2011] also studied the movement of Twitter users.

Modeling User Political Orientation

The political orientation of the users can also be predicted as part of their profiles. Prediction voting intentions can be based on the political profiles of a large number of users, without necessarily modeling each user in detail, as discussed in Section 4.4; but user-centric approaches can provide more useful information [Lampos et al., 2013], for example about which users are more influential [Lampos et al., 2014], to direct political messages to them, since they have many followers; or to detect users that are not yet decided for a political party, to try to convince them to vote for a specific candidate.

Existing models for social media personal analytics assume access to thousands of messages per user, even though most users author post content only sporadically over time. Given this sparsity, one possibility is to leverage content from the local neighborhood of a user; another possibility is to evaluate batch models based on the size and the amount of messages in various types of neighborhoods. Volkova et al. [2014] estimated the amount of time and tweets required for a dynamic model to predict user political preferences. They showed that even when limited or no self-authored data is available, messages from friends, retweets, and user mention communications provide sufficient evidence for prediction. When updating models over time based on Twitter, they found that political preference can be often be predicted using approximately 100 tweets per user.

User's identity, which can be predicted by textual evidence, can also shape a user's political orientation. Shoemark et al. [2017] specifically investigated the correlation between Scottish identity and support for Scottish independence. Using Twitter's Streaming API, the researchers sampled over six million tweets from 2013 and 2014, the year before the UK referendum on Scottish independence. Filtering by geography and inclusion of hashtags related to the referendum, they distilled a final dataset of 60,000 tweets from 18,000 distinct users. The researchers then generated a list of Scottish linguistic traits, including proper nouns referencing Scottish places, Scottish spelling variants of English words, and words from the Scottish vocabulary. To indicate political orientation, they looked for tweets that included polarized hashtags either in favor of or opposition to the Scottish independence referendum. Thus, users were divided into either pro- or anti-independence groups. The difference between the groups' average probability of using Scottish terms was statistically significant.

Automatic political orientation prediction from social media posts has proven successful in distinguishing between publicly declared liberals and conservatives in the U.S. Preotiuc-Pietro et al. [2017] also propose to examine users' political ideology at a finer-grained level. They aim to identify politically moderate and neutral users, since these groups can be of particular interest to political scientists and pollsters. Using a dataset with political ideology labels self-reported through surveys, they characterize the groups of politically engaged users through language use on Twitter and build a fine-grained model (7-point scale) that predicts political ideology of unseen users. Their results identify differences in political leaning and engagement and the extent to which each group tweets using political keywords. They improve ideology prediction accuracy by exploiting the relationships between the user groups.

Modeling User's Life Events

Modeling major life events, such as weddings and graduations, was explored by Li et al. [2014c]. Information from the social network structure can be used to guess current and past jobs, for example when a user has many friends from a similar work place. The same applies to schools or universities that the user attended. Using the text of the messages might be used to strengthen such predictions, in a small way.

Modeling multiple topics at the same time can also be done using the above models or complex models that consider multiple latent attributes in the same time. Rao et al. [2010] presented a study that shows that there are differences between the language usage of the users based on gender, age, region of origin, and political orientation. Another work that modeled multiple topics (extracting information about spousal relations, education and job) was presented by Li et al. [2014d].

Modeling User Income

The automatic inference of income is particularly useful for social and market research. Preotiuc-Pietro et al. sought to determine what factors could be useful in inferring age from social media posts, specifically Twitter data. To gather data for this task, the researchers queried Twitter's API for users whose self-reported job titles could be closely matched with a list of official job titles generated by the UK government. From this set of users, they collected 10 million tweets, and examined the relationship between user features and the average income for the official job titles. The researchers then learned word embeddings using Word2Vec built on 10% of the entire Twitter feed from January 2 to February 28, 2011. These word vectors were then clustered to model different topics, and the topic distribution for each tweet was used as a feature for income classification. To predict income, the researchers compared both a logistic regression and an SVM model. In all cases, the SVM outperformed the logistic regression model. The SVM with only the topic distributions as its feature set achieved a mean average error of £9,835. This only slightly underperformed an SVM that included topic features, as well as psychological and demographic features extracted from the users' profiles. The model that included all of these features achieved a mean average error of £9,652.

4.9   APPLICATIONS FOR ENTERTAINMENT

Media and the entertainment industry have a big challenge in keeping the pace as social media grow. Social media are changing users' expectations and their behavior. For these reasons, media and entertainment companies have adopted new approaches toward content creation, distribution, operations, technology, and user interaction. This industry needs to ensure they participate actively in the growth of future platforms for online videos, social media, and mobile media to bring the information to the user and to interact with them. This is a serious issue for the media and entertainment industry since advertisers spend less on traditional paid media and require more resources for digital social media and e-marketing. Electronic gaming companies invest massively in increasing the number of users on digital platforms. Both Microsoft and Sony have made integrated video sharing a focal point of their next generation consoles.

This industry is using the benefit of innovation in search, online video advertising, and advanced methods of social media analysis. Social media dramatically enhances the interaction between providers and users. Fans can follow their popular stars and express their admiration. For example, Harry Potter's Facebook page recorded nearly 29 million likes during the run up to unveiling of one of the films in the series. In the week leading to the premiere, Harry Potter's Facebook page gained nearly 100,000 friends per day.[16]

The sentiment analysis of major entertainment events such as the Oscars, or sentiment related to the movie's premium, are the active application in social media analysis. Sinha et al. [2014] studied the sentiment analysis of Wimbledon tweets by analyzing a set of tweets of the Roger Federer and Novak "Nole" Djokovic semifinals match at Wimbledon 2012. In the absence of textual metadata for annotating videos, they assumed that the live video coverage of an event and the time-correlated textual microblog streams about the same event can act as an important source for such annotation. The intensity of sentiment is used to detect peaks of sentiments toward players as well, and can tag best moments in the game.

The trusted measurement of movie and TV programming ranking is one of the important indicators regarding the popularity of a program or a movie in the entertainment industry. Entertainment and media marketing take great interest in the impact of social media on TV and film ratings. For example, Netflix, a provider of on-demand Internet streaming media, uses the popularity of a movie on Facebook as a proposed feature for consumers. Predicting TV audience ratings with social media was studied by Hsieh et al. [2013]. They exploited the network structure and the number of posts, likes, comments, and shares on the fan pages of various TV dramas to try to find their relationships to ratings. Their results showed that using Facebook fan page data to perform ratings forecasts for non-broadcast programs could be feasible.

Another application, based on event monitoring and geo-location detection, is Tilofy,[17] in which the mobile application curates entertainment events from pop-up concerts to celebrity sightings using dynamic streams of text, photos, and videos close to the location of interest.

---

[16]http://www.mediaweek.co.uk/article/1082526/sector-analysis-cinema-gears-social-networks
[17]http://tilofy.com/

4.10   NLP-BASED INFORMATION VISUALIZATION FOR SOCIAL MEDIA

Realizing the value of social media requires innovation in visualizing the automatically acquired information in order to present it to users and decision makers. Information visualization for social media analysis has become important in order to explore the full potential of social media data. Information visualization is a research topic which presents significant challenges with the growing availability of big social data. Data analytics and visualization tools are needed to represent the extracted topics and draw relationships between these elements. Applying NLP techniques on social media data gives us the power of transforming the noisy data into structured information, but it is still difficult to discern meaning by extracting information piece by piece. The link inference and visualizing the content could make the analyzed information more apparent and meaningful to present to users and decision makers.

In Section 3.2, we mentioned that geo-location detection from social content, such as blog posts or tweets, is possible thanks to NLP methods. The locations themselves might not be relevant, but the projection of the locations on the map of the world, tracking the events on specific timeline and connecting with other name entity and sentiment analysis can bring another dimension toward a "big picture" visualization. Such visualization provides an intuitive way to summarize the information in order to make it easier to understand and interact with.

A few applications focused specifically on visualization of social media data. Shahabi et al. [2010] developed GeoDec: a framework to visualize and search geospatial data for decision-making. In this platform, first the geo-location of interest was simulated and the relevant geospatial data were fused and embedded in the virtualized model. Then, users could interactively formulate abstract decision-making queries in order to verify decisions in the virtual world prior to executing the decisions in the real world. This effort was pursued by Kim et al. [2014] with MediaQ: Mobile Media Management Framework which is an online media management system to collect, organize, share, and search mobile multimedia contents. MediaQ visualizes the user-generated video using automatically tagged geospatial data. Kotval and Burns [2013] studied the visualization of entities within social media by analyzing user needs. To understand user needs and preferences, the authors developed 14 social media data visualization concepts and conducted a user evaluation of these concepts by measuring the usefulness of the underlying data relationships and the usability of each data visualization concept. However, they reported a divergence and a strong preference for the "big picture" visualization among the users. Diakopoulos et al. [2010] studied the visualization of opinions extracted from social media.

4.11   GOVERNMENT COMMUNICATION

Social media has become an increasingly popular platform for communication between governments and citizens. Through this immediate and voluminous source of feedback, governments can better track the effectiveness of and the response to government services. Thus, the pressure exists for governments to capture and understand social media interactions in real-time.

Wan et al. [2015] developed a social media monitoring prototype, Vizie, which could help improve government services based on published user requirements for Facebook, Twitter, Flickr, and YouTube. The study analyzed nearly 200 registered users across 17 government departments. The results suggested that Vizie was able to explore data and facilitate relevance judgments of online community. Finally, the researchers conducted case studies illustrating query maintenance strategies for three social media monitoring scenarios.

4.12   RUMOR DETECTION

Rumors have existed in newspapers and magazines since their inception but more issues have been noticed since the advancement of social media. The ease of distribution and an increase in the digital audience allows rumors to propagate at a large scale. This poses a real threat to the veracity of the information and hence automatic rumor detection has become necessary. As the volume of news generated daily has drastically increased, traditional methods for rumor detection are not quite scalable. There is a need for new methodologies.

Gorrell et al. [2018] discussed the seventh task of the SemEval 2019 called RumorEval task. This edition consisted in two subtasks: rumor stance prediction (task A) and rumor verification (task B). The dataset consisted of Twitter and Reddit posts.

For both the tasks, Li et al. [2019] implemented an ensemble of classifiers (SVM, Random Forest, and Logistic Regression), including a neural network with three connected layers, where individual post representations were created using an attention-based LSTM. For stance prediction (subtask A), they considered a range of other features and word embeddings generated from the messages and a postprocessing module to find similarities between source tweets. For rumor verification (subtask B), they analyzed information in different dimensions like rumor content, source credibility, user credibility, user stance, event propagation path, etc. For subtask B, this was the best performing model among all submissions for this subtask, giving a macro-average F-score of 0.5776, while it ranked third for subtask A with a macro-average F-score of 0.5776.

The best performing system in subtask A was developed by Yang et al. [2019] and proposed an inference chain-based system, where the conversation thread started with a source tweet, followed by replies, in which each one responded to an earlier one in the time sequence. The authors took each conversation thread as an inference chain and concentrated on utilizing it to solve the problem of class imbalance in subtask A and of training data scarcity in subtask B. They also have augmented the training data with external public datasets. Using OpenAI GPT [Radford et al., 2018] that was pretrained on BooksCorpus [Zhu et al., 2015], they achieved a macro-average F-score of 0.6187 for subtask A and 0.2525 for subtask B, ranking fourth.

4.13   RECOMMENDER SYSTEMS

Recommender systems (RS) have become a vital aspect of e-commerce websites. These systems provide recommendations for a product, based on the available user and product data. Recommender systems are beneficial for both sellers and consumers. The seller's aim is to make their products accessible to interested clients and to get consumer satisfaction and loyalty. While consumers save time and money by receiving a list of products that are most useful for them.

Alharthi et al. [2018] survey the existing book recommender systems and how these could be useful in libraries and schools, and on e-learning portals. The vast amount of e-books that are available online helps readers get access to inexpensive resources with little effort, which could increase the skill of reading among these users. Alharthi et al. [2018] majorly focused on collaborative filtering algorithms and content-based recommenders, categorizing the book RSs into six classes depending on the features that they deployed. The classes discussed were traditional recommendation methods, recommendations based on library loans, stylometry-based recommendations, e-book recommendations, recommendations based on textual reviews, and recommendations based on social media. Offline and online experiments were conducted to evaluate the systems and they were measured on the basis of prediction of usage, ratings, and ranking of books in the RS. Offline experiments measure the predictive power of a system, while online experiments evaluate the effect of recommendations on users of real-time applications. They also discuss the future scope of these recommender systems, like using the systems for other textual items such as news articles, micro-blogs, movie plots, and scientific papers; recommending books to readers based on their mood or interest; recommending books for non-readers; and audiobook recommendations. A direct application that leverages social media information is based on topic detection from comments from the Goodreads forum, to model the topics of interest to new users [Alharthi et al., 2017].

Priyadharsini and Felciah created an e-commerce website and used a stochastic learning algorithm which performed sentiment analysis on the product reviews, ratings, and emoticons, and classified each product as negative, positive, and neutral. When a user searched for a product, positive products according to the rating and review analysis were displayed in the recommendation panel. The proposed system also discovered fake product reviews with the help of the MAC address of the system along with review posting patterns.

Lee and Lee [2019] implemented a collaborative filtering algorithm based on deep neural networks that used a supervised learning architecture. They used batch normalization on each layer to prevent overfitting of the neural network. This model's performance was better than conventional collaborative filtering algorithms like user-based collaborative filtering and SVD, and it can be extended to online collaborative filtering.

4.14   PREVENTING SEXUAL HARASSMENT

#MeToo is a movement mainly launched by actress Alyssa Milano in October 2017 against the famous film producer Harvey Weinstein's sexual assault allegations on several actresses. This movement called on all women who have been sexually assaulted to speak up about their painful experience to arouse social attention. In recent years with the rise and development of the #MeToo movement, Twitter became a platform on which women could speak about their experience of sexual harassment. Inspired by this phenomenon, Ghosh Chowdhury et al. [2019] presented the Disclosure Language Model (DLM), which is based on the ULMFiT deep learning architecture [Howard and Ruder, 2018]. The basic construction of the DLM is a 3-layer AWD-LSTM, and Ghosh Chowdhury et al. [2019] tuned dropout hyperparameters. Compared with other eight baseline models (RNNs, LSTMs, CNNs, etc.), the DLM presented a better result (accuracy: 96%, precision: 0.95, F-score: 0.96) on the sexual harassment task based on a Twitter dataset which was annotated carefully by some experts.

4.15   SUMMARY

In this chapter, we demonstrated some of the applications for social media analysis that require natural language processing and semantic analysis of textual social data. Social media analyzing applications are increasingly in demand with the growth of social media data and user generated content in various platforms. There are lots of challenges to understand the large social media data environments, including architecture, security, integrity, management, scalability, artificial intelligence, NLP techniques, distribution, and visualization. Therefore, there is a great opportunity for new small businesses in Silicon Valley and other parts of the globe to develop new applications, including mobile apps. The sky is the limit!

CHAPTER 5

Data Collection, Annotation, and Evaluation

5.1 INTRODUCTION

In this chapter, we discuss different complementary aspects of social media text analysis. The results of the information analysis could be influenced by the quality of collected input data. In order to use empirical methods of natural language processing or statistical machine learning algorithms, we need to build or acquire data for training or development, and for testing. These data sets need to be annotated. At least the test data needs to be annotated, so that we can evaluate the algorithms. The training data needs to be labeled in case the algorithms are supervised learning algorithms, while unsupervised learning algorithms can use the data as it is, without additional annotations (though they could benefit from a small annotated development data set). Avoiding social media spam in the process of data collection is another challenge that we discuss.

Some information available on social media is public and some is private. We will briefly discuss the privacy of user information and how the massive volume of publicly available information can be used as open intelligence to help the population, such as online victimization and cyberbullying prevention in schools. It is important to mention the ethics of information technology and business using social media data. At the end of this chapter, we will discuss the current benchmarks that are available for evaluating social media applications and NLP tasks.

5.2 DISCUSSION ON DATA COLLECTION AND ANNOTATION

The growing popularity of social media and the enormous quantities of user-created Web content provide the opportunity to access publicly available data. However, the collection and annotation of social data from online microblogs and other social textual data pose a challenge for natural language processing applications.

Data Collection from Social Media

Social data collection depends on the intended task and application. Textual data from social media can be collected in various forms such as microblog messages, image descriptions, commented posts, video narrations, and metadata [Ford and Voegtlin, 2003]. We may also be interested in interconnecting data, for example connections between social media platforms (e.g., Twitter and Instagram) or linking Tweets to news [Guo et al., 2013].

The social media service's application programming interface (API) allows other applications to integrate with their platforms. However, collecting data from social media has some restrictions. For example, microblogging services, such as Twitter, offer an API Rate Limit[1] per user or per application; this allows for limited requests per rate limit window. For larger usages of Twitter data, there is paid access to support bigger message volumes, in the thousands or higher per hour.

Annotation Tags for Social Media

The annotation of social media content is a challenging task. Annotation tasks can be performed semi-automatically by using intelligent interfaces between the annotations and the users. For example, GATE (General Architecture for Text Engineering) and TwitIE, its social media component, is an interesting tool for annotation [Bontcheva et al., 2013]. Some researchers have attempted to automatically generate annotation tags to label Twitter users' interests by applying text ranking such as TF-IDF and TextRank (graph-based text ranking models) to extract keywords from Tweets to tag each user [Wu et al., 2010]. Other researchers applied supervised machine learning to annotate Twitter datasets with argumentation classes [Llewellyn et al., 2014]. There are cases when the users themselves annotated their posts, and such labels were sued as tags for supervised machine learning. An example is the mood labels in the LiveJournal platform [Mishne, 2005]. Researches are still trying to find some new approaches to annotate social media. Scheffler et al. [2019] studied a new Penn Discourse Treebank (PDTB)-style annotation method on English Tweets by annotating shallow discourse relations in Twitter conversations.

5.3   SPAM AND NOISE DETECTION

When it comes to choosing resources for social media data collection and analysis, the simple act of listening or crawling the millions of daily social conversations is not sufficient. With billions of active users on social media in the world, the volume of user-generated content has grown astronomically. The number of Tweets jumped from 5,000 daily Tweets in 2007[2] to 500,000,000 Tweets per day in 2013,[3] and it has maintained its popularity to this day.

Selecting the strategy that best supports your objectives and metrics is key in applying the appropriate NLP-based methods and analytic approaches. The significant amount of spam and noise in social media gave rise to the debate surrounding the validity and value of social media data, where this data closely depends on time and location.

---

[1]https://dev.twitter.com/rest/public/rate-limiting
[2]https://blog.twitter.com/2010/measuring-tweets
[3]https://blog.twitter.com/2013/new-tweets-per-second-record-and-how

Social Media Noise

New means of communication, from text messaging to social media, have changed how we use language. Some of the innovative linguistic forms have been used in online communication, for example many Persian users (Farsi language) or Middle Eastern and North African users (Arabic language with different dialects) express themselves on social media by applying the Latin character with the same pronunciation of the word in the original language (a form of transliteration). In English, words such as LOL (laugh out loud), OMG (Oh my God), or TTYL (talk to you later) became very popular. Some new words have even been entered in the dictionaries, such as retweet (verb), in 2011, and selfie (noun), in 2013, which were added to the Oxford Dictionary.

There are several reasons for social media noise to cause disturbance for natural language processing tasks such as machine translation, information retrieval, and opinion mining. For example, misspelled words are quite present on social media. As we mentioned in Section 2.2, the normalization task can partially remove irregularities of the language featured.

Baldwin et al. [2013] analyzed social media noise by applying linguistic and statistical analysis to the corpora collected from social media, and compared them to each other and to a reference corpus. They analyzed the lexical composition and relative occurrence of out-of-vocabulary (OOV) words, and the parsing of sentences to see how ungrammatical they are. Eisenstein et al. [2010] studied regional linguistic variations by modeling the relationship between words and geographical regions. They mentioned that for some topics, such as sports or the weather, slang is rendered differently depending on the region. For example, a sports-related topic will be rendered differently in New York vs. California.

Detecting Real Information

When checking information on social media, it is important to know and trust the source. The main challenge is to find the original source, which could be identified and authenticated using NLP methods and social network analysis. Barbier et al. [2013] studied provenance data associated with a social media statement, which can help dispel rumors, clarify opinions, and confirm facts. In this book, they proposed three steps: analyzing provenance attributes, provenance via network information, and searching provenance data using the value and network. Another concern is collecting data that contains enough information rather than almost no content. There are attempts to classify social media messages into informative or not, based on the text and/or the user's history, especially for Twitter data [Efron, 2011, Imran et al., 2013].

There are attempts to automatically detect rumors (fake information) in social media. Ma et al. [2017] analyze micro-blog posts based on their propagation structure. They model the posts' diffusion with propagation trees, in order to encode how each original message was transmitted and developed over time. Then they use a kernel-based method called Propagation Tree Kernel to capture high-order patterns differentiating different types of rumors by evaluating the similarities between their propagation tree structures. The experimental results on two real-world datasets demonstrate that the approach can detect rumors more quickly and accurately than other automatic rumor detection models. Zhou et al. [2019] introduced an effective method which can detect rumors early. Their team applied reinforcement learning on the data stream of social media such as Twitter. They created an early rumor detection system (ERD) which has two modules: (1) a classifier which can detect whether an event is a rumor; and (2) a checkpoint module that determines when to wake up the rumor detection action. The ERD has been evaluated on two datasets (Twitter and Weibo), and this new system performs better than up-to-date rumor detection systems.

Spam Detection

Social media and online blogs create an opportunity for readers to comment and ask questions. However, it is important for people to read online opinions and reviews for different purposes, such as buying new products or services, finding a restaurant or hotel, or consulting a doctor. For these reasons, comment reviews have become an important marketing tool. Positive opinions can result in significant success for target businesses, organizations, and individuals. Unfortunately, this situation also attracts fake social network postings and opinion spamming, which mislead readers or automated semantic analysis systems.

A form of false advertisement called clickbait has become a menace on social media. It can be in the form of an image, tweet, or teaser which hardly reveals its advertised content so that the target audience is tempted to visit the original webpage. Although clickbait is evidently an effective marketing tool, it is also an effective mechanism of manipulation. For example, in order to spread false information, fake news can be propagated through clickbait [Potthast et al., 2018].

Fake "positive" reviews and fake "negative" reviews could both have a serious impact. Spam detection or trustworthiness of online opinions can help detect fake negative reviews to avoid damage to reputations[4] and also to avoid colleting spam from social media in data collection and training. Research has shown that 20–30% of Yelp reviews are fake [Liu, 2012, Luca and Zervas, 2014]. Manipulating online reviews and fake opinions are likely to be illegal under consumer protection legislation and the Federal Trade Commission (FTC). Jindal and Liu [2008] studied the deceptive opinion problem. They trained models using supervised learning with manually labeled training examples, based on the review text, reviewer, and product, in order to identify deceptive opinions. Li et al. [2014a] studied the problem of detecting campaign promoters on Twitter, promoting certain target products, services, ideas, or messages, based on Markov Random Fields. Li et al. [2014b] analyzed the difference of language usage between online deceptive opinions and truthful reviews based on a gold standard dataset, which is comprised of data from three different domains (hotels, restaurants, and doctors).

---

[4]See, for example, the BBC story about Samsung probed in Taiwan over "fake Web reviews" in April 2013 http://www.bbc.com/news/technology-22166606.

Nowadays, more and more people acknowledge the news from social media. Many online news websites have their own official social media account and post news on it. However, there are some social media accounts which just look like "official" but are actually "fake." These accounts may spread fake news through social media and bring negative effects. Pérez-Rosas et al. [2018] presented the computational resource and model for the task of fake news detection. They used the datasets which are collected by combining them with manual and crowdsourced annotation methods and then created an automatic fake news detection system based on the linguistic features.

Another source of spam can be created by spambots. A spambot is an automated computer program designed to assist in the sending of spam. Spambots usually create fake accounts and send spam using them. There are also password-cracking spambots that are able to send spam using other people's accounts. In many cases it would be obvious to a human reader that a spambot is sending the messages, but if the data is collected automatically, such spam could be included in the data.

5.4   PRIVACY AND DEMOCRACY IN SOCIAL MEDIA

Social media plays an important role in interactive relationships between individuals, organizations, and societies. Consequently, all of the content shared in social media has an impact on the privacy for end-users. Published information can also present some difficulties when circumstances change.

There are several concerns about privacy in social media regarding user misunderstandings, the bugs in the development of social media platforms allowing unauthorized access, or lack of ethics in marketing. Some privacy research focused on concerns about data protection by establishing metrics, such as privacy scales, for evaluating these concerns [Wang et al., 2013]. However, there is little guidance or research on how to protect the information. In the previous chapter, we mentioned some concerns about privacy in healthcare (Section 4.2).

The American Bar Association[5] provides an overview of privacy and social media in America and how privacy intrusions can be captured by legislations and jurisdictions. Stutzman et al. [2011] studied the evolution of privacy and disclosure on Facebook. They reported the significant and negative association between privacy attitudes and disclosures practices. Vallor [2012] presented a philosophical reflection on the ethics of personal identities and communities on social networking services. This research draws our attention to virtual types of ethically social roles such as friend-to-friend, parent-to-child, co-worker-to-co-worker, employer-to-employee, teacher-to-student, neighbor-to-neighbor, seller-to-buyer, and doctor-to-patient. Moreover, social media revolutionizes liberal democracies and human rights. Social media platforms provide a raised bed for political community and allow expressing democratic values for liberals, progressives, moderates, and independents.

[5]http://www.americanbar.org/publications/blt/2014/01/03a_claypoole.html

In 2009, the *Washington Times*[6] coined the term *Iran's Twitter revolution* to protest against the rigged election in Iran and required permissions for news coverage. The Iranian election protests were a series of protests following the 2009 Iranian presidential election against the disputed victory of Iranian President Mahmoud Ahmadinejad and in support of opposition candidates Mir-Hossein Mousavi and Mehdi Karroubi. The protests were described using the term Twitter Revolution because the Western journalists who could not reach people on the ground in Iran scrolled through the tweets posted with hashtag #iranelection. After President Ahmadinejad's victory, in many different cities around the world, Iranians protested against the "stolen election." Although many supporters including Iranian-Americans were not even eligible to vote, they changed their Facebook profile picture to "Where is My Vote?" Also, in view of recent mobilizations, social media has played a key role in other events, such as the Arab Spring (2010–2012), which referred to the large-scale conflicts in Middle East and North Africa, and in Canada Printemps Erable (Maple Spring) 2012, which was a series of protests and widespread student strikes against the provincial government in Quebec. Many researchers study the long-term evolution of political systems via social media networks.

5.5   EVALUATION BENCHMARKS

We briefly mentioned different evaluation methods and quality measures used in the applications described in the previous three chapters. They are used for standard NLP tasks in evaluations campaigns such as SemEval,[7] TREC,[8] DUC/TAC,[9] CLEF,[10] etc. In addition to the study and standardization of the evaluation measures, these institutions provide benchmark datasets for NLP tasks.

A few tracks in these evaluation campaigns already-built benchmarks for social media data, for example for Twitter or blog data. Here are some of them.

The microblog retrieval task at TREC 2013, 2012, and 2011[11] contains queries and a list of document names that are expected answers to these queries (relevance judgments). The documents are from a large collection of over one million Twitter messages collected in 2011.

The opinion summarization in blogs,[12] a pilot task at TAC 2008 had as its goal the generation of well-organized, fluent summaries of opinions about specified targets found in a set of blog documents.

The Twitter sentiment analysis task at SemEval 2013[13] and a second edition at SemEval 2014[14] contain Twitter messages annotated with opinion labels.

---

[6]http://www.washingtontimes.com/news/2009/jun/16/irans-twitter-revolution/
[7]http://aclweb.org/aclwiki/index.php?title=SemEval_Portal
[8]http://trec.nist.gov
[9]http://duc.nist.gov/pubs.html, http://www.nist.gov/tac/
[10]http://www.clef-initiative.eu/
[11]https://github.com/lintool/twitter-tools/wiki
[12]http://www.nist.gov/tac/2008/summarization/op.summ.08.guidelines.html
[13]http://www.cs.york.ac.uk/semeval-2013/task2/
[14]http://alt.qcri.org/semeval2014/task9/

The Making Sense of Microposts workshops had shared tasks. In 2014, the task of the challenge was to automatically extract entities from English microposts, and link them to the corresponding English DBpedia v3.9 resources (if the linkage exists). At linking stage, the aim was to disambiguate expressions that are formed by discrete (and typically short) sequences of words. This is the entity extraction and linking task discussed in Section 3.3. The dataset is availble[15] and it consists of 3,500 tweets extracted from a much larger collection of over 18 million tweets. The collection covers event-annotated tweets collected for the period of July 15, 2011 to August 15, 2011 (31 days). It extends over multiple noteworthy events including the death of Amy Winehouse, the London Riots, and the Oslo bombing. Since the task of this challenge was to automatically extract and link entities, the dataset was built considering both event and non-event tweets. While event tweets are more likely to contain entities, non-event tweets enable the task to evaluate the performance of the systems in avoiding false positives in the entity extraction phase. In 2013, the task was to extract entity concepts from micropost data, characterized by a type and a value, restricting the classification to four entity types: persons, locations, organization, and miscellaneous (this task is similar to the named entity extraction task discussed in Section 2.6). The dataset is available[16] and it contains 4,341 manually annotated microposts, on a variety of topics, including comments on the news and politics, collected from the end of 2010 to the beginning of 2011.

There was a shared task for Twitter message language identification. Two datasets were used in the task: one development set composed of 15,000 tweets, and one test set composed of 15,000 tweets.[17] A script is provided to collect the data based on Twitter ID messages. The languages included are English, Basque, Catalan, Galician, Spanish, and Portuguese. Another shared task was about code switching in Twitter messages at EMNLP 2014.[18] The data included messages that switch back and forth between two languages, for the following pairs: Spanish-English, Modern Standard Arabic and Arabic dialects, Chinese-English, and Nepalese-English.

Shared tasls for detecting issues related to mental health from social media were organized by the Workshop on Computational Linguistics and Clinical Psychology—From Linguistic Signal to Clinical Reality at NAACL 2015, NAACL 2016, and ACL 2017. In 2015, the CLPsych shared task focused on tweets annotated for depression and PTSD. The 2016[19] and 2017[20] shared tasks focused on forum posts from ReachOut.com.

In this section, we also want to stress the need for more publicly available corpora and test benchmarks for social media text data, in order to allow a more comprehensive evaluation

---

[15]http://www.scc.lancs.ac.uk/microposts2014/challenge/index.html
[16]http://oak.dcs.shef.ac.uk/msm2013/challenge.html
[17]http://komunitatea.elhuyar.org/tweetlid/resources/
[18]http://emnlp2014.org/workshops/CodeSwitch/call.html
[19]http://clpsych.org/shared-task-2016/
[20]http://clpsych.org/shared-task-2017/

of performance and an objective comparison of different approaches to various tasks and applications.

5.6   SUMMARY

In this chapter, we first discussed data collection and annotation on the challenges of data collection for different social media platforms and corpus annotation efforts. Then, we presented the efforts on online spam opinion and noise detection, legal restrictions in sharing social media datasets, privacy and democracy in social media. Finally, we presented evaluation benchmarks for natural language processing tasks on social media data. In the next chapter, we conclude and discuss future perspectives for applications based on social media data.

CHAPTER 6

Conclusion and Perspectives

6.1 CONCLUSION

In this book, we investigated and highlighted the relevant NLP tools for social media data with the purpose of integrating them into real-world applications, by reviewing the latest in NLP innovative methods for social media analysis.

After a short introduction to the challenges of processing social media data, this book took a detailed view of key NLP tasks such as corpus annotation, linguistic pre-processing and normalization, part-of-speech tagging, parsing, information extraction, named-entity recognition, and multilingualism in social media texts. We presented the current methods for social media text applications using NLP algorithms tailored to social media, and more specifically for geo-localization, opinion mining, emotion analysis, event and topic detection, summarization, machine translation, and healthcare applications.

An example of real-world application is presented in Appendix A. It can be used to monitor information about events of interest and where in the world people are posting about these events. Such systems are important because, over the last decade, the semantic analysis of text in social media monitoring has become a primary form of business intelligence in order to help identify and predict behavior, and to respond to consumers. Also, it could provide better intelligent visual presentation and reporting for decision-makers to improve awareness, communication, planning, problem solving, or prevention. By using the methods that we discussed in this book and integrating them in decision making systems, the industry can manage, measure, and analyze social media marketing initiatives.

The semantic analysis of social media is an emerging area of scientific and technological opportunity. It is a new and rapidly growing interdisciplinary field (Economics, Sociology, Psychology, and Artificial Intelligence) addressing the development of automated tools and algorithms based on Natural Language Processing to monitor, capture, and analyze big data collected from publicly available social networks. We look more into the future of this area in the next section.

6.2 PERSPECTIVES

Advancements in social networks have increasingly focused on mobile communications; the volume of social media data dramatically increased and the messages and communications became shorter. The mobile-driven adoption of social media is a growing market which has included mobile app developers, location-based services, mobile bookmarking and content sharing, and mobile analytics. The high potential for research, given the analysis of end-users' social media needs arising from gathering and mining social media content to information visualization, requires new algorithms and NLP-based methods.

Considering the volume of social media data, exploring new online algorithms could prove very promising. The online algorithms can process its input piece-by-piece in a serial fashion, in the order that the input is fed to the algorithm, without having the entire input available from the source. For example, online algorithms can be applied for social media monitoring tasks for a specific event and they can process the information in relation with a contrasting event, while an offline algorithm is given the whole collection of tweets crawled from Twitter and is required to output an answer which solves the problem at hand. Online algorithms for data mining (supervised learning, clustering, etc.) can be adapted to text mining from social media streams.

The evaluation of NLP tasks for social media remains a challenge because of the lack of human-annotated NLP corpora of social media content, references, and availability of evaluation datasets. Although evaluation campaigns started to propose shared tasks based on social media texts, they are still few and the datasets are small (since manual annotation is needed). Developing more datasets remains a priority. The datasets need manual annotations for testing the performance of NLP tools and applications, but also large amounts of annotated data are needed for training, especially for part-of-speech taggers and parsers. Alternatively, more semi-supervised learning can be exploited in order to leverage the large amounts of unannotated social media data.

In addition to information extraction from social media using the NLP tools and applications that we focused on, there are many more directions of studies. Some of them concern using similar techniques for other applications in order to detect other kids of information from social media. Other directions can be related to socio-linguistic investigations [Danescu-Niculescu-Mizil et al., 2013]. In the future, researchers could investigate deeper in order to answer questions such as the following.

- What do people talk about on social media?

    - What are the topics and entities that people refer to?

    - What is an effective way to summarize contributions in social media or around a newsworthy event that offer a lens into the society's perceptions?

    - How do cultures interpret any situation in local contexts and support them in their variable observations on a social medium?

    - What are the dynamics of conversations in social communities?

    - How are emotion, mood, and affect expressed in social media?

- How do they express themselves?

- What does language tell us about the community or about individual members and their allegiances to group practices?

- Can users be meaningfully grouped in terms of their language use (e.g., stylistic properties)?

• Why do they write on social media?

- What is the underlying motivation for generating and sharing content on social media?

- How are community structures and roles evidenced via language usage? Can content analysis shed more light on network properties of community such as link-based diffusion models?

• Natural language processing techniques for social media analysis.

- How can existing NLP techniques be better adapted to this medium?

- How to develop more benchmarks for social media applications?

- How to do deeper semantic analysis for texts from social networks?

- How to improve machine translation for social media?

• Language and network structure: How do language and social network properties interact?

- What is the relation between network properties and the language that flows through them?

• Semantic Web/ontologies/domain models to aid in social data understanding.

- Given the recent interest in the Semantic Web and Linked Open Data[1] community to expose models of a domain, how can we utilize these public knowledge bases to serve as priors in linguistic analysis?

• Language across verticals.

- What challenges and opportunities in processing language on social media are common or different across industry or topic or language verticals?

- What differences appear in how users ask for or share information when they interact with a company vs. with friends?

- What language signals on social media are relevant to public health and crisis management?

• Characterize participants via linguistic analysis.

---

[1]http://linkeddata.org/

- Can we infer the relation between the participants via properties of language used in dyadic interactions?

- Do we see differences in how users self-present on this new form of digital media?

- What effect do participants have on an evolving conversation?

- Security, identity, and privacy issues from linguistic analysis over social media.

• Language, social media, and human behavior.

- What can language in social media tell us about human behavior?

- How does language in social media reflect human conditions such as power relations, emotional states, distress, mental conditions?

Finding answers to the above questions will help our society in general and require analysis in several multi-disciplinary fields. From the point of view of Computer Science and the Internet, we could say that social media is the current killer application, in the same way the Web (WWW) was in the recent past, and email was in the early years of the Internet (starting from 1969 when the Internet was born). The scale of the Web and social media continues to grow. These two reasons make automatic techniques for information extraction of crucial importance in the future.

In the future, the rapid advancement of technology will change the way humans and machines operate. The predicted rise of wearable technologies, such as glasses, smart watches, healthcare devices, fitness trackers, sleeping monitors, and other devices will influence social media and communication. For example, healthcare applications are among the focus areas of wearable technologies. Microsoft, Google, and Apple have released their own health platforms, in which doctors and other healthcare professionals can monitor the data, text, and voice collected via the patient's wearable technology. It seems that NLP techniques and applications will be more and more necessary to analyze data in the future, integrated with multi-media processing techniques.

APPENDIX A

TRANSLI: a Case Study for Social Media Analytics and Monitoring

A.1   TRANSLI ARCHITECTURE

NLP Technologies[1] has developed TRANSLI[2] Social Media Analytics and Monitoring which is an online visual analytics system designed to provide social intelligence from news and other events from Twitter. TRANSLI[3] is composed several application of Natural Language Processing tasks as we explained in chapter 4. The system features an intuitive user interface and is designed to browse and visualise the results of the semantic analysis of social discussion on specific events from Twitter. The user can obtain the information not only limited to the main event of interest [Farzindar and Khreich, 2013] but also to the information about the sub events where the system helps users find further details.

For example a journalist monitoring an event like the *Montreal Jazz Festival* is not only interested in the event schedule, but also in all the social interaction and information around this subject. The social media discussions may shift the attention to the number of bike accidents during the summer festival, which leads to the possibility of writing a new article on the security of cyclists. With Geolocation function, it is possible to monitor an event in a specific area [Inkpen et al., 2015]. The statistical machine translation module, which is trained on Twitter data to translate 140 characters, considering the short links and hashtags, can translate multilingual tweets [Sadat et al., 2014b], [Gotti et al., 2013]. These features can be used for social media analytics in various industry applications and market analysis, for example for consumer feedback on a product or service, for market strategic activities for a new product launched by competitors, or for brand reputation in a specific geographic location using social media.

Here we provide a brief description of the tool consisting of the major components that are part of the TRANSLI Social Media Analytics application. Figure A.1 represents the general architecture of the system which includes different modules such as Geo-Localization, Topic Classification, Sentiment Analysis and Machine Translation. These modules are deployed as

---

[1]http://www.nlptechnologies.ca
[2]In fact named TRANSLI™
[3]http://www.nlptechnologies.ca/en/social-networks

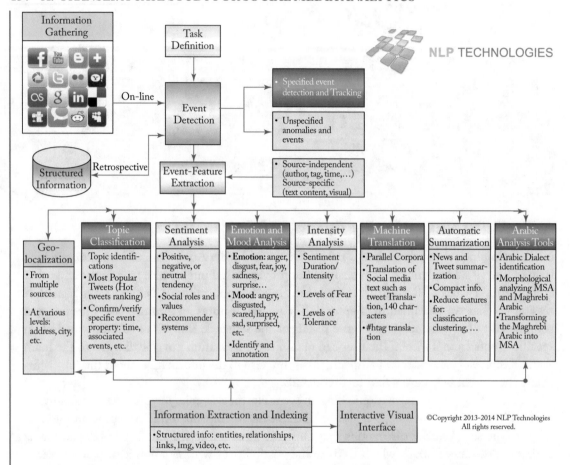

Figure A.1: TRANSLI Social Media Analytics and monitoring module architecture.

Web services cloud computing infrastructure, having proper Application Programming Interfaces (APIs), which can be accessed via HTTP requests by the user interface components for Visualization and Analytical Graphs.

A.2 USER INTERFACE

The user interface of the system includes the view for different modules of the system including the event creation, event browsing and event presentation modules. Figures A.2 and A.3 illustrate the UI for the event creation and event browsing modules.

In order to create an event, the event information should be provided, which includes its name, description, search keywords, language, and the start and the end date for capturing

Create an event

Event name   Ex: Sochi Winter Olyi

Event description

Search keywords
Put each set of keywords that need to be present
at the same time on a new line.
Use quotation marks to indicate an exact
expression.

Languages
Select each language you want the collected   ☐English ☐French
tweets to be in.

Start date
When you want the coverage to begin   2014-05-22

End date
When you want the coverage to end   2014-05-29

Create event

Figure A.2: TRANSLI user interface for event creation module.

Figure A.3: TRANSLI user interface for event browsing module.

tweets. Therefore in the browsing events, the provided information for each event is presented correspondingly.

Data visualisation in TRANSLI present the results of semantic analysis modules on social media data that have been shown in some graphic forms and abstracted the information Figure A.4. This interface consists of a dashboard with a number of components based on natural language processing which help the decision makers visualise the business intelligence from social media data. The results of semantic analysis processing are stored and indexed in data base. The visualisation dashboard includes a search toolbar at the top, most relevant pictures and videos and word cloud, giving larger context for the monitored event, on the left, the highly related tweets on the right, and the analysis on the bottom. On the right hand side of this interface, a number of tabs are provided which represent the profiles of people associated with the event, the locations associated with the event, and the automatic translation from English to French and vice versa. The analysis section include the trends in terms of volume of tweets, and top words associated with the event on the left and the most prominent hashtags and sentiment analysis in different levels associated with the event on the right.

Figure A.4: TRANSLI user interface to present an event. Components are identified with their IDs.

Glossary

Automatic summarization Reducing a text in order to summarize the major points of the original document in a manner sensitive to the application or user's need.

CNN Convolutional Neural Networks are a class of deep neural networks, most commonly applied to image analysis. Each part of the input data is passed through a series of convolution layers / filters.

CRF Conditional Random Fields, a classifier used for sequence labelling tasks, when the next class to be predicted depends on the classes chosen for the previous items in the sequence.

Deep Learning The application of artificial neural networks to learning tasks that contain more than one hidden layer. Deep learning is part of a broader family of machine learning methods based on learning data representations, as opposed to task-specific algorithms.

Information extraction The automatic extraction of structured information such as entities, relations or events from unstructured documents.

LSTM Long short-term memory networks are a class of recurrent neural networks that can provide a sequence output rather than a single value output and can capture long-distance dependencies.

Microblogging A broadcast medium in the form of blogging featuring small content allowing users to exchange small elements such as short sentences, individual images, or video links.

Naïve Bayes classifier A machine leaning algorithm that computes the probabilities of the features relative to each class, by making the simplification assumption that features are independent of each other.

NMT Neural machine translation is the use of neural network models to predict the likelihood of a sequence of words for translation.

RNN Recurrent neural networks are a class of deep neural networks where connections between nodes form a directed graph along a temporal sequence.

Semantic analysis in social media (SASM) Linguistic processing of the social media messages enhanced with semantics, and possibly also combining this with the meta-data from the social networks. In a larger sense, we refer to analyzing, understanding and enabling social networks using natural language interfaces and human behaviour on the web, e-learning environments, cyber communities and educational or online shared workspaces.

Social computing A term for an area of computer science that is concerned with the intersection of social behaviour and computational systems.

Social event A planned public or social event that can be broadly defined as any occurrence unfolding over some spatial and temporal scope. A social event is planned by people, attended by people, and the media providing the event are captured by people.

Social event detection Discovers social events and identifies related media items.

Social event summarization Extraction of social media text representatives of some real-world events. In practice, the aim is not to summarize any and all events, but only events of interest.

Social media Computer-mediated tools that allow people to create, share or exchange information, ideas, pictures and videos in virtual communities and networks.

Social media data Data available in social media, in the form of text messages, images, videos, preferences, links, and other kinds of data.

Social media information Information that can be extracted from social media data.

Social media intelligence Using information extraction from social media for specific purposes, after further distillation.

Social media summarization Automatic summarization from multiple social media sources aiming to reduce and aggregate the amount of information presented to users.

Social media text A written content posted on social media platforms.

Social network A social structure made up of a set of social actors (such as individuals or organizations) and a set of the dyadic ties between these actors.

Social networking service A Web-based platform to build social networks among people who share interests and activities.

SMT Statistical Machine Translation, that learns probabilities of translation from parallel bilingual data.

SVM Support Vector Machines, a binary classifier that learns the best separation margin between two classes.

TF-IDF Term frequency / inverse document frequency, calculated as $tf * logN/df$, where tf is the term frequency in the document, N is the number of documents in the corpus, and df is the number of documents that contain the term. The intuition behind the fromula is that frequent terms are considered important as long as they do not appear in most of the documents in a collection, and terms that appear in fewer documents are considered more discriminating.

Bibliography

Muhammad Abdul-Mageed and Lyle Ungar. Emonet: Fine-grained emotion detection with gated recurrent neural networks. In *Proceedings of the 55th Annual Meeting of the Association for Computational Linguistics (Volume 1: Long Papers)*, pages 718–728, Vancouver, Canada, July 2017. Association for Computational Linguistics. http://aclweb.org/anthology/P17-1067. DOI: 10.18653/v1/p17-1067 59

Eugene Agichtein, Carlos Castillo, Debora Donato, Aristides Gionis, and Gilad Mishne. Finding high-quality content in social media. In *Proceedings of the 2008 International Conference on Web Search and Data Mining*, Stanford, CA, USA, 11-12 February 2008, pages 183–194. ACM, 2008. DOI: 10.1145/1341531.1341557 80

Gustavo Aguilar, Suraj Maharjan, Adrian Pastor López-Monroy, and Thamar Solorio. A multi-task approach for named entity recognition in social media data. In *Proceedings of the 3rd Workshop on Noisy User-generated Text*, pages 148–153, Copenhagen, Denmark, September 2017. Association for Computational Linguistics. https://www.aclweb.org/anthology/W17-4419. DOI: 10.18653/v1/W17-4419 30

Gustavo Aguilar, Adrian Pastor López-Monroy, Fabio González, and Thamar Solorio. Modeling noisiness to recognize named entities using multitask neural networks on social media. In *Proceedings of the 2018 Conference of the North American Chapter of the Association for Computational Linguistics: Human Language Technologies, Volume 1 (Long Papers)*, pages 1401–1412, New Orleans, Louisiana, June 2018. Association for Computational Linguistics. https://www.aclweb.org/anthology/N18-1127. DOI: 10.18653/v1/N18-1127 30

Md Shad Akhtar, Utpal Kumar Sikdar, and Asif Ekbal. IITP: Hybrid approach for text normalization in Twitter. In *Proceedings of the Workshop on Noisy User-generated Text*, pages 106–110, Beijing, China, July 2015. Association for Computational Linguistics. http://www.aclweb.org/anthology/W15-4316. DOI: 10.18653/v1/w15-4316 xvii, 19

Galeb H. Al-Gaphari and M. Al-Yadoumi. A method to convert Sana'ani accent to Modern Standard Arabic. *International Journal of Information Science & Management*, 8(1), 2010. 85

Haifa Alharthi, Diana Inkpen, and Stan Szpakowicz. Unsupervised topic modelling in a book recommender system for new users. In *Proceedings of the SIGIR 2017 Workshop On eCommerce co-located with the 40th International ACM SIGIR Conference on Research and Development in Information Retrieval, eCOM@SIGIR 2017*, Tokyo, Japan, August 2017. 119

Haifa Alharthi, Diana Inkpen, and Stan Szpakowicz. A survey of book recommender systems. *Journal of Intelligent Information Systems*, 51(1):139–160, 2018. DOI: 10.1007/s10844-017-0489-9 8, 119

Tanveer Ali, Marina Sokolova, Diana Inkpen, and David Schramm. Can I hear you? opinion learning from medical forums. *Proceedings of the 6th International Joint Conference on Natural Language Processing (IJCNLP 2013)*, 2013. http://www.aclweb.org/anthology/I13-1077. 88

James Allan. *Topic Detection and Tracking: Event-based Information Organization*, volume 12. Springer, Norwell, MA, USA, 2002. DOI: 10.1007/978-1-4615-0933-2 69

James Allan, Victor Lavrenko, Daniella Malin, and Russell Swan. Detections, bounds, and timelines: UMASS and TDT-3. In *Proceedings of Topic Detection and Tracking Workshop (TDT-3)*, pages 167–174. Vienna, VA, 2000. 64

Kristen Allen, Shrey Bagroy, Alex Davis, and Tamar Krishnamurti. ConvSent at CLPsych 2019 task a: Using post-level sentiment features for suicide risk prediction on Reddit. In *Proceedings of the Sixth Workshop on Computational Linguistics and Clinical Psychology*, pages 182–187, Minneapolis, Minnesota, June 2019. Association for Computational Linguistics. https://www.aclweb.org/anthology/W19-3024. 96

Cecilia Ovesdotter Alm, Dan Roth, and Richard Sproat. Emotions from text: Machine learning for text-based emotion prediction. In *Proceedings of the Human Language Technology Conference on Empirical Methods in Natural Language Processing(HLT/EMNLP 2005)*, pages 579–586. ACL, 2005. DOI: 10.3115/1220575.1220648 58

Saima Aman and Stan Szpakowicz. Identifying expressions of emotion in text. In *Text, Speech and Dialogue*, pages 196–205. Springer, 2007. DOI: 10.1007/978-3-540-74628-7_27 58, 59, 62

Ashwin Karthik Ambalavanan, Pranjali Dileep Jagtap, Soumya Adhya, and Murthy Devarakonda. Using contextual representations for suicide risk assessment from Internet forums. In *Proceedings of the Sixth Workshop on Computational Linguistics and Clinical Psychology*, pages 172–176, Minneapolis, Minnesota, June 2019. Association for Computational Linguistics. https://www.aclweb.org/anthology/W19-3022. DOI: 10.18653/v1/w19-3022 96

Paul André, Michael Bernstein, and Kurt Luther. Who gives a tweet?: Evaluating microblog content value. In *Proceedings of the ACM 2012 conference on Computer Supported Cooperative Work(CSCW 2012)*, Bellevue, Washington, USA, 11-15 February 2012, pages 471–474, 2012. DOI: 10.1145/2145204.2145277. 10

Ron Artstein and Massimo Poesio. Inter-coder agreement for computational linguistics. *Computational Linguistics*, 34:553–596, 2008. http://cswww.essex.ac.uk/research/nle/arrau/icagr.pdf. DOI: 10.1162/coli.07-034-r2 15

Ravi Arunachalam and Sandipan Sarkar. The new eye of government: Citizen sentiment analysis in social media. In *Proceedings of the IJCNLP 2013 Workshop on Natural Language Processing for Social Media (SocialNLP)*, pages 23–28, Nagoya, Japan, October 2013. Asian Federation of Natural Language Processing. http://www.aclweb.org/anthology/W13-4204. 100

Atanas Atanasov, Gianmarco De Francisci Morales, and Preslav Nakov. Predicting the role of political trolls in social media. In *Proceedings of the 23rd Conference on Computational Natural Language Learning (CoNLL)*, 2019. DOI: 10.18653/v1/k19-1096 101

Neela Avudaiappan, Alexander Herzog, Sneha Kadam, Yuheng Du, Jason Thatcher, and Ilya Safro. Detecting and summarizing emergent events in microblogs and social media streams by dynamic centralities. 2016. https://arxiv.org/abs/1610.06431. DOI: 10.1109/big-data.2017.8258097 72

Stefano Baccianella, Andrea Esuli, and Fabrizio Sebastiani. Sentiwordnet 3.0: An enhanced lexical resource for sentiment analysis and opinion mining. In *Proceedings of the Seventh International Conference on Language Resources and Evaluation (LREC'10)*, Valletta, Malta, May 2010. European Language Resources Association (ELRA). URL http://lrec.elra.info/proceedings/lrec2010/pdf/769_Paper.pdf. 57

Lars Backstrom, Eric Sun, and Cameron Marlow. Find me if you can: Improving geographical prediction with social and spatial proximity. In *Proceedings of the 19th international conference on World Wide Web*, pages 61–70. ACM, 2010. DOI: 10.1145/1772690.1772698 44, 45, 47

Dzmitry Bahdanau, Kyunghyun Cho, and Yoshua Bengio. Neural machine translation by jointly learning to align and translate. In Yoshua Bengio and Yann LeCun, editors, *3rd International Conference on Learning Representations, ICLR 2015, San Diego, CA, USA, May 7-9, 2015, Conference Track Proceedings*, 2015. http://arxiv.org/abs/1409.0473. 78

Hitham Abo Bakr, Khaled Shaalan, and Ibrahim Ziedan. A hybrid approach for converting written Egyptian colloquial dialect into diacritized Arabic. In *The 6th International Conference on Informatics and Systems, INFOS2008. Cairo University*, 2008. http://infos2008.fci.cu.edu.eg/infos/NLP_05_P027-033.pdf. 84

Ramnath Balasubramanyan, William W. Cohen, Doug Pierce, and David P. Redlawsk. What pushes their buttons? Predicting comment polarity from the content of political blog posts. In *Proceedings of the Workshop on Language in Social Media (LSM 2011)*, pages 12–19, Portland, Oregon, June 2011. Association for Computational Linguistics. http://www.aclweb.org/anthology/W11-0703. 100

Timothy Baldwin, Paul Cook, Marco Lui, Andrew MacKinlay, and Li Wang. How noisy social media text, how diffrnt social media sources? In *Proceedings of the Sixth International Joint Conference on Natural Language Processing*, pages 356–364. Asian Federation of Natural Language Processing, 2013. http://aclweb.org/anthology/I13-1041. 123

Tyler Baldwin and Yunyao Li. An in-depth analysis of the effect of text normalization in social media. In *Proceedings of the 2015 Conference of the North American Chapter of the Association for Computational Linguistics: Human Language Technologies*, pages 420–429, Denver, Colorado, May–June 2015. Association for Computational Linguistics. http://www.aclweb.org/anthology/N15-1045. DOI: 10.3115/v1/n15-1045 xvii, 19, 20

Georgios Balikas and Massih-Reza Amini. TwiSE at SemEval-2016 task 4: Twitter sentiment classification. In *Proceedings of the 10th International Workshop on Semantic Evaluation (SemEval-2016)*, pages 85–91, San Diego, California, June 2016. Association for Computational Linguistics. http://www.aclweb.org/anthology/S16-1010. DOI: 10.18653/v1/s16-1010 60

Geoffrey Barbier, Zhuo Feng, Pritam Gundecha, and Huan Liu. *Provenance Data in Social Media*. Synthesis Lectures on Data Mining and Knowledge Discovery. Morgan & Claypool Publishers, 2013. DOI: 10.2200/S00496ED1V01Y201304DMK007 1, 123

Francesco Barbieri, Horacio Saggion, and Francesco Ronzano. Modelling sarcasm in Twitter, a novel approach. In *Proceedings of the 5th Workshop on Computational Approaches to Subjectivity, Sentiment and Social Media Analysis*, pages 50–58, Baltimore, Maryland, June 2014. Association for Computational Linguistics. http://www.aclweb.org/anthology/W/W14/W14-2609. DOI: 10.3115/v1/w14-2609 61

Utsab Barman, Amitava Das, Joachim Wagner, and Jennifer Foster. Code mixing: A challenge for language identification in the language of social media. In *Proceedings of the First Workshop on Computational Approaches to Code Switching*, pages 13–23, Doha, Qatar, October 2014. Association for Computational Linguistics. http://www.aclweb.org/anthology/W14-3902. DOI: 10.3115/v1/w14-3902 33

Marco Baroni, Francis Chantree, Adam Kilgarriff, and Serge Sharoff. Cleaneval: A competition for cleaning web pages. In *Proceedings of the Sixth International Conference on Language Resources and Evaluation (LREC'08)*, Marrakech, Morocco, May 2008. European Language Resources Association (ELRA). 22

Valerio Basile, Cristina Bosco, Elisabetta Fersini, Debora Nozza, Viviana Patti, Francisco Manuel Rangel Pardo, Paolo Rosso, and Manuela Sanguinetti. SemEval-2019 task 5: Multilingual detection of hate speech against immigrants and women in twitter. In *Proceedings of the 13th International Workshop on Semantic Evaluation*, pages 54–63, Minneapolis, Minnesota, USA, June 2019. Association for Computational Linguistics. https://www.aclweb.org/anthology/S19-2007. DOI: 10.18653/v1/s19-2007 103

Leonard E. Baum and Ted Petrie. Statistical inference for probabilistic functions of finite state Markov chains. *The Annals of Mathematical Statistics*, pages 1554–1563, 1966. http://www.jstor.org/stable/2238772. DOI: 10.1214/aoms/1177699147 16, 22

Hila Becker, Feiyang Chen, Dan Iter, Mor Naaman, and Luis Gravano. Automatic identification and presentation of Twitter content for planned events. In *Proceedings of the 5th International AAAI Conference on Weblogs and Social Media (ICWSM)*, pages 655–656, 2011a. 68

Hila Becker, Mor Naaman, and Luis Gravano. Beyond trending topics: Real-world event identification on Twitter. In *Proceedings of the 5th International AAAI Conference on Weblogs and Social Media (ICWSM)*, pages 438–441, 2011b. 65, 71

Hila Becker, Mor Naaman, and Luis Gravano. Selecting quality Twitter content for events. In *Proceedings of the 5th International AAAI Conference on Weblogs and Social Media (ICWSM)*, pages 443–445, 2011c. 68

Hila Becker, Dan Iter, Mor Naaman, and Luis Gravano. Identifying content for planned events across social media sites. In *Proceedings of the fifth ACM international conference on Web search and data mining*, pages 533–542. ACM, 2012. DOI: 10.1145/2124295.2124360 68

Abdelghani Bellaachia and Mohammed Al-Dhelaan. HG-Rank: A hypergraph-based keyphrase extraction for short documents in dynamic genre. In *4th Workshop on Making Sense of Microposts (#Microposts2014)*, pages 42–49, 2014. http://ceur-ws.org/Vol-1141/paper_06.pdf. 53

Edward Benson, Aria Haghighi, and Regina Barzilay. Event discovery in social media feeds. In *Proceedings of the 49th Annual Meeting of the Association for Computational Linguistics:Human Language Technologies*, Portland, Oregon, USA, 19-24 June 2011, volume 1, pages 389–398, 2011. http://dl.acm.org/citation.cfm?id=2002472.2002522. 67, 71

Adrian Benton, Margaret Mitchell, and Dirk Hovy. Multitask learning for mental health conditions with limited social media data. In *Proceedings of the 15th Conference of the European Chapter of the Association for Computational Linguistics: Volume 1, Long Papers*, pages 152–162, Valencia, Spain, April 2017. Association for Computational Linguistics. http://www.aclweb.org/anthology/E17-1015. DOI: 10.18653/v1/e17-1015 93

Adam L. Berger, Vincent J. Della Pietra, and Stephen A. Della Pietra. A maximum entropy approach to natural language processing. *Computational Linguistics*, 22(1):39–71, March 1996. http://dl.acm.org/citation.cfm?id=234285.234289. 17

Shane Bergsma, Paul McNamee, Mossaab Bagdouri, Clayton Fink, and Theresa Wilson. Language identification for creating language-specific Twitter collections. In *Proceedings of the Second Workshop on Language in Social Media*, pages 65–74, Montréal, Canada, June 2012. Association for Computational Linguistics. http://www.aclweb.org/anthology/W12-2108. 33

Adam Bermingham and Alan Smeaton. On using Twitter to monitor political sentiment and predict election results. In *Proceedings of the Workshop on Sentiment Analysis where AI meets Psychology (SAAIP 2011)*, pages 2–10, Chiang Mai, Thailand, November 2011. Asian Federation of Natural Language Processing. http://www.aclweb.org/anthology/W11-3702. 100

Gary Beverungen and Jugal Kalita. Evaluating methods for summarizing Twitter posts. *Proceedings of the 5th AAAI ICWSM*, 2011. 9, 11

Li Bing, Keith C.C. Chan, and Carol Ou. Public sentiment analysis in Twitter data for prediction of a company's stock price movements. In *e-Business Engineering (ICEBE), 2014 IEEE 11th International Conference on*, pages 232–239, Nov 2014. DOI: 10.1109/ICEBE.2014.47 98

Christian Bizer, Tom Heath, and Tim Berners-Lee. Linked data-the story so far. *International journal on semantic web and information systems*, 5(3):1–22, 2009. DOI: 10.4018/978-1-60960-593-3.ch008 52

David M. Blei, Andrew Y. Ng, and Michael I. Jordan. Latent Dirichlet Allocation. *Journal of Machine Learning Research*, 3:993–1022, 2003. http://dl.acm.org/citation.cfm?id=944919.944937. 66

Su Lin Blodgett, Johnny Wei, and Brendan O'Connor. Twitter universal dependency parsing for African-American and mainstream American English. In *Proceedings of the 56th Annual Meeting of the Association for Computational Linguistics (Volume 1: Long Papers)*, pages 1415–1425, Melbourne, Australia, July 2018. Association for Computational Linguistics. https://www.aclweb.org/anthology/P18-1131. DOI: 10.18653/v1/p18-1131 7

Victoria Bobicev, Marina Sokolova, Yasser Jafer, and David Schramm. Learning sentiments from tweets with personal health information. In *Advances in Artificial Intelligence*, pages 37–48. Springer, 2012. DOI: 10.1007/978-3-642-30353-1_4 88

Johan Bollen, Huina Mao, and Alberto Pepe. Modeling public mood and emotion: Twitter sentiment and socio-economic phenomena. In *Proceedings of the Fifth International AAAI Conference on Weblogs and Social Media (ICWSM)*, pages 450–453, July 2011. http://arxiv.org/abs/0911.1583. 59

Jonah Bollen, Huina Mao, and Xiao-Jun Zeng. Twitter mood predicts the stock market. *Computing Research Repository (CoRR)*, abs/1010.3003, 2010. http://arxiv.org/abs/1010.3003. DOI: 10.1016/j.jocs.2010.12.007 97

Kalina Bontcheva, Leon Derczynski, Adam Funk, Mark Greenwood, Diana Maynard, and Niraj Aswani. Twitie: An open-source information extraction pipeline for microblog text.

In *Proceedings of the International Conference Recent Advances in Natural Language Processing RANLP 2013*, pages 83–90. INCOMA Ltd. Shoumen, BULGARIA, 2013. http://aclweb.org/anthology/R13-1011. 122

Rahma Boujelbane, Meriem Ellouze Khemekhem, and Lamia Hadrich Belguith. Mapping rules for building a Tunisian dialect lexicon and generating corpora. *International Joint Conference on Natural Language Processing*, pages 419–429, October 2013. http://www.aclweb.org/anthology/I13-1048. 85

Danah Boyd and Nicole Ellison. Social network sites: Definition, history, and scholarship. *Journal of Computer-Mediated Communication*, 13(1):210–230, 2007. DOI: 10.1111/j.1083-6101.2007.00393.x 1

Margaret M. Bradley and Peter J. Lang. Affective norms for English words (ANEW): Instruction manual and affective ratings. Technical report c-1, University of Florida, 1999. The Center for Research in Psychophysiology. 59

Richard Brantingham and Aleem Hossain. Crowded: A crowd-sourced perspective of events as they happen. In *SPIE*, volume 8758, 2013. URL http://spie.org/Publications/Proceedings/Paper/10.1117/12.2016596. DOI: 10.1117/12.2016596 107

Chris Brew. Classifying reachout posts with a radial basis function svm. In *Proceedings of the Third Workshop on Computational Linguistics and Clinical Psychology*, pages 138–142, San Diego, CA, USA, June 2016. Association for Computational Linguistics. http://www.aclweb.org/anthology/W16-0315. DOI: 10.18653/v1/w16-0315 95

Ralf D. Brown. Selecting and weighting n-grams to identify 1100 languages. In Ivan Habernal and Vaclav Matousek, editors, *Text, Speech, and Dialogue*, volume 8082 of *Lecture Notes in Computer Science*, pages 475–483. Springer, 2013. DOI: 10.1007/978-3-642-40585-3_60 34

Tim Buckwalter. Buckwalter Arabic morphological analyzer version 2.0. LDC catalog number LDC2004L02. Technical report, University of Pennsylvania, 2004. http://catalog.ldc.upenn.edu/LDC2004L02. 37, 84

Clinton Burfoot, Steven Bird, and Timothy Baldwin. Collective classification of congressional floor-debate transcripts. In *Proceedings of the 49th Annual Meeting of the Association for Computational Linguistics: Human Language Technologies*, pages 1506–1515, Portland, Oregon, USA, June 2011. Association for Computational Linguistics. http://www.aclweb.org/anthology/P11-1151. 100

Cornelia Caragea, Adrian Silvescu, and Andrea H. Tapia. Identifying informative messages in disaster events using convolutional neural networks. In *Proceedings of the ISCRAM 2016 Conference*, Rio de Janeiro, Brazil, May 2016. http://www.cse.unt.edu/~ccaragea/papers/iscram16a.pdf. 108

Jean Carletta. Assessing agreement on classification tasks: The kappa statistic. *Comput. Linguist.*, 22(2):249–254, June 1996. http://dl.acm.org/citation.cfm?id=230386.230390. 15

Simon Carter, Manos Tsagkias, and Wouter Weerkamp. Twitter hashtags: Joint translation and clustering. In *Proceedings of the ACM WebSci'11*, pages 1–3, 2011. 83

Simon Carter, Wouter Weerkamp, and Manos Tsagkias. Microblog language identification: Overcoming the limitations of short, unedited and idiomatic text. *Language Resources and Evaluation*, 47(1):195–215, March 2013. DOI: 10.1007/s10579-012-9195-y 33

William B. Cavnar and John M. Trenkle. N-gram-based text categorization. In *Proceedings of SDAIR-94, 3rd Annual Symposium on Document Analysis and Information Retrieval*, pages 161–175, 1994. 34

Fabio Celli. Unsupervised personality recognition for social network sites. In *The Sixth International Conference on Digital Society ICDS 2012*, January 2012. http://www.worldcat.org/isbn/978-1-61208-176-2. 110

Daniel Cer, Yinfei Yang, Sheng-yi Kong, Nan Hua, Nicole Limtiaco, Rhomni St. John, Noah Constant, Mario Guajardo-Cespedes, Steve Yuan, Chris Tar, Yun-Hsuan Sung, Brian Strope, and Ray Kurzweil. Universal sentence encoder. *CoRR*, abs/1803.11175, 2018. http://arxiv.org/abs/1803.11175. 103

Chen Chen, Wu Dongxing, Hou Chunyan, and Yuan Xiaojie. Exploiting social media for stock market prediction with factorization machine. In *2014 IEEE/WIC/ACM International Joint Conferences on Web Intelligence (WI) and Intelligent Agent Technologies (IAT)*, volume 2, pages 142–149, August 2014a. DOI: 10.1109/WI-IAT.2014.91 98

Chien Chin Chen and Meng Chang Chen. Tscan: A novel method for topic summarization and content anatomy. In *Proceedings of the 31st annual international ACM SIGIR conference on Research and development in information retrieval*, pages 579–586, New York, NY, USA, 2008. ACM. DOI: 10.1145/1390334.1390433. 69

Danqi Chen and Christopher Manning. A fast and accurate dependency parser using neural networks. In *Proceedings of the 2014 Conference on Empirical Methods in Natural Language Processing (EMNLP)*, pages 740–750, Doha, Qatar, October 2014. Association for Computational Linguistics. https://www.aclweb.org/anthology/D14-1082. DOI: 10.3115/v1/D14-1082 25

Hailiang Chen, Prabuddha De, Yu Hu, and Byoung-Hyoun Hwang. Sentiment revealed in social media and its effect on the stock market. In *Statistical Signal Processing Workshop (SSP), 2011 IEEE*, pages 25–28, June 2011. DOI: 10.1109/SSP.2011.5967675 98

Hailiang Chen, Prabuddha De, Yu Hu, and Byoung-Hyoun Hwang. Wisdom of crowds: The value of stock opinions transmitted through social media, 2014b. URL https://academic.oup.com/rfs/article-abstract/27/5/1367/1581938/Wisdom-of-Crowds-The-Value-of-Stock-Opinions?redirectedFrom=fulltext. DOI: 10.1093/rfs/hhu001 98

Zheng Chen and Xiaoqing Du. Study of stock prediction based on social network. In *Social Computing (SocialCom), 2013 International Conference on*, pages 913–916, Sept 2013. DOI: 10.1109/SocialCom.2013.141 98

Zhiyuan Cheng, James Caverlee, and Kyumin Lee. You are where you tweet: A content-based approach to geo-locating Twitter users. In *Proceedings of the 19th ACM international conference on Information and knowledge management*, pages 759–768. ACM, 2010. DOI: 10.1145/1871437.1871535. 44, 46, 47, 49

Jorge Ale Chilet, Cuicui Chen, and Yusan Lin. Analyzing social media marketing in the high-end fashion industry using named entity recognition. In *2016 IEEE/ACM International Conference on Advances in Social Networks Analysis and Mining (ASONAM)*, 2016. http://ieeexplore.ieee.org/abstract/document/7752300/. DOI: 10.1109/asonam.2016.7752300 102

Jishnu Ray Chowdhury, Cornelia Caragea, , and Doina Caragea. On identifying hashtags in disaster twitter data. In *Proceedings of the Thirty-Fourth AAAI Conference on Artificial Intelligence (AAAAI 2020)*, New York City, NY, USA, February 2020. 108

Freddy Chong Tat Chua and Sitaram Asur. Automatic summarization of events from social media. Technical report, HP Labs, 2012. URL http://www.hpl.hp.com/research/scl/papers/socialmedia/tweet_summary.pdf. 11

Camille Cobb, Ted McCarthy, Annuska Perkins, Ankitha Bharadwaj, Jared Comis, Brian Do, and Kate Starbird. Designing for the deluge: Understanding and supporting the distributed, collaborative work of crisis volunteers. In *Proceedings of the 17th ACM Conference on Computer Supported Cooperative Work and Social Computing*, CSCW '14, pages 888–899. ACM, 2014. DOI: 10.1145/2531602.2531712. 71

Richard Colbaugh and Kristin Glass. Estimating sentiment orientation in social media for intelligence monitoring and analysis. In *Intelligence and Security Informatics (ISI), 2010 IEEE International Conference on*, pages 135–137, May 2010. DOI: 10.1109/ISI.2010.5484760 105

Glen Coppersmith, Mark Dredze, and Craig Harman. Measuring post traumatic stress disorder in Twitter. In *Proceedings of the 7th International AAAI Conference on Weblogs and Social Media (ICWSM).*, volume 2, pages 23–45, 2014a. 92

Glen Coppersmith, Mark Dredze, and Craig Harman. Quantifying mental health signals in Twitter. In *Proceedings of the Workshop on Computational Linguistics and Clinical Psychol-*

ogy: From Linguistic Signal to Clinical Reality, pages 51–60, 2014b. http://www.aclweb.org/anthology/W/W14/W14-3207. DOI: 10.3115/v1/w14-3207 92, 111

Glen Coppersmith, Mark Dredze, Craig Harman, and Kristy Hollingshead. From ADHD to SAD: Analyzing the language of mental health on Twitter through self-reported diagnoses. In *Proceedings of the 2nd Workshop on Computational Linguistics and Clinical Psychology: From Linguistic Signal to Clinical Reality*, pages 1–10, Denver, Colorado, June 5 2015a. Association for Computational Linguistics. http://www.aclweb.org/anthology/W15-1201. DOI: 10.3115/v1/w15-1201 93

Glen Coppersmith, Mark Dredze, Craig Harman, Kristy Hollingshead, and Margaret Mitchell. CLPsych 2015 shared task: Depression and PTSD on Twitter. In *Proceedings of the 2nd Workshop on Computational Linguistics and Clinical Psychology: From Linguistic Signal to Clinical Reality*, pages 31–39, 2015b. DOI: 10.3115/v1/w15-1204 92

Mário Cordeiro. Twitter event detection: Combining wavelet analysis and topic inference summarization. In *Doctoral Symposium on Informatics Engineering, DSIE*, 2012. 66

Corinna Cortes and Vladimir Vapnik. Support-vector networks. *Machine Learning*, 20(3): 273–297, 1995. DOI: 10.1007/BF00994018 16

S. Cucerzan. Large-scale named entity disambiguation based on Wikipedia data. In *Proceedings of EMNLP-CoNLL 2007*, pages 708–716, 2007. http://www.aclweb.org/anthology/D/D07/D07-1074. 51

Hamish Cunningham, Diana Maynard, Kalina Bontcheva, and Valentin Tablan. A framework and graphical development environment for robust NLP tools and applications. In *Proceedings of the 40th Anniversary Meeting of the Association for Computational Linguistics (ACL'02)*. Association for Computational Linguistics, 2002. 30, 48

Cristian Danescu-Niculescu-Mizil, Robert West, Dan Jurafsky, Jure Leskovec, and Christopher Potts. No country for old members: User lifecycle and linguistic change in online communities. In *Proceedings of WWW*, 2013. http://dl.acm.org/citation.cfm?id=2488388.2488416. DOI: 10.1145/2488388.2488416 130

Hal Daumé, III and Jagadeesh Jagarlamudi. Domain adaptation for machine translation by mining unseen words. In *Proceedings of the 49th Annual Meeting of the Association for Computational Linguistics: Human Language Technologies: Short Papers - Volume 2*, HLT '11, pages 407–412. Association for Computational Linguistics, 2011. http://dl.acm.org/citation.cfm?id=2002736.2002819. 80

Dmitry Davidov, Oren Tsur, and Ari Rappoport. Semi-supervised recognition of sarcasm in Twitter and Amazon. In *Proceedings of the Fourteenth Conference on Computational Natural*

Language Learning, pages 107–116, Uppsala, Sweden, July 2010. Association for Computational Linguistics. http://www.aclweb.org/anthology/W10-2914. 61

Munmun De Choudhury, Scott Counts, and Eric Horvitz. Social media as a measurement tool of depression in populations. *WebSci '13: Proceedings of the 5th Annual ACM Web Science Conference*, pages 47–56, 2013a. DOI: 10.1145/2464464.2464480 91

Munmun De Choudhury, Michael Gamon, Scott Counts, and Eric Horvitz. Predicting depression via social media. In *Proceedings of the Seventh International AAAI Conference on Weblogs and Social Media*, volume 2, pages 128–137, 2013b. ISBN 9781450313315. http://www.aaai.org/ocs/index.php/ICWSM/ICWSM13/paper/viewFile/6124/6351. 92

Pragna Debnath, Saniul Haque, Somprakash Bandyopadhyay, and Siuli Roy. Post-disaster situational analysis from whatsapp group chats of emergency response providers. In *Proceedings of the ISCRAM 2016 Conference*, Rio de Janeiro, Brazil, May 2016. URL http://idl.iscram.org/files/pragnadebnath/2016/1393_PragnaDebnath_etal2016.pdf. 109

Jean-Yves Delort and Enrique Alfonseca. Description of the Google update summarizer. In *Proceedings of the Text Analysis Conference 2011 (TAC2011)*, 2011. URL http://www.nist.gov/tac/publications/2011/participant.papers/GOOGLE.proceedings.pdf. 73

Seniz Demir. Context tailoring for text normalization. In *Proceedings of TextGraphs-10: the Workshop on Graph-based Methods for Natural Language Processing*, pages 6–14, San Diego, CA, USA, June 2016. Association for Computational Linguistics. http://www.aclweb.org/anthology/W16-1402. DOI: 10.18653/v1/w16-1402 18

Leon Derczynski and Kalina Bontcheva. Passive-aggressive sequence labeling with discriminative post-editing for recognising person entities in tweets. In *Proceedings of the 14th Conference of the European Chapter of the Association for Computational Linguistics, volume 2: Short Papers*, pages 69–73, Gothenburg, Sweden, April 2014. Association for Computational Linguistics. http://www.aclweb.org/anthology/E14-4014. DOI: 10.3115/v1/e14-4014 31

Leon Derczynski, Diana Maynard, Niraj Aswani, and Kalina Bontcheva. Microblog-genre noise and impact on semantic annotation accuracy. In *Proceedings of the 24th ACM Conference on Hypertext and Social Media*, pages 21–30, Paris, France, May 2013a. ACM. http://derczynski.com/sheffield/papers/ner_issues.pdf. DOI: 10.1145/2481492.2481495 30, 32

Leon Derczynski, Alan Ritter, Sam Clark, and Kalina Bontcheva. Twitter part-of-speech tagging for all: Overcoming sparse and noisy data. In *Proceedings of the International Conference on Recent Advances in Natural Language Processing*, Hissar, Bulgaria, 7-13 September 2013. ACL, 2013b. 18, 22, 24, 30, 32

Leon Derczynski, Diana Maynard, Giuseppe Rizzo, Marieke van Erp, Genevieve Gorrell, Raphael Troncy, Johann Petrak, and Kalina Bontcheva. Analysis of named entity recognition and linking for tweets. In *Information Processing and Management*, pages 32–49, 2014. URL http://www.sciencedirect.com/science/article/pii/S0306457314001034. DOI: 10.1016/j.ipm.2014.10.006 54

Jan Deriu, Maurice Gonzenbach, Fatih Uzdilli, Aurelien Lucchi, Valeria De Luca, and Martin Jaggi. SwissCheese at SemEval-2016 task 4: Sentiment classification using an ensemble of convolutional neural networks with distant supervision. In *Proceedings of the 10th International Workshop on Semantic Evaluation (SemEval-2016)*, pages 1124–1128, San Diego, California, June 2016. Association for Computational Linguistics. http://www.aclweb.org/anthology/S16-1173. DOI: 10.18653/v1/s16-1173 60

Mona Diab, Nizar Habash, Owen Rambow, Mohamed Altantawy, and Yassine Benajiba. Colaba: Arabic dialect annotation and processing. In *LREC Workshop on Semitic Language Processing*, pages 66–74, 2010. 35

Nicholas Diakopoulos, Mor Naaman, and Funda Kivran-Swaine. Diamonds in the rough: Social media visual analytics for journalistic inquiry. In *2010 IEEE Symposium on Visual Analytics Science and Technology (VAST)*, pages 115–122, Oct 2010. DOI: 10.1109/VAST.2010.5652922 102, 117

Štefan Dlugolinský, Peter Krammer, Marek Ciglan, Michal Laclavík, and Ladislav Hluchý. Combining named entity recognition methods for concept extraction in Microposts. In *4th Workshop on Making Sense of Microposts (#Microposts2014)*, pages 34–41, 2014. http://ceurws.org/Vol-1141/paper_09.pdf. 53

Peter Sheridan Dodds and Christopher M Danforth. Measuring the happiness of large-scale written expression: Songs, blogs, and presidents. *Journal of Happiness Studies*, 11(4):441–456, 2010. DOI: 10.1007/s10902-009-9150-9 56

Mark Dredze, Nicholas Andrews, and Jay DeYoung. Twitter at the Grammys: A social media corpus for entity linking and disambiguation. In *Proceedings of The Fourth International Workshop on Natural Language Processing for Social Media*, pages 20–25, Austin, TX, USA, November 2016. Association for Computational Linguistics. http://aclweb.org/anthology/W16-6204. DOI: 10.18653/v1/w16-6204 54

Yajuan Duan, Long Jiang, Tao Qin, Ming Zhou, and Heung-Yeung Shum. An empirical study on learning to rank of tweets. In *Proceedings of the 23rd International Conference on Computational Linguistics*, COLING 2010, pages 295–303, Stroudsburg, PA, USA, 2010. Association for Computational Linguistics. http://dl.acm.org/citation.cfm?id=1873781.1873815. 72

Ted Dunning. Statistical identification of language. Technical report, Computing Research Laboratory, New Mexico State University, 1994. 37

Miles Efron. Information search and retrieval in microblogs. *Journal of American Society for Information Science and Technology*, 62(6):996–1008, June 2011. DOI: 10.1002/asi.21512 123

Jacob Eisenstein. Phonological factors in social media writing. In *Proceedings of the Workshop on Language Analysis in Social Media*, pages 11–19, Atlanta, Georgia, June 2013a. Association for Computational Linguistics. http://www.aclweb.org/anthology/W13-1102. 11, 18

Jacob Eisenstein. What to do about bad language on the Internet. In *Proceedings of the 2013 Conference of the North American Chapter of the Association for Computational Linguistics: Human Language Technologies*, pages 359–369, Atlanta, Georgia, June 2013b. Association for Computational Linguistics. http://www.aclweb.org/anthology/N13-1037. 18

Jacob Eisenstein. *Introduction to Natural Language Processing*. MIT Press, 2019. 16

Jacob Eisenstein, Brendan O'Connor, Noah A Smith, and Eric P Xing. A latent variable model for geographic lexical variation. In *Proceedings of the 2010 Conference on Empirical Methods in Natural Language Processing*, pages 1277–1287. ACL, 2010. http://dl.acm.org/citation.cfm?id=1870658.1870782. 47, 49, 123

Jacob Eisenstein, Noah A. Smith, and Eric P. Xing. Discovering sociolinguistic associations with structured sparsity. In *Proceedings of the 49th Annual Meeting of the Association for Computational Linguistics: Human Language Technologies*, pages 1365–1374, Portland, Oregon, USA, June 2011. Association for Computational Linguistics. http://www.aclweb.org/anthology/P11-1137. 18

Paul Ekman. An argument for basic emotions. *Cognition and Emotion*, 6(3-4):169–200, 1992. DOI: 10.1080/02699939208411068 58, 59

Heba Elfardy and Mona Diab. Sentence level dialect identification in Arabic. In *Proceedings of the 51st Annual Meeting of the Association for Computational Linguistics (Volume 2: Short Papers)*, pages 456–461, Sofia, Bulgaria, August 2013. Association for Computational Linguistics. http://www.aclweb.org/anthology/P13-2081. 41

Brian Eriksson, Paul Barford, Joel Sommers, and Robert Nowak. A learning-based approach for IP geolocation. In *Passive and Active Measurement*, pages 171–180. Springer, 2010. http://dl.acm.org/citation.cfm?id=1889324.1889342. DOI: 10.1007/978-3-642-12334-4_18 44, 45

Atefeh Farzindar and Diana Inkpen, editors. *Proceedings of the Workshop on Semantic Analysis in Social Media*. Association for Computational Linguistics, Avignon, France, April 2012. http://www.aclweb.org/anthology/W12-06. 5

Atefeh Farzindar and Wael Khreich. A survey of techniques for event detection in Twitter. *Computational Intelligence*, 2013. DOI: 10.1111/coin.12017 62, 74, 101, 133

154 BIBLIOGRAPHY

Atefeh Farzindar, Michael Gamon, Diana Inkpen, Meena Nagarajan, and Cristian Danescu-Niculescu-Mizil, editors. *Proceedings of the Workshop on Language Analysis in Social Media.* Association for Computational Linguistics, Atlanta, Georgia, June 2013. http://www.aclweb.org/anthology/W13-11. 5

Atefeh Farzindar, Diana Inkpen, Michael Gamon, and Meena Nagarajan, editors. *Proceedings of the 5th Workshop on Language Analysis for Social Media (LASM).* Association for Computational Linguistics, Gothenburg, Sweden, April 2014. http://www.aclweb.org/anthology/W14-13. 5

Paolo Ferragina and Ugo Scaiella. TAGME: on-the-fly annotation of short text fragments (by Wikipedia entities). *Computing Research Repository (CoRR)*, abs/1006.3498, 2010. http://arxiv.org/abs/1006.3498. DOI: 10.1145/1871437.1871689 53

Antske Fokkens, Marieke van Erp, Marten Postma, Ted Pedersen, Piek Vossen, and Nuno Freire. Offspring from reproduction problems: What replication failure teaches us. In *Proceedings of the 51st Annual Meeting of the Association for Computational Linguistics*, volume 1, pages 1691–1701, Sofia, Bulgaria, August 2013. ACL. http://www.aclweb.org/anthology/P13-1166. 22

Dominey Peter Ford and Thomas Voegtlin. Learning word meaning and grammatical constructions from narrated video events. In *Proceedings of the HLT-NAACL 2003 Workshop on Learning Word Meaning from Non Linguistic Data*, 2003. http://aclweb.org/anthology/W03-0606. DOI: 10.3115/1119212.1119218 121

Eric N. Forsyth and Craig H. Martell. Lexical and discourse analysis of online chat dialog. In *Semantic Computing, 2007. ICSC 2007. International Conference on*, pages 19–26. IEEE, 2007. DOI: 10.1109/ICSC.2007.54 24

George Foster, Cyril Goutte, and Roland Kuhn. Discriminative instance weighting for domain adaptation in statistical machine translation. In *Proceedings of the 2010 Conference on Empirical Methods in Natural Language Processing*, pages 451–459, Cambridge, MA, October 2010. Association for Computational Linguistics. http://www.aclweb.org/anthology/D10-1044. 80

Jennifer Foster, Ozlem Cetinoglu, Joachim Wagner, Joseph Le Roux, Joakim Nivre, Deirdre Hogan, and Josef van Genabith. From news to comment: Resources and benchmarks for parsing the language of Web 2.0. In *Proceedings of 5th International Joint Conference on Natural Language Processing*, pages 893–901, Chiang Mai, Thailand, November 2011. Asian Federation of Natural Language Processing. http://www.aclweb.org/anthology/I11-1100. 27

Dieter Fox, Dirk Schulz, Gaetano Borriello, Jeffrey Hightower, and Lin Liao. Bayesian filtering for location estimation. *IEEE pervasive computing*, 2(3):24–33, 2003. DOI: 10.1109/MPRV.2003.1228524 68

Jerome H Friedman. Greedy function approximation: A gradient boosting machine. *Annals of Statistics*, pages 1189–1232, 2001. 66

Jonas Gehring, Michael Auli, David Grangier, Denis Yarats, and Yann Dauphin. Convolutional sequence to sequence learning. In *Proceedings of the 34th International Conference on Machine Learning (ICML 2017)*, Sydney, Australia, 05 2017. 17, 78

Spandana Gella, Paul Cook, and Timothy Baldwin. One sense per tweeter ... and other lexical semantic tales of Twitter. In *Proceedings of the 14th Conference of the European Chapter of the Association for Computational Linguistics, volume 2: Short Papers*, pages 215–220, Gothenburg, Sweden, April 2014. Association for Computational Linguistics. http://www.aclweb.org/anthology/E14-4042. DOI: 10.3115/v1/e14-4042 54

Diman Ghazi, Diana Inkpen, and Stan Szpakowicz. Hierarchical versus flat classification of emotions in text. In *Proceedings of the NAACL HLT 2010 workshop on computational approaches to analysis and generation of emotion in text*, pages 140–146, Los Angeles, CA, June 2010. Association for Computational Linguistics. http://www.aclweb.org/anthology/W10-0217. 59, 62, 105

Diman Ghazi, Diana Inkpen, and Stan Szpakowicz. Prior and contextual emotion of words in sentential context. *Computer Speech & Language*, 28(1):76–92, 2014. DOI: 10.1016/j.csl.2013.04.009 xix, 59, 62, 63

Arijit Ghosh Chowdhury, Ramit Sawhney, Puneet Mathur, Debanjan Mahata, and Rajiv Ratn Shah. Speak up, fight back! detection of social media disclosures of sexual harassment. In *Proceedings of the 2019 Conference of the North American Chapter of the Association for Computational Linguistics: Student Research Workshop*, pages 136–146, Minneapolis, Minnesota, June 2019. Association for Computational Linguistics. https://www.aclweb.org/anthology/N19-3018. DOI: 10.18653/v1/n19-3018 120

Gonzalo Blazquez Gil, Antonio Berlanga de Jesus, and Jose M. Molina Lopez. Combining machine learning techniques and natural language processing to infer emotions using Spanish Twitter corpus. In *PAAMS (Workshops)*, pages 149–157, 2013. DOI: 10.1007/978-3-642-38061-7_15 111

Kevin Gimpel, Nathan Schneider, Brendan O'Connor, Dipanjan Das, Daniel Mills, Jacob Eisenstein, Michael Heilman, Dani Yogatama, Jeffrey Flanigan, and Noah A. Smith. Part-of-speech tagging for Twitter: Annotation, features, and experiments. In *Proceedings of the ACL 2011 Conference Short Papers, Portland, Oreg., USA, 19-24 June 2011, volume 2 of HLT '11*, pages 42–47, Stroudsburg, PA, USA, 2011. Association for Computational Linguistics. http://dl.acm.org/citation.cfm?id=2002736.2002747. DOI: 10.21236/ada547371 xix, 25, 26, 27, 77

George Gkotsis, Anika Oellrich, Tim Hubbard, Richard Dobson, Maria Liakata, Sumithra Velupillai, and Rina Dutta. The language of mental health problems in social media. In *Proceedings of the Third Workshop on Computational Linguistics and Clinical Psychology*, pages 63–73, San Diego, CA, USA, June 2016. Association for Computational Linguistics. http://www.aclweb.org/anthology/W16-0307. DOI: 10.18653/v1/w16-0307 93, 94

Alec Go, Richa Bhayani, and Lei Huang. Twitter sentiment classification using distant supervision. Technical Report CS224N, Stanford University, 2009. DOI: 10.1109/icisim.2017.8122138 57, 62

Moises Goldszmidt, Marc Najork, and Stelios Paparizos. Boot-strapping language identifiers for short colloquial postings. In Hendrik Blockeel, Kristian Kersting, Siegfried Nijssen, and Filip Zelezny, editors, *Machine Learning and Knowledge Discovery in Databases*, volume 8189 of *Lecture Notes in Computer Science*, pages 95–111. Springer Berlin Heidelberg, 2013. DOI: 10.1007/978-3-642-40991-2_7 33, 34

Roberto González-Ibáñez, Smaranda Muresan, and Nina Wacholder. Identifying sarcasm in Twitter: A closer look. In *Proceedings of the 49th Annual Meeting of the Association for Computational Linguistics: Human Language Technologies*, pages 581–586, Portland, Oregon, USA, June 2011. Association for Computational Linguistics. http://www.aclweb.org/anthology/P11-2102. 61

Genevieve Gorrell, Kalina Bontcheva, Leon Derczynski, Elena Kochkina, Maria Liakata, and Arkaitz Zubiaga. Rumoureval 2019: Determining rumour veracity and support for rumours. *CoRR*, abs/1809.06683, 2018. http://arxiv.org/abs/1809.06683. DOI: 10.18653/v1/s19-2147 118

Fabrizio Gotti, Philippe Langlais, and Atefeh Farzindar. Translating government agencies' tweet feeds: Specificities, problems and (a few) solutions. In *Proceedings of the Workshop on Language Analysis in Social Media*, pages 80–89, Atlanta, Georgia, June 2013. Association for Computational Linguistics. http://www.aclweb.org/anthology/W13-1109. 80, 81, 133

Fabrizio Gotti, Phillippe Langlais, and Atefeh Farzindar. Hashtag occurrences, layout and translation: A corpus-driven analysis of tweets published by the Canadian government. In *Proceedings of the Ninth International Conference on Language Resources and Evaluation (LREC'14)*, Reykjavik, Iceland, May 2014. European Language Resources Association (ELRA). xix, 81, 82, 83, 86

Hansu Gu, Xing Xie, Qin Lv, Yaoping Ruan, and Li Shang. Etree: Effective and efficient event modeling for real-time online social media networks. In *Web Intelligence and Intelligent Agent Technology (WI-IAT), 2011 IEEE/WIC/ACM International Conference on*, volume 1, pages 300–307. IEEE, 2011. DOI: 10.1109/WI-IAT.2011.126 69

Pedro Calais Guerra, Wagner Meira, Jr., and Claire Cardie. Sentiment analysis on evolving social streams: How self-report imbalances can help. In *Proceedings of the 7th ACM International Conference on Web Search and Data Mining*, WSDM '14, pages 443–452, New York, NY, USA, 2014. ACM. DOI: 10.1145/2556195.2556261. 56

Tao Gui, Qi Zhang, Jingjing Gong, Minlong Peng, Di Liang, Keyu Ding, and Xuanjing Huang. Transferring from formal newswire domain with hypernet for twitter POS tagging. In *Proceedings of the 2018 Conference on Empirical Methods in Natural Language Processing*, pages 2540–2549, Brussels, Belgium, October-November 2018. Association for Computational Linguistics. https://www.aclweb.org/anthology/D18-1275. DOI: 10.18653/v1/D18-1275 25

Weiwei Guo, Hao Li, Heng Ji, and Mona Diab. Linking tweets to news: A framework to enrich short text data in social media. In *Proceedings of the 51st Annual Meeting of the Association for Computational Linguistics (Volume 1: Long Papers)*, pages 239–249. Association for Computational Linguistics, 2013. http://aclweb.org/anthology/P13-1024. 102, 122

Nizar Habash. Introduction to Arabic natural language processing. *Synthesis Lectures on Human Language Technologies*, 3(1):1–187, 2010. DOI: 10.1162/COLI_r_00066 35

Nizar Habash and Owen Rambow. Magead: A morphological analyzer and generator for the Arabic dialects. In *Proceedings of the 21st International Conference on Computational Linguistics and 44th Annual Meeting of the Association for Computational Linguistics*, Sydney, Australia, 17-21 July 2006, pages 681–688, 2006. DOI: 10.3115/1220175.1220261 37

Nizar Habash, Owen Rambow, and Ryan Roth. Mada+tokan: A toolkit for Arabic tokenization, diacritization, morphological disambiguation, POS tagging, stemming and lemmatization. In *Proceedings of the 2nd International Conference on Arabic Language Resources and Tools (MEDAR)*, pages 102–109, Cairo, Egypt, 2009. 37

Sherzod Hakimov, Salih Atilay Oto, and Erdogan Dogdu. Named entity recognition and disambiguation using linked data and graph-based centrality scoring. In *Proceedings of the 4th International Workshop on Semantic Web Information Management*, SWIM '12, pages 4:1–4:7, New York, NY, USA, 2012. ACM. DOI: 10.1145/2237867.2237871. 53

Bo Han and Timothy Baldwin. Lexical normalisation of short text messages: Makn sens a# Twitter. In *Proceedings of the 49th Annual Meeting of the Association for Computational Linguistics:Human Language Technologies*, Portland, Oregon, USA, 19-24 June 2011, volume 1, pages 368–378, 2011. http://dl.acm.org/citation.cfm?id=2002472.2002520. 18, 30

Bo Han, Paul Cook, and Timothy Baldwin. Geolocation prediction in social media data by finding location indicative words. In *Proceedings of COLING 2012*, pages 1045–1062, Mumbai, India, December 2012. The COLING 2012 Organizing Committee. http://www.aclweb.org/anthology/C12-1064. 46

Bo Han, Paul Cook, and Timothy Baldwin. Text-based Twitter user geolocation prediction. *Artificial Intelligence Research*, 49(1):451–500, January 2014. http://dl.acm.org/citation.cfm?id=2655713.2655726. DOI: 10.1613/jair.4200 47, 49

Sanda Harabagiu and Andrew Hickl. Relevance modeling for microblog summarization. In *International AAAI Conference on Weblogs and Social Media*, 2011. URL http://www.aaai.org/ocs/index.php/ICWSM/ICWSM11/paper/view/2863. 74

Phillip G. Harrison, S. Abney, E. Black, D. Flickinger, C. Gdaniec, R. Grishman, D. Hindle, R. Ingria, M. Marcus, B. Santorini, and T. Strzalkowski. Evaluating syntax performance of parsers/grammars of English. In *Proceedings of the Workshop on Evaluating Natural Language Processing Systems*, pages 71–77, Berkley, CA, 1991. ACL. 26

Vasileios Hatzivassiloglou and Kathleen R. McKeown. Predicting the semantic orientation of adjectives. In *Proceedings of the 35th Annual Meeting of the Association for Computational Linguistics and Eighth Conference of the European Chapter of the Association for Computational Linguistics*, ACL '98, pages 174–181, Stroudsburg, PA, USA, 1997. Association for Computational Linguistics. DOI: 10.3115/976909.979640 58

Hangfeng He and Xu Sun. F-score driven max margin neural network for named entity recognition in Chinese social media. In *Proceedings of the 15th Conference of the European Chapter of the Association for Computational Linguistics: Volume 2, Short Papers*, pages 713–718, Valencia, Spain, April 2017. Association for Computational Linguistics. http://www.aclweb.org/anthology/E17-2113. DOI: 10.18653/v1/e17-2113 29

Wu He, Shenghua Zha, and Ling Li. Social media competitive analysis and text mining: A case study in the pizza industry. *International Journal of Information Management*. DOI: 10.1016/j.ijinfomgt.2013.01.001 72

Brent Hecht, Lichan Hong, Bongwon Suh, and Ed H. Chi. Tweets from Justin Bieber's heart: The dynamics of the location field in user profiles. In *Proceedings of the SIGCHI Conference on Human Factors in Computing Systems*, CHI '11, pages 237–246. ACM, 2011. DOI: 10.1145/1978942.1978976. 44, 45, 113

Verena Henrich and Alexander Lang. Audience segmentation in social media. In *Proceedings of the Software Demonstrations of the 15th Conference of the European Chapter of the Association for Computational Linguistics*, pages 53–56, Valencia, Spain, April 2017. Association for Computational Linguistics. http://aclweb.org/anthology/E17-3014. DOI: 10.18653/v1/e17-3014 103

Bahareh Rahmanzadeh Heravi and Ihab Salawdeh. Tweet location detection. In *Computation + Journalism Symposium*, Columbia University, New York, US, October 2015. http://cj2015.brown.columbia.edu/papers/tweet-location.pdf. 44

Vu Cong Duy Hoang, Philipp Koehn, Gholamreza Haffari, and Trevor Cohn. Iterative back-translation for neural machine translation. In *Proceedings of the 2nd Workshop on Neural Machine Translation and Generation*, pages 18–24, Melbourne, Australia, July 2018. Association for Computational Linguistics. https://www.aclweb.org/anthology/W18-2703. DOI: 10.18653/v1/W18-2703 78

Sepp Hochreiter and Jürgen Schmidhuber. Long short-term memory. *Neural Computation*, 9: 1735–80, 12 1997. DOI: 10.1162/neco.1997.9.8.1735 16

Johannes Hoffart, Mohamed Amir Yosef, Ilaria Bordino, Hagen Fürstenau, Manfred Pinkal, Marc Spaniol, Bilyana Taneva, Stefan Thater, and Gerhard Weikum. Robust disambiguation of named entities in text. In *Proceedings of the 2011 Conference on Empirical Methods in Natural Language Processing*, pages 782–792, Edinburgh, Scotland, UK., July 2011. Association for Computational Linguistics. http://www.aclweb.org/anthology/D11-1072. 55

Johannes Hoffart, Stephan Seufert, Dat Ba Nguyen, Martin Theobald, and Gerhard Weikum. Kore: Keyphrase overlap relatedness for entity disambiguation. In *Proceedings of the 21st ACM International Conference on Information and Knowledge Management*, CIKM '12, pages 545–554, New York, NY, USA, 2012. ACM. DOI: 10.1145/2396761.2396832. 55

Lars E. Holzman and William M. Pottenger. Classification of emotions in Internet chat: An application of machine learning using speech phonemes. *Retrieved November*, 27:2011, 2003. 58

Tobias Horsmann and Torsten Zesch. LTL-UDE at EmpiriST 2015: Tokenization and PoS tagging of social media text. In *Proceedings of the 10th Web as Corpus Workshop*, pages 120–126, Berlin. Germany, August 2016. Association for Computational Linguistics. http://aclweb.org/anthology/W16-2615. DOI: 10.18653/v1/w16-2615 21, 24

Jeremy Howard and Sebastian Ruder. Universal language model fine-tuning for text classification. In *Proceedings of the 56th Annual Meeting of the Association for Computational Linguistics (Volume 1: Long Papers)*, pages 328–339, Melbourne, Australia, July 2018. Association for Computational Linguistics. https://www.aclweb.org/anthology/P18-1031. DOI: 10.18653/v1/P18-1031 120

Christine Howes, Matthew Purver, and Rose McCabe. Linguistic indicators of severity and progress in online text-based therapy for depression. In *Workshop on Computational Linguistics and Clinical Psychology*, number 611733, pages 7–16, 2014. ISBN 978-1-941643-16-7. DOI: 10.3115/v1/w14-3202 91

Wen-Tai Hsieh, Seng-cho T. Chou, Yu-Hsuan Cheng, and Chen-Ming Wu. Predicting tv audience rating with social media. In *Proceedings of the IJCNLP 2013 Workshop on Natural Language Processing for Social Media (SocialNLP)*, pages 1–5, Nagoya, Japan, October 2013.

Asian Federation of Natural Language Processing. http://www.aclweb.org/anthology/W13-4201. 116

Meishan Hu, Aixin Sun, and Ee-Peng Lim. Comments-oriented blog summarization by sentence extraction. In *Proceedings of the ACM 16th Conference on Information and Knowledge Management (CIKM 2007)*, Lisbon, Portugal, 6-9 November 2007, pages 901–904. ACM, 2007a. DOI: 10.1145/1321440.1321571. 11

Meishan Hu, Aixin Sun, and Ee-Peng Lim. Comments-oriented blog summarization by sentence extraction. In *Proceedings of the sixteenth ACM conference on Conference on information and knowledge management*, pages 901–904. ACM, 2007b. DOI: 10.1145/1321440.1321571. 72

Minqing Hu and Bing Liu. Mining and summarizing customer reviews. In *Proceedings of the 10th ACM SIGKDD Conference on Knowledge Discovery and Data Mining*, Seattle, Wash., 22-25 August 2004, pages 168–177. ACM, 2004. DOI: 10.1145/1014052.1014073. 57

Xiaohua Hu, Xiaodan Zhang, Daniel Wu, Xiaohua Zhou, and Peter Rumm. Text mining the biomedical literature for identification of potential virus/bacterium as bio-terrorism weapons. In Hsinchun Chen, Edna Reid, Joshua Sinai, Andrew Silke, and Boaz Ganor, editors, *Terrorism Informatics*, volume 18 of *Integrated Series In Information Systems*, pages 385–406. Springer US, 2008. DOI: 10.1007/978-0-387-71613-8_18 107

Fei Huang. Improved arabic dialect classification with social media data. In *Proceedings of the 2015 Conference on Empirical Methods in Natural Language Processing*, pages 2118–2126, Lisbon, Portugal, September 2015. Association for Computational Linguistics. http://aclweb.org/anthology/D15-1254. DOI: 10.18653/v1/d15-1254 35

Wenyi Huang, Ingmar Weber, and Sarah Vieweg. Inferring nationalities of Twitter users and studying inter-national linking. In *Proceedings of the 25th ACM Conference on Hypertext and Social Media*, HT '14, pages 237–242, New York, NY, USA, 2014. ACM. DOI: 10.1145/2631775.2631825. 112

Xiaolei Huang and Michael J. Paul. Neural user factor adaptation for text classification: Learning to generalize across author demographics. In *Proceedings of the Eighth Joint Conference on Lexical and Computational Semantics (*SEM 2019)*, pages 136–146, Minneapolis, Minnesota, June 2019. Association for Computational Linguistics. https://www.aclweb.org/anthology/S19-1015. DOI: 10.18653/v1/s19-1015 109, 112

Muhammad Imran, Shady Mamoon Elbassuoni, Carlos Castillo, Fernando Diaz, and Patrick Meier. Extracting information nuggets from disaster-related messages in social media. In *ISCRAM*, Baden-Baden, Germany, 2013. 108, 123

Vijayasaradhi Indurthi, Bakhtiyar Syed, Manish Shrivastava, Nikhil Chakravartula, Manish Gupta, and Vasudeva Varma. FERMI at SemEval-2019 task 5: Using sentence embeddings to identify hate speech against immigrants and women in twitter. In *Proceedings of the 13th International Workshop on Semantic Evaluation*, pages 70–74, Minneapolis, Minnesota, USA, June 2019. Association for Computational Linguistics. https://www.aclweb.org/anthology/S19-2009. DOI: 10.18653/v1/s19-2009 103

Diana Inkpen, Ji Liu, Atefeh Farzindar, Farzaneh Kazemi, and Diman Ghazi. Location detection and disambiguation from Twitter messages. In *Proceedings of the 16th International Conference on Intelligent Text Processing and Computational Linguistics (CICLing 2015), LNCS 9042*, pages 321–332, Cairo, Egypt, 2015. DOI: 10.1007/978-3-319-18117-2_24 xix, 48, 49, 50, 51, 133

David Inouye and Jougal K. Kalita. Comparing Twitter summarization algorithms for multiple post summaries. In *Privacy, Security, Risk and Trust (PASSAT) and 2011 IEEE Third Inernational Conference on Social Computing (SocialCom), 2011 IEEE Third International Conference on*, pages 298–306, Oct 2011. DOI: 10.1109/PASSAT/SocialCom.2011.31 72

Caroll E. Izard. *The Face of Emotion*. Appleton-Century-Crofts, 1971. 58

Kokil Jaidka, Niyati Chhaya, and Lyle Ungar. Diachronic degradation of language models: Insights from social media. In *Proceedings of the 56th Annual Meeting of the Association for Computational Linguistics (Volume 2: Short Papers)*, pages 195–200, Melbourne, Australia, July 2018. Association for Computational Linguistics. https://www.aclweb.org/anthology/P18-2032. DOI: 10.18653/v1/p18-2032 7

Zunaira Jamil, Diana Inkpen, Prasadith Buddhitha, and Kenton White. Monitoring tweets for depression to detect at-risk users. In *Proceedings of the Fourth Workshop on Computational Linguistics and Clinical Psychology — From Linguistic Signal to Clinical Reality*, pages 32–40, Vancouver, BC, August 2017. Association for Computational Linguistics. http://www.aclweb.org/anthology/W17-3104. DOI: 10.18653/v1/w17-3104 93

Laura Jehl, Felix Hieber, and Stefan Riezler. Twitter translation using translation-based cross-lingual retrieval. In *Proceedings of the Seventh Workshop on Statistical Machine Translation*, pages 410–421. ACL, 2012. http://dl.acm.org/citation.cfm?id=2393015.2393074. 78

Laura Elisabeth Jehl. Machine translation for Twitter. Master's thesis, The University of Edinburgh, 2010. http://hdl.handle.net/1842/5317. 78

Jyun-Yu Jiang, Xue Sun, Wei Wang, and Sean Young. Enhancing air quality prediction with social media and natural language processing. In *Proceedings of the 57th Annual Meeting of the Association for Computational Linguistics*, pages 2627–2632, Florence, Italy, July 2019. Association for Computational Linguistics. https://www.aclweb.org/anthology/P19-1251. DOI: 10.18653/v1/P19-1251 96

Xiaotian Jin, Defeng Guo, and Hongjian Liu.   Enhanced stock prediction using so-cial network and statistical model.   In *Advanced Research and Technology in Industry Applications (WARTIA), 2014 IEEE Workshop on*, pages 1199–1203, Sept 2014. DOI: 10.1109/WARTIA.2014.6976495 98

Nitin Jindal and Bing Liu. Opinion spam and analysis. In *Proceedings of the International Conference on Web Search and Web Data Mining, WSDM 2008, Palo Alto, California, USA, February 11-12, 2008*, pages 219–230, 2008. DOI: 10.1145/1341531.1341560. 124

Kristen Johnson, Di Jin, and Dan Goldwasser. Leveraging behavioral and social information for weakly supervised collective classification of political discourse on Twitter. In *Proceedings of the 55th Annual Meeting of the Association for Computational Linguistics (Volume 1: Long Papers)*, pages 741–752, Vancouver, Canada, July 2017. Association for Computational Linguistics. http://aclweb.org/anthology/P17-1069. DOI: 10.18653/v1/p17-1069 100

Joel Judd and Jugal Kalita. Better Twitter summaries? In *Proceedings of the 2013 Conference of the North American Chapter of the Association for Computational Linguistics: Human Language Technologies*, pages 445–449, Atlanta, Georgia, June 2013. Association for Computational Linguistics. http://www.aclweb.org/anthology/N13-1047. 72

Yuchul Jung, Hogun Park, and SungHyon Myaeng. A hybrid mood classification approach for blog text. In Qiang Yang and Geoff Webb, editors, *PRICAI 2006: Trends in Artificial Intelligence*, volume 4099 of *Lecture Notes in Computer Science*, pages 1099–1103. Springer Berlin Heidelberg, 2006. DOI: 10.1007/978-3-540-36668-3_141 59

Lisa Kaati, Amendra Shrestha, Katie Cohen, and Sinna Lindquist. Automatic detection of xenophobic narratives: A case study on swedish alternative media.   In *2016 IEEE Conference on Intelligence and Security Informatics (ISI)*, Tucson, AZ, USA, September 2016.   URL https://www.researchgate.net/publication/308784964_Automatic_detection_of_xenophobic_narratives_A_case_study_on_Swedish_alternative_media. DOI: 10.1109/isi.2016.7745454 104

Ranjitha Kashyap and Ani Nahapetian. Tweet analysis for user health monitoring. In *Advances in Personalized Healthcare Services, Wearable Mobile Monitoring, and Social Media Pervasive Technologies*. IEEE, 12 2014. DOI: 10.4108/icst.mobihealth.2014.257537 111

Fazel Keshtkar and Diana Inkpen. A hierarchical approach to mood classification in blogs. *Natural Language Engineering*, 18(1):61–81, 2012. DOI: 10.1017/S1351324911000118 xix, 60, 62, 63, 105

Elham Khabiri, James Caverlee, and Chiao-Fang Hsu. Summarizing user-contributed comments. In *International AAAI Conference on Weblogs and Social Media*, 2011. URL http://www.aaai.org/ocs/index.php/ICWSM/ICWSM11/paper/view/2865/3257. 72

Mohammad Khan, Markus Dickinson, and Sandra Kuebler. Does size matter? Text and grammar revision for parsing social media data. In *Proceedings of the Workshop on Language Analysis in Social Media (LASM 2013), NAACL-HLT 2013*, pages 1–10, Atlanta, GA, USA, June 2013. ACL. http://www.aclweb.org/anthology/W13-1101. 27

Hyun Duk Kim and ChengXiang Zhai. Generating comparative summaries of contradictory opinions in text. In *Proceedings of the 18th ACM Conference on Information and Knowledge Management*, CIKM '09, pages 385–394, New York, NY, USA, 2009. ACM. DOI: 10.1145/1645953.1646004. 75

Seon Ho Kim, Ying Lu, Giorgos Constantinou, Cyrus Shahabi, Guanfeng Wang, and Roger Zimmermann. Mediaq: mobile multimedia management system. In *Multimedia Systems Conference 2014, MMSys '14, Singapore, March 19-21, 2014*, pages 224–235, 2014. DOI: 10.1145/2557642.2578223. 117

Sheila Kinsella, Vanessa Murdock, and Neil O'Hare. "i'm eating a sandwich in glasgow": Modeling locations with tweets. In *Proceedings of the 3rd International Workshop on Search and Mining User-generated Contents*, SMUC '11, pages 61–68, New York, NY, USA, 2011. ACM. DOI: 10.1145/2065023.2065039. 114

Prasadith Kirinde Gamaarachchige and Diana Inkpen. Multi-task, multi-channel, multi-input learning for mental illness detection using social media text. In *Proceedings of the Tenth International Workshop on Health Text Mining and Information Analysis (LOUHI 2019)*, pages 54–64, Hong Kong, November 2019. Association for Computational Linguistics. https://www.aclweb.org/anthology/D19-6208. DOI: 10.18653/v1/D19-6208 93

Athanasios Kokkos and Theodoros Tzouramanis. A robust gender inference model for online social networks and its application to LinkedIn and Twitter. *First Monday*, 2014. http://firstmonday.org/ojs/index.php/fm/article/view/5216. DOI: 10.5210/fm.v19i9.5216 112

Lingpeng Kong, Nathan Schneider, Swabha Swayamdipta, Archna Bhatia, Chris Dyer, and Noah A. Smith. A dependency parser for tweets. In *Proceedings of the 2014 Conference on Empirical Methods in Natural Language Processing (EMNLP)*, pages 1001–1012, Doha, Qatar, October 2014. Association for Computational Linguistics. http://www.aclweb.org/anthology/D14-1108. DOI: 10.3115/v1/d14-1108 27

Xerxes P. Kotval and Michael J. Burns. Visualization of entities within social media: Toward understanding users' needs. *Bell Labs Technical Journal*, 17(4):77–102, March 2013. DOI: 10.1002/bltj.21576 117

John D. Lafferty, Andrew McCallum, and Fernando C. N. Pereira. Conditional Random Fields: Probabilistic models for segmenting and labeling sequence data. In *Proceedings of the Eighteenth International Conference on Machine Learning*, ICML '01, pages 282–289, San Francisco, CA, USA, 2001. Morgan Kaufmann Publishers Inc. http://dl.acm.org/citation.cfm?id=645530.655813. 17, 22, 24

Vasileios Lampos, Daniel Preotiuc-Pietro, and Trevor Cohn. A user-centric model of voting intention from social media. In *Proceedings of the 51st Annual Meeting of the Association for Computational Linguistics (Volume 1: Long Papers)*, pages 993–1003, Sofia, Bulgaria, August 2013. Association for Computational Linguistics. http://www.aclweb.org/anthology/P13-1098. 99, 114

Vasileios Lampos, Nikolaos Aletras, Daniel Preotiuc-Pietro, and Trevor Cohn. Predicting and characterising user impact on Twitter. In *Proceedings of the 14th Conference of the European Chapter of the Association for Computational Linguistics*, pages 405–413, Gothenburg, Sweden, April 2014. Association for Computational Linguistics. http://www.aclweb.org/anthology/E14-1043. DOI: 10.3115/v1/e14-1043 114

Victor Lavrenko and W Bruce Croft. Relevance based language models. In *Proceedings of the 24th annual international ACM SIGIR conference on Research and development in information retrieval*, pages 120–127, New York, NY, USA, 2001. ACM. DOI: 10.1145/383952.383972. 69

Yann LeCun, Y. Bengio, and Geoffrey Hinton. Deep learning. *Nature*, 521:436–44, 05 2015. DOI: 10.1038/nature14539 7, 16

Hyeungill Lee and Jungwoo Lee. Scalable deep learning-based recommendation systems. *ICT Express*, 5(2):84–88, 2019. DOI: 10.1016/j.icte.2018.05.003 119

Ryong Lee and Kazutoshi Sumiya. Measuring geographical regularities of crowd behaviors for Twitter-based geo-social event detection. In *Proceedings of the 2nd ACM SIGSPATIAL International Workshop on Location Based Social Networks*, pages 1–10. ACM, 2010. DOI: 10.1145/1867699.1867701. 68, 70

Will Lewis. Haitian Creole: how to build and ship an MT engine from scratch in 4 days, 17 hours, & 30 minutes. In *EAMT 2010: Proceedings of the 14th Annual conference of the European Association for Machine Translation*, 2010. 78

Chenliang Li, Jianshu Weng, Qi He, Yuxia Yao, Anwitaman Datta, Aixin Sun, and Bu-Sung Lee. Twiner: Named entity recognition in targeted Twitter stream. In *Proceedings of the 35th International ACM SIGIR Conference on Research and Development in Information Retrieval*, SIGIR '12, pages 721–730, New York, NY, USA, 2012a. ACM. DOI: 10.1145/2348283.2348380. 30

Huayi Li, Arjun Mukherjee, Bing Liu, Rachel Kornfield, and Sherry Emery. Detecting campaign promoters on Twitter using Markov Random Fields. In *Proceedings of the IEEE Inter-*

national Conference on Data Mining (ICDM'14). IEEE, 2014a. URL http://www.cs.uic.edu/~liub/publications/twitter-promoters-paper531.pdf. DOI: 10.1109/icdm.2014.59 124

Jiwei Li, Sujian Li, Xun Wang, Ye Tian, and Baobao Chang. Update summarization using a multi-level hierarchical Dirichlet process model. In *Proceedings of the International Conference on Computational Linguistics COLING 2012*, pages 1603–1618, Mumbai, India, December 2012b. http://www.aclweb.org/anthology/C12-1098. 73

Jiwei Li, Myle Ott, Claire Cardie, and Eduard Hovy. Towards a general rule for identifying deceptive opinion spam. In *Proceedings of the 52nd Annual Meeting of the Association for Computational Linguistics (Volume 1: Long Papers)*, pages 1566–1576. Association for Computational Linguistics, 2014b. http://aclweb.org/anthology/P14-1147. DOI: 10.3115/v1/p14-1147 124

Jiwei Li, Alan Ritter, Claire Cardie, and Eduard Hovy. Major life event extraction from Twitter based on congratulations/condolences speech acts. In *Proceedings of the 2014 Conference on Empirical Methods in Natural Language Processing (EMNLP)*, pages 1997–2007. Association for Computational Linguistics, 2014c. http://aclweb.org/anthology/D14-1214. DOI: 10.3115/v1/d14-1214 115

Jiwei Li, Alan Rittrer, and Eduard H. Hovy. Weakly supervised user profile extraction from Twitter. In *Proceedings of the 52nd Annual Meeting of the Association for Computational Linguistics, ACL 2014, June 22-27, 2014, Baltimore, MD, USA, Volume 1: Long Papers*, pages 165–174, 2014d. http://aclweb.org/anthology/P/P14/P14-1016.pdf. DOI: 10.3115/v1/p14-1016 115

Quanzhi Li, Qiong Zhang, and Luo Si. eventAI at SemEval-2019 task 7: Rumor detection on social media by exploiting content, user credibility and propagation information. In *Proceedings of the 13th International Workshop on Semantic Evaluation*, pages 855–859, Minneapolis, Minnesota, USA, June 2019. Association for Computational Linguistics. https://www.aclweb.org/anthology/S19-2148. DOI: 10.18653/v1/s19-2148 118

Nut Limsopatham and Nigel Collier. Adapting phrase-based machine translation to normalise medical terms in social media messages. In *Proceedings of the 2015 Conference on Empirical Methods in Natural Language Processing*, pages 1675–1680, Lisbon, Portugal, September 2015. Association for Computational Linguistics. http://aclweb.org/anthology/D15-1194. DOI: 10.18653/v1/d15-1194 79

Chin-Yew Lin and Eduard Hovy. Automatic evaluation of summaries using n-gram co-occurrence statistics. In *Proceedings of the Human Language Technology Conference of the North American Chapter of the Association for Computational Linguistics,* Edmonton, Alberta, Canada, 27 May -1 June 2003, volume 1, pages 71–78. ACL, 2003. DOI: 10.3115/1073445.1073465 76

Hui Lin, Jeff Bilmes, and Shasha Xie. Graph-based submodular selection for extractive summarization. In *The eleventh biannual IEEE workshop on Automatic Speech Recognition and Understanding (ASRU 2009)*, pages 381–386. IEEE, 2009. DOI: 10.1109/asru.2009.5373486 11

Wang Ling, Guang Xiang, Chris Dyer, Alan Black, and Isabel Trancoso. Microblogs as parallel corpora. In *Proceedings of the 51st Annual Meeting of the Association for Computational Linguistics (Volume 1: Long Papers)*, pages 176–186, Sofia, Bulgaria, August 2013. Association for Computational Linguistics. http://www.aclweb.org/anthology/P13-1018. 77

Alex Liu, Anna Farzindar, and Mingbo Gong, editors. *Transforming Healthcare with Big Data and AI*. IAP Information Age Publishing, 2019a. 96

Bing Liu. *Sentiment Analysis and Opinion Mining*. Synthesis Lectures on Human Language Technologies. Morgan & Claypool Publishers, 2012. 55, 124

Fei Liu, Maria Vasardani, and Timothy Baldwin. Automatic identification of locative expressions from social media text: A comparative analysis. In *Proceedings of the 4th International Workshop on Location and the Web*, LocWeb '14, pages 9–16, New York, NY, USA, 2014. ACM. DOI: 10.1145/2663713.2664426. 48, 51

Hugo Liu and Push Singh. Conceptnet: A practical commonsense reasoning toolkit. *BT Technology Journal*, 22:211–226, 2004. DOI: 10.1023/B:BTTJ.0000047600.45421.6d 59

Ji Liu and Diana Inkpen. Estimating user locations on social media: A deep learning approach. In *Proceedings of the NAACL 2015 Workshop on Vector Space Modeling for NLP*, Denver, Colorado, 2015. xix, 47, 49, 50

Ping Liu, Wen Li, and Liang Zou. NULI at SemEval-2019 task 6: Transfer learning for offensive language detection using bidirectional transformers. In *Proceedings of the 13th International Workshop on Semantic Evaluation*, pages 87–91, Minneapolis, Minnesota, USA, June 2019b. Association for Computational Linguistics. https://www.aclweb.org/anthology/S19-2011. DOI: 10.18653/v1/s19-2011 104

Wendy Liu and Derek Ruths. What's in a name? using first names as features for gender inference in Twitter. In *AAAI Spring Symposium: Analyzing Microtext*, volume SS-13-01 of *AAAI Technical Report*. AAAI, 2013. URL http://dblp.uni-trier.de/db/conf/aaaiss/aaaiss2013-01.html#LiuR13. 88, 112

Xiaohua Liu, Yitong Li, Furu Wei, and Ming Zhou. Graph-based multi-tweet summarization using social signals. In *Proceedings of the International Conference on Computational Linguistics COLING 2012*, pages 1699–1714, Mumbai, India, December 2012a. http://www.aclweb.org/anthology/C12-1104. 74

Xiaohua Liu, Ming Zhou, Furu Wei, Zhongyang Fu, and Xiangyang Zhou. Joint inference of named entity recognition and normalization for tweets. In *Proceedings of the 50th Annual Meeting of the Association for Computational Linguistics: Long Papers*, volume 1, pages 526–535. ACl, 2012b. http://dl.acm.org/citation.cfm?id=2390524.2390598. 30

Clare Llewellyn, Claire Grover, Jon Oberlander, and Ewan Klein. Re-using an argument corpus to aid in the curation of social media collections. In *Proceedings of the Ninth International Conference on Language Resources and Evaluation (LREC'14)*, Reykjavik, Iceland, may 2014. European Language Resources Association (ELRA). URL http://www.lrec-conf.org/proceedings/lrec2014/pdf/84_Paper.pdf. 122

Rui Long, Haofen Wang, Yuqiang Chen, Ou Jin, and Yong Yu. Towards effective event detection, tracking and summarization on microblog data. In *Web-Age Information Management*, pages 652–663. Springer, 2011. http://dl.acm.org/citation.cfm?id=2035562.2035636. DOI: 10.1007/978-3-642-23535-1_55 65

Uta Lösch and David Müller. Mapping microblog posts to encyclopedia articles. In *Tagungsband Informatik 2011*, Berlin, October 2011. GI-Edition. 53

Michael Luca and Georgios Zervas. Fake it till you make it: Reputation, competition, and yelp review fraud. Technical report, Harvard Business School NOM Unit Working Paper No. 14-006, 2014. DOI: 10.2139/ssrn.2293164 124

Marco Lui and Timothy Baldwin. langid.py: An off-the-shelf language identification tool. In *Proceedings of the ACL 2012 System Demonstrations*, pages 25–30, Jeju Island, Korea, July 2012. Association for Computational Linguistics. http://www.aclweb.org/anthology/P12-3005. 34

Marco Lui and Timothy Baldwin. Accurate language identification of Twitter messages. In *Proceedings of the 5th Workshop on Language Analysis for Social Media (LASM)*, pages 17–25, Gothenburg, Sweden, April 2014. Association for Computational Linguistics. http://www. aclweb.org/anthology/W14-1303. DOI: 10.3115/v1/w14-1303 33, 34

Stephanie Lukin and Marilyn Walker. Really? Well. Apparently bootstrapping improves the performance of sarcasm and nastiness classifiers for online dialogue. In *Proceedings of the Workshop on Language Analysis in Social Media*, pages 30–40, Atlanta, Georgia, June 2013. Association for Computational Linguistics. http://www.aclweb.org/anthology/W13-1104. 61

Jing Ma, Wei Gao, and Kam-Fai Wong. Detect rumors in microblog posts using propagation structure via kernel learning. In *Proceedings of the 55th Annual Meeting of the Association for Computational Linguistics (Volume 1: Long Papers)*, pages 708–717, Vancouver, Canada, July 2017. Association for Computational Linguistics. http://aclweb.org/anthology/P17-1066. DOI: 10.18653/v1/p17-1066 123

Stuart Mackie, Richard McCreadie, Craig Macdonald, and Iadh Ounis. On choosing an effective automatic evaluation metric for microblog summarisation. In *Proceedings of the 5th Information Interaction in Context Symposium*, IIiX '14, pages 115–124, New York, NY, USA, 2014. ACM. DOI: 10.1145/2637002.2637017. 77

Tushar Maheshwari, Aishwarya N. Reganti, Samiksha Gupta, Anupam Jamatia, Upendra Kumar, Björn Gambäck, and Amitava Das. A societal sentiment analysis: Predicting the values and ethics of individuals by analysing social media content. In *Proceedings of the 15th Conference of the European Chapter of the Association for Computational Linguistics: Volume 1, Long Papers*, pages 731–741, Valencia, Spain, April 2017. Association for Computational Linguistics. http://www.aclweb.org/anthology/E17-1069. DOI: 10.18653/v1/e17-1069 110

Jalal Mahmud, Jeffrey Nichols, and Clemens Drews. Home location identification of Twitter users. *ACM Trans. Intell. Syst. Technol.*, 5(3):1–21, July 2014. DOI: 10.1145/2528548. 113

Emmanouil Manousogiannis, Sepideh Mesbah, Alessandro Bozzon, Selene Baez, and Robert Jan Sips. Give it a shot: Few-shot learning to normalize ADR mentions in social media posts. In *Proceedings of the Fourth Social Media Mining for Health Applications (#SMM4H) Workshop & Shared Task*, pages 114–116, Florence, Italy, August 2019. Association for Computational Linguistics. https://www.aclweb.org/anthology/W19-3219. DOI: 10.18653/v1/W19-3219 90

Huina Mao and Johan Bollen. Computational economic and finance gauges: Polls, search, and Twitter. *The National Bureau of Economic Research(NBER) Working Papers*, Nov 2011. 96

Micol Marchetti-Bowick and Nathanael Chambers. Learning for microblogs with distant supervision: Political forecasting with Twitter. In *Proceedings of the 13th Conference of the European Chapter of the Association for Computational Linguistics*, pages 603–612, Avignon, France, April 2012. Association for Computational Linguistics. http://www.aclweb.org/anthology/E12-1062. 100

Adam Marcus, Michael S. Bernstein, Osama Badar, David R. Karger, Samuel Madden, and Robert C. Miller. Twitinfo: aggregating and visualizing microblogs for event exploration. In *Proceedings of the International Conference on Human Factors in Computing Systems, CHI 2011, Vancouver, BC, Canada, May 7-12, 2011*, pages 227–236, 2011. DOI: 10.1145/1978942.1978975. 102

Mitchell P Marcus, Mary Ann Marcinkiewicz, and Beatrice Santorini. Building a large annotated corpus of English: The Penn Treebank. *Computational linguistics*, 19(2):313–330, 1993. http://dl.acm.org/citation.cfm?id=972470.972475. DOI: 10.21236/ada273556 17, 22

Vincent Martin. Predicting the French stock market using social media analysis. In *Semantic and Social Media Adaptation and Personalization (SMAP), 2013 8th International Workshop on*, pages 3–7, Dec 2013. DOI: 10.1109/SMAP.2013.22 98

Kamran Massoudi, Manos Tsagkias, Maarten de Rijke, and Wouter Weerkamp. Incorporating query expansion and quality indicators in searching microblog posts. In *Advances in Information Retrieval*, volume 6611 of *Lecture Notes in Computer Science*, pages 362–367. Springer Berlin Heidelberg, 2011. DOI: 10.1007/978-3-642-20161-5_36 68

Michael Mathioudakis and Nick Koudas. Twittermonitor: Trend detection over the Twitter stream. In *Proceedings of the 2010 ACM SIGMOD International Conference on Management of data*, pages 1155–1158. ACM, 2010. DOI: 10.1145/1807167.1807306. 64

Uwe F. Mayer. Bootstrapped language identification for multi-site Internet domains. In *Proceedings of the 18th ACM SIGKDD International Conference on Knowledge Discovery and Data Mining*, KDD 2012, pages 579–585, New York, NY, USA, 2012. ACM. DOI: 10.1145/2339530.2339622. 33

Diana Maynard, Kalina Bontcheva, and Dominic Rout. Challenges in developing opinion mining tools for social media. In *Proceedings of NLP can u tag #usergeneratedcontent?! Workshop at LREC 2012*, Istanbul, Turkey, 2012. URL https://gate.ac.uk/sale/lrec2012/ugc-workshop/opinion-mining-extended.pdf. 56

Chandler McClellan, Mir M Ali, Ryan Mutter, Larry Kroutil, and Justin Landwehr. Using social media to monitor mental health discussions – evidence from Twitter. *Journal of American Medical Informatics Association*. DOI: 10.1093/jamia/ocw133 91

Edgar Meij, Wouter Weerkamp, and Maarten de Rijke. Adding semantics to microblog posts. In *Proceedings of the Fifth ACM International Conference on Web Search and Data Mining*, WSDM '12, pages 563–572, New York, NY, USA, 2012. ACM. DOI: 10.1145/2124295.2124364. 53

Prem Melville, Vikas Sindhwani, and Richard D. Lawrence. Social media analytics: Channeling the power of the blogosphere for marketing insight, 2009. 5

Donald Metzler, Susan Dumais, and Christopher Meek. Similarity measures for short segments of text. In *Advances in Information Retrieval*, volume 4425 of *Lecture Notes in Computer Science*, pages 16–27. Springer Berlin Heidelberg, 2007. DOI: 10.1007/978-3-540-71496-5_5 10

Donald Metzler, Congxing Cai, and Eduard Hovy. Structured event retrieval over microblog archives. In *Proceedings of the 2012 Conference of the North American Chapter of the Association for Computational Linguistics: Human Language Technologies*, pages 646–655. ACL, 2012. http://dl.acm.org/citation.cfm?id=2382029.2382138. 69, 70

Tomas Mikolov, Kai Chen, Greg Corrado, and Jeffrey Dean. Efficient estimation of word representations in vector space. In Yoshua Bengio and Yann LeCun, editors, *1st International Conference on Learning Representations, ICLR 2013*, Scottsdale, Arizona, USA, May 2-4, 2013, *Workshop Track Proceedings*, 2013. http://arxiv.org/abs/1301.3781. 17

Gilad Mishne. Experiments with mood classification in blog posts. In *Proceedings of ACM SIGIR 2005 Workshop on Stylistic Analysis of Text for Information Access*, volume 19, 2005. URL http://staff.science.uva.nl/~{}gilad/pubs/style2005-blogmoods.pdf. 60, 62, 122

Margaret Mitchell, Kristy Hollingshead, and Glen Coppersmith. Quantifying the language of schizophrenia in social media. In *Proceedings of the 2nd Workshop on Computational Linguistics and Clinical Psychology: From Linguistic Signal to Clinical Reality*, pages 11–20, Denver, Colorado, June 5, 2015. Association for Computational Linguistics. https://www.aclweb.org/anthology/W15-1202. DOI: 10.3115/v1/W15-1202 92

Shamima Mithun. *Exploiting Rhetorical Relations in Blog Summarization*. PhD thesis, Concordia University, 2012. DOI: 10.1007/978-3-642-13059-5_53 75

Samaneh Moghaddam and Fred Popowich. Opinion polarity identification through adjectives. *Computing Research Repository (CoRR)*, abs/1011.4623, 2010. http://arxiv.org/abs/1011.4623. 58

Saif M. Mohammad and Svetlana Kiritchenko. Using hashtags to capture fine emotion categories from tweets. *Computational Intelligence*, 2014. DOI: 10.1111/coin.12024 59, 62

Saif M. Mohammad and Peter D. Turney. Crowdsourcing a word–emotion association lexicon. *Computational Intelligence*, 29(3):436–465, 2013. http://arxiv.org/abs/1308.6297. DOI: 10.1111/j.1467-8640.2012.00460.x 59

Saif M. Mohammad, Svetlana Kiritchenko, and Xiaodan Zhu. NRC-Canada: Building the state-of-the-art in sentiment analysis of tweets. In *Second Joint Conference on Lexical and Computational Semantics (*SEM), Volume 2: Proceedings of the Seventh International Workshop on Semantic Evaluation (SemEval 2013)*, pages 321–327, Atlanta, Georgia, USA, June 2013. ACL. http://www.aclweb.org/anthology/S13-2053. 58, 62

Saif M. Mohammad, Xiaodan Zhu, Svetlana Kiritchenko, and Joel Martin. Sentiment, emotion, purpose, and style in electoral tweets. *Information Processing & Management*, pages –, 2014. URL http://www.sciencedirect.com/science/article/pii/S0306457314000880. DOI: 10.1016/j.ipm.2014.09.003 100

Ehsan Mohammady and Aron Culotta. Using county demographics to infer attributes of twitter users. In *Proceedings of the Joint Workshop on Social Dynamics and Personal Attributes in Social Media*, pages 7–16, Baltimore, Maryland, June 2014. Association for Computational Linguistics. http://www.aclweb.org/anthology/W14-2702. DOI: 10.3115/v1/w14-2702 112

George Mohay, Alison Anderson, Byron Collie, Olivier de Vel, and Rodney McKemmi. *Computer and Intrusion Forensics*. Artech House, Boston, 2003. 104

Seungwhan Moon, Leonardo Neves, and Vitor Carvalho. Multimodal named entity recognition for short social media posts. In *Proceedings of the 2018 Conference of the North American Chapter of the Association for Computational Linguistics: Human Language Technologies, Volume 1 (Long Papers)*, pages 852–860, New Orleans, Louisiana, June 2018. Association for Computational Linguistics. https://www.aclweb.org/anthology/N18-1078. DOI: 10.18653/v1/N18-1078 54

Andrea Moro, Alessandro Raganato, and Alessandro Navigli. Entity linking meets word sense disambiguation: A unified approach. *Transactions of the ACL*, 2:231–243, 2014. URL https://tacl2013.cs.columbia.edu/ojs/index.php/tacl/article/view/291. DOI: 10.1162/tacl_a_00179 53, 55

Sai Moturu. *Quantifying the Trustworthiness of User-Generated Social Media Content*. PhD thesis, Arizona State University, 2009. DOI: 10.1007/s10619-010-7077-0 3

Hamdy Mubarak and Kareem Darwish. Using Twitter to collect a multi-dialectal corpus of Arabic. In *Proceedings of the EMNLP 2014 Workshop on Arabic Natural Language Processing (ANLP)*, pages 1–7, Doha, Qatar, October 2014. Association for Computational Linguistics. http://www.aclweb.org/anthology/W14-3601. DOI: 10.3115/v1/w14-3601 41

Robert Munro. Crowdsourced translation for emergency response in Haiti: The global collaboration of local knowledge. In *AMTA Workshop on Collaborative Crowdsourcing for Translation*, 2010. 77

Mor Naaman, Hila Becker, and Luis Gravano. Hip and trendy: Characterizing emerging trends on Twitter. *Journal of the American Society for Information Science and Technology*, 62(5):902–918, 2011. DOI: 10.1002/asi.21489 64, 65

Meenakshi Nagarajan, Karthik Gomadam, Amit P. Sheth, Ajith Ranabahu, Raghava Mutharaju, and Ashutosh Jadhav. Spatio-temporal-thematic analysis of citizen sensor data: Challenges and experiences. In *Web Information Systems Engineering - WISE 2009, 10th International Conference, Poznan, Poland, October 5-7, 2009. Proceedings*, pages 539–553, 2009. DOI: 10.1007/978-3-642-04409-0_52 101

Preslav Nakov, Alan Ritter, Sara Rosenthal, Fabrizio Sebastiani, and Veselin Stoyanov. SemEval-2016 task 4: Sentiment analysis in Twitter. In *Proceedings of the 10th International Workshop on Semantic Evaluation (SemEval-2016)*, pages 1–18, San Diego, California, June 2016. Association for Computational Linguistics. http://www.aclweb.org/anthology/S16-1001. DOI: 10.18653/v1/s16-1001 59

Ramesh Nallapati, Ao Feng, Fuchun Peng, and James Allan. Event threading within news topics. In *Proceedings of the Thirteenth ACM International Conference on Information and Knowledge Management*, CIKM '04, pages 446–453, New York, NY, USA, 2004. ACM. DOI: 10.1145/1031171.1031258. 10

Alena Neviarouskaya, Helmut Prendinger, and Mitsuru Ishizuka. Compositionality principle in recognition of fine-grained emotions from text. In *Proceedings of 3th International AAAI Conference on Weblogs and Social Media (ICWSM 2009)*, 2009. URL https://www.aaai.org/ocs/index.php/ICWSM/09/paper/viewFile/197/525. 58, 59

Dong Nguyen and A. Seza Doğruöz. Word level language identification in online multilingual communication. In *Proceedings of the 2013 Conference on Empirical Methods in Natural Language Processing*, pages 857–862, Seattle, Washington, USA, October 2013. Association for Computational Linguistics. http://www.aclweb.org/anthology/D13-1084. 33

Azadeh Nikfarjam. *Health Information Extraction from Social Media*. PhD thesis, Arizona State University, 2016. xviii, 89, 90

Azadeh Nikfarjam, Abeed Sarker, Karen O'Connor, Rachel Ginn, and Graciela Gonzalez. Pharmacovigilance from social media: mining adverse drug reaction mentions using sequence labeling with word embedding cluster features. *Journal of the American Medical Informatics Association*, 22(3):671–681, 2015. DOI: 10.1093/jamia/ocu041 xvii, 88, 89

Alex Nikolov and Victor Radivchev. Nikolov-radivchev at SemEval-2019 task 6: Offensive tweet classification with BERT and ensembles. In *Proceedings of the 13th International Workshop on Semantic Evaluation*, pages 691–695, Minneapolis, Minnesota, USA, June 2019. Association for Computational Linguistics. https://www.aclweb.org/anthology/S19-2123. DOI: 10.18653/v1/s19-2123 104

Eric Nunes, Ahmad Diab, Andrew Gunn, Ericsson Marin, Vineet Mishra, Vivin Paliath, John Robertson, Jana Shakarian, Amanda Thart, and Paulo Shakarian. Darknet and Deepnet mining for proactive cybersecurity threat intelligence. 2016. https://arxiv.org/pdf/1607.08583.pdf. DOI: 10.1109/isi.2016.7745435 106

Jon Oberlander and Scott Nowson. Whose thumb is it anyway?: Classifying author personality from weblog text. In *Proceedings of COLING/ACL 2006 (Posters)*, pages 627–634. Association for Computational Linguistics, 2006. http://www.aclweb.org/anthology/P06-2081.pdf. DOI: 10.3115/1273073.1273154 110

Brendan O'Connor, Michel Krieger, and David Ahn. Tweetmotif: Exploratory search and topic summarization for Twitter. In *ICWSM*, 2010. 22

Myle Ott, Sergey Edunov, David Grangier, and Michael Auli. Scaling neural machine translation. *CoRR*, abs/1806.00187, 2018. http://arxiv.org/abs/1806.00187. DOI: 10.18653/v1/w18-6301 78

Lilja Ovrelid and Arne Skjærholt. Lexical categories for improved parsing of web data. In *Proceedings of the International Conference on Computational Linguistics COLING 2012 (Posters)*, pages 903–912, Mumbai, India, December 2012. http://www.aclweb.org/anthology/C12-2088. 27

Olutobi Owoputi, Brendan O'Connor, Chris Dyer, Kevin Gimpel, Nathan Schneider, and Noah A. Smith. Improved part-of-speech tagging for online conversational text with word clusters. In *Proceedings of Human Language Technologies 2013: The Conference of the North American Chapter of the Association for Computational Linguistics*, Atlanta, GA, USA, 9-15 June 2013, pages 380–390. ACL, 2013. http://www.aclweb.org/anthology/N13-1039. 25, 32

Julia Pajzs, Ralf Steinberger, Maud Ehrmann, Mohamed Ebrahim, Leonida Della Rocca, Eszter Simon, Stefano Bucci, and Tamas Varadi. Media monitoring and information extraction for the highly inflected agglutinative language hungarian. In *LREC 2014 Proceedings*, pages 2040–2056, Reykjavik, Iceland, 2014. URL http://www.lrec-conf.org/proceedings/lrec2014/pdf/449_Paper.pdf. 101

Alexander Pak and Patrick Paroubek. Twitter based system: Using Twitter for disambiguating sentiment ambiguous adjectives. In *Proceedings of the 5th International Workshop on Semantic Evaluation*, pages 436–439. Association for Computational Linguistics, 2010a. http://aclweb.org/anthology/S10-1097. 58

Alexander Pak and Patrick Paroubek. Twitter as a corpus for sentiment analysis and opinion mining. In *Proceedings of the Seventh conference on International Language Resources and Evaluation (LREC'10)*. European Languages Resources Association (ELRA), 2010b. http://aclweb.org/anthology/L10-1263. 58

Elisavet Palogiannidi, Athanasia Kolovou, Fenia Christopoulou, Filippos Kokkinos, Elias Iosif, Nikolaos Malandrakis, Haris Papageorgiou, Shrikanth Narayanan, and Alexandros Potamianos. Tweester at SemEval-2016 task 4: Sentiment analysis in Twitter using semantic-affective model adaptation. In *Proceedings of the 10th International Workshop on Semantic Evaluation (SemEval-2016)*, pages 155–163, San Diego, California, June 2016. Association for Computational Linguistics. http://www.aclweb.org/anthology/S16-1023. DOI: 10.18653/v1/s16-1023 60

Georgios Paltoglou and Mike Thelwall. Twitter, MySpace, Digg: Unsupervised sentiment analysis in social media. *ACM Transactions on Intelligent Systems and Technology (TIST)*, 3(4):66, 2012. DOI: 10.1145/2337542.2337551. 56

Bo Pang and Lillian Lee. Opinion mining and sentiment analysis. *Foundations and trends in information retrieval*, 2(1-2):1–135, 2008. DOI: 10.1561/1500000011 55

Kartikey Pant, Venkata Himakar Yanamandra, Alok Debnath, and Radhika Mamidi. SmokEng: Towards fine-grained classification of tobacco-related social media text. In *Proceedings of the 5th Workshop on Noisy User-generated Text (W-NUT 2019)*, pages 181–190,

Hong Kong, China, November 2019. Association for Computational Linguistics. https://www.aclweb.org/anthology/D19-5524. DOI: 10.18653/v1/D19-5524 91

Kishore Papineni, Salim Roukos, Todd Ward, and Wei-Jing Zhu. Bleu: A method for automatic evaluation of machine translation. In *Proceedings of the 40th Annual Meeting of the Association for Computational Linguistics,* Philadelphia, Penn., 7-12 July 2002, pages 311–318. ACL, 2002. DOI: 10.3115/1073083.1073135 85

Deepa Paranjpe. Learning document aboutness from implicit user feedback and document structure. In *Proceedings of the 18th ACM conference on Information and knowledge management*, pages 365–374. ACM, 2009. DOI: 10.1145/1645953.1646002. 67

Minsu Park, Chiyoung Cha, and Meeyoung Cha. Depressive moods of users portrayed in Twitter. In *ACM SIGKDD Workshop on Healthcare Informatics (HI-KDD)*, pages 1–8, 2012. ISBN 9781450315487. 91

Desmond Upton Patton, Jamie MacBeth, Sarita Schoenebeck, Katherine Shear, and Kathleen McKeown. Accommodating grief on twitter: An analysis of expressions of grief among gang involved youth on twitter using qualitative analysis and natural language processing. *Biomedical Informatics Insights*, 10:1178222618763155, 2018. DOI: 10.1177/1178222618763155 5

Michael Paul, ChengXiang Zhai, and Roxana Girju. Summarizing contrastive viewpoints in opinionated text. In *Proceedings of the 2010 Conference on Empirical Methods in Natural Language Processing*, pages 66–76, Cambridge, MA, October 2010. Association for Computational Linguistics. http://www.aclweb.org/anthology/D10-1007. 75

Fuchun Peng and Dale Schuurmans. Combining Naïve Bayes and n-gram language models for text classification. *Advances in Information Retrieval*, pages 335–350, 2003. DOI: 10.1007/3-540-36618-0_24 37, 38

Nanyun Peng and Mark Dredze. Multi-task domain adaptation for sequence tagging. 2016. https://arxiv.org/abs/1608.02689. DOI: 10.18653/v1/w17-2612 29, 30

James W. Pennebaker, Roger J. Booth, and Martha E. Francis. Operator's manual: Linguistic inquiry and word count (LIWC2007). Technical report, Austin, Texas, LIWC.net, 2007. 57

Juan Manuel Pérez and Franco M. Luque. Atalaya at SemEval 2019 task 5: Robust embeddings for tweet classification. In *Proceedings of the 13th International Workshop on Semantic Evaluation*, pages 64–69, Minneapolis, Minnesota, USA, June 2019. Association for Computational Linguistics. https://www.aclweb.org/anthology/S19-2008. DOI: 10.18653/v1/s19-2008 103

Verónica Pérez-Rosas, Bennett Kleinberg, Alexandra Lefevre, and Rada Mihalcea. Automatic detection of fake news. In *Proceedings of the 27th International Conference on Computational Linguistics*, pages 3391–3401, Santa Fe, New Mexico, USA, August 2018. Association for Computational Linguistics. https://www.aclweb.org/anthology/C18-1287. 125

Isaac Persing and Vincent Ng. Vote prediction on comments in social polls. In *Proceedings of the 2014 Conference on Empirical Methods in Natural Language Processing (EMNLP)*, pages 1127–1138, Doha, Qatar, October 2014. Association for Computational Linguistics. http://www.aclweb.org/anthology/D14-1119. DOI: 10.3115/v1/d14-1119 100

Sasha Petrovic, Miles Osborne, and Victor Lavrenko. Streaming first story detection with application to Twitter. In *Proceedings of Human Language Technologies 2010: The Conference of the North American Chapter of the Association for Computational Linguistics*, Los Angeles, Cal., 2-4 June 2010, pages 181–189. ACL, 2010. http://dl.acm.org/citation.cfm?id=1857999.1858020. 64

Swit Phuvipadawat and Tsuyoshi Murata. Breaking news detection and tracking in Twitter. In *Web Intelligence and Intelligent Agent Technology (WI-IAT), 2010 IEEE/WIC/ACM International Conference on*, volume 3, pages 120–123. IEEE, 2010. DOI: 10.1109/WI-IAT.2010.205 64

Ferran Pla and Lluís-F. Hurtado. Political tendency identification in Twitter using sentiment analysis techniques. In *Proceedings of the 25th International Conference on Computational Linguistics COLING 2014*, pages 183–192, Dublin, Ireland, August 2014. Dublin City University and Association for Computational Linguistics. http://www.aclweb.org/anthology/C14-1019. 100

Robert Plutchik and Henry Kellerman. *Emotion: Theory, Research and Experience. Vol. 1, Theories of Emotion*. Academic Press, 1980. http://www.jstor.org/stable/1422757. 59

Ingmar Poese, Steve Uhlig, Mohamed Ali Kaafar, Benoit Donnet, and Bamba Gueye. IP geolocation databases: Unreliable? *ACM SIGCOMM Computer Communication Review*, 41(2): 53–56, 2011. DOI: 10.1145/1971162.1971171. 44

Adrian Popescu and Gregory Grefenstette. Mining user home location and gender from flickr tags. In *Proceedings of the International Conference on Weblogs and Social Media (ICWSM)*, 2010. URL http://www.aaai.org/ocs/index.php/ICWSM/ICWSM10/paper/viewFile/1477/1881. 47

Ana-Maria Popescu and Oren Etzioni. Extracting product features and opinions from reviews. In *Proceedings of the Conference on Human Language Technology and Empirical Methods in Natural Language Processing*, HLT '05, pages 339–346, Stroudsburg, PA, USA, 2005. Association for Computational Linguistics. DOI: 10.3115/1220575.1220618 56

Ana-Maria Popescu and Marco Pennacchiotti. Detecting controversial events from Twitter. In *Proceedings of the 19th ACM international conference on Information and knowledge management*, pages 1873–1876. ACM, 2010. DOI: 10.1145/1871437.1871751. 66, 70

Ana-Maria Popescu, Marco Pennacchiotti, and Deepa Paranjpe. Extracting events and event descriptions from Twitter. In *Proceedings of the 20th international conference companion on World Wide Web*, pages 105–106. ACM, 2011. DOI: 10.1145/1963192.1963246. 67

Alexander Popov. Deep learning architecture for part-of-speech tagging with word and suffix embeddings. In *Proceedings of Artificial Intelligence: Methodology, Systems, and Applications: 17th International Conference, AIMSA 2016*, pages 68–77, Varna, Bulgaria, 09 2016. ISBN 978-3-319-44747-6. DOI: 10.1007/978-3-319-44748-3_7 24

Alexabder Porshnev, Ilyia Redkin, and Alexey Shevchenko. Machine learning in prediction of stock market indicators based on historical data and data from Twitter sentiment analysis. In *Data Mining Workshops (ICDMW), 2013 IEEE 13th International Conference on*, pages 440–444, Dec 2013. DOI: 10.1109/ICDMW.2013.111 97

Martin Potthast, Tim Gollub, Kristof Komlossy, Sebastian Schuster, Matti Wiegmann, Erika Patricia Garces Fernandez, Matthias Hagen, and Benno Stein. Crowdsourcing a large corpus of clickbait on twitter. In *Proceedings of the 27th International Conference on Computational Linguistics*, pages 1498–1507, Santa Fe, New Mexico, USA, August 2018. Association for Computational Linguistics. https://www.aclweb.org/anthology/C18-1127. 124

Robert Power, Bella Robinson, and David Ratcliffe. Finding fires with Twitter. In *Australasian Language Technology Association Workshop*, pages 80–89, 2013. http://www.aclweb.org/anthology/U/U13/U13-1011.pdf. 108

G. Prapula, Soujanya Lanka, and Kamalakar Karlapalem. TEA: Episode analytics on short messages. In *4th Workshop on Making Sense of Microposts (#Microposts2014)*, pages 11–18, 2014. http://ceur-ws.org/Vol-1141/paper_08.pdf. 53

Daniel Preoţiuc-Pietro and Lyle Ungar. User-level race and ethnicity predictors from twitter text. In *Proceedings of the 27th International Conference on Computational Linguistics*, pages 1534–1545, Santa Fe, New Mexico, USA, August 2018. Association for Computational Linguistics. https://www.aclweb.org/anthology/C18-1130. 113

Daniel Preotiuc-Pietro, Svitlana Volkova, Vasileios Lampos, Yoram Bachrach, and Nikolaos Aletras. Studying user income through language, behaviour and affect in social media. *PLOS ONE*. DOI: 10.1371/journal.pone.0138717 115

Daniel Preotiuc-Pietro, Maarten Sap, H. Andrew Schwartz, and Lyle Ungar. Mental illness detection at the world well-being project for the CLPsych 2015 shared task. In *Proceedings of the 2nd Workshop on Computational Linguistics and Clinical Psychology: From Linguistic Signal to Clinical Reality*, pages 40–45, 2015. DOI: 10.3115/v1/w15-1205 92

Daniel Preotiuc-Pietro, Ye Liu, Daniel Hopkins, and Lyle Ungar. Beyond binary labels: Political ideology prediction of Twitter users. In *Proceedings of the 55th Annual Meeting of the Association for Computational Linguistics (Volume 1: Long Papers)*, pages 729–740, Vancouver, Canada, July 2017. Association for Computational Linguistics. http://aclweb.org/anthology/P17-1068. DOI: 10.18653/v1/p17-1068 114

Reid Priedhorsky, Aron Culotta, and Sara Y. Del Valle. Inferring the origin locations of tweets with quantitative confidence. In *Proceedings of the 17th ACM Conference on Computer Supported Cooperative Work & Social Computing (CSCW '14)*, pages 1523–1536, New York, USA, February 2014. ACM Press. http://dl.acm.org/citation.cfm?id=2531602.2531607. DOI: 10.1145/2531602.2531607 47

R Lydia Priyadharsini and M Lovelin Ponn Felciah. Recommendation system in e-commerce using sentiment analysis. DOI: 10.14445/22315381/ijett-v49p269 119

Alec Radford, Karthik Narasimhan, Tim Salimans, and Ilya Sutskever. Improving language understanding by generative pre-training. https://s3-us-west-2.amazonaws.com/openai-assets/research-covers/language-unsupervised/language_understanding_paper.pdf, 2018 118

Daniel Ramage, David Hall, Ramesh Nallapati, and Christopher D. Manning. Labeled LDA: A supervised topic model for credit attribution in multi-labeled corpora. In *Proceedings of the 2009 Conference on Empirical Methods in Natural Language Processing*, Singapore, 6-7 August 2009, volume 1, pages 248–256, 2009. http://dl.acm.org/citation.cfm?id=1699510.1699543. DOI: 10.3115/1699510.1699543 30

Gabriele Ranco, Darko Aleksovski, Guido Caldarelli, Miha Grcar, and Igor Mozetic. The effects of Twitter sentiment on stock price returns. *PLOS ONE*. DOI: 10.1371/journal.pone.0138441 97

Delip Rao, David Yarowsky, Abhishek Shreevats, and Manaswi Gupta. Classifying latent user attributes in Twitter. In *Proceedings of the 2Nd International Workshop on Search and Mining User-generated Contents*, SMUC '10, pages 37–44, New York, NY, USA, 2010. ACM. DOI: 10.1145/1871985.1871993. 112, 115

Delip Rao, Michael J. Paul, Clayton Fink, David Yarowsky, Timothy Oates, and Glen Coppersmith. Hierarchical Bayesian models for latent attribute detection in social media. In *Proceedings of the Fifth International Conference on Weblogs and Social Media, Barcelona, Catalonia, Spain, July 17-21, 2011*, 2011. URL http://www.aaai.org/ocs/index.php/ICWSM/ICWSM11/paper/view/2881. 112

Amir H. Razavi, Diana Inkpen, Dmitry Brusilovsky, and Lana Bogouslavski. General topic annotation in social networks: A Latent Dirichlet Allocation approach. In Osmar R. Zaiane and Sandra Zilles, editors, *Advances in Artificial Intelligence*, volume 7884 of *Lecture Notes in Computer Science*, pages 293–300. Springer Berlin Heidelberg, 2013. DOI: 10.1007/978-3-642-38457-8_29 104

Amir H. Razavi, Diana Inkpen, Rafael Falcon, and Rami Abielmona. Textual risk mining for maritime situational awareness. In *Cognitive Methods in Situation Awareness and Decision Support (CogSIMA), 2014 IEEE International Inter-Disciplinary Conference on*, pages 167–173. IEEE, 2014. DOI: 10.1109/CogSIMA.2014.6816558 106

Majid Razmara, George Foster, Baskaran Sankaran, and Anoop Sarkar. Mixing multiple translation models in statistical machine translation. In *Proceedings of the 50th Annual Meeting of the Association for Computational Linguistics (Volume 1: Long Papers)*, pages 940–949, Jeju Island, Korea, July 2012. Association for Computational Linguistics. http://www.aclweb.org/anthology/P12-1099. 80

Philip Resnik, William Armstrong, Leonardo Claudino, Thang Nguyen, Viet-an Nguyen, and Jordan Boyd-graber. Beyond LDA: Exploring supervised topic modeling for depression-related language in Twitter. In *Proceedings of the 2nd Workshop on Computational Linguistics and Clinical Psychology: From Linguistic Signal to Clinical Reality*, volume 1, pages 99–107, 2015. DOI: 10.3115/v1/w15-1212 92, 93

Matthew Riemer, Sophia Krasikov, and Harini Srinivasan. A deep learning and knowledge transfer based architecture for social media user characteristic determination. In *Proceedings of the third International Workshop on Natural Language Processing for Social Media*, pages 39–47, Denver, Colorado, June 2015. Association for Computational Linguistics. http://www.aclweb.org/anthology/W15-1705. DOI: 10.3115/v1/w15-1705 113

Ellen Riloff, Ashequl Qadir, Prafulla Surve, Lalindra De Silva, Nathan Gilbert, and Ruihong Huang. Sarcasm as contrast between a positive sentiment and negative situation. In *Proceedings of the 2013 Conference on Empirical Methods in Natural Language Processing*, pages 704–714, Seattle, Washington, USA, October 2013. Association for Computational Linguistics. http://www.aclweb.org/anthology/D13-1066. 61

Alan Ritter, Sam Clark, Mausam, and Oren Etzioni. Named entity recognition in tweets: An experimental study. In *Proceedings of the Conference on Empirical Methods in Natural Language Processing*, EMNLP'11, pages 1524–1534, Edinburgh, Scotland, UK., July 2011. ACL. http://www.aclweb.org/anthology/D11-1141. 17, 24, 27, 30, 32

Bella Robinson, Robert Power, and Mark Cameron. A sensitive Twitter earthquake detector. In *Proceedings of the 22nd international conference on World Wide Web companion*, pages 999–1002. International World Wide Web Conferences Steering Committee, 2013. http://www2013.org/companion/p999.pdf. DOI: 10.1145/2487788.2488101 108

Stephen Roller, Michael Speriosu, Sarat Rallapalli, Benjamin Wing, and Jason Baldridge. Supervised text-based geolocation using language models on an adaptive grid. In *Proceedings of the 2012 Joint Conference on Empirical Methods in Natural Language Processing and Computational Natural Language Learning*, pages 1500–1510. Association for Computational Linguistics, July 2012. http://dl.acm.org/citation.cfm?id=2390948.2391120. 46, 47, 50

Sara Rosenthal, Preslav Nakov, Svetlana Kiritchenko, Saif M. Mohammad, Alan Ritter, and Veselin Stoyanov. SemEval-2015 task 10: Sentiment analysis in Twitter. In *Proceedings of the ninth international workshop on Semantic Evaluation Exercises (SemEval-2015)*, Denver, Colorado, June 2015. Association for Computational Linguistics. DOI: 10.18653/v1/s15-2078 58

Dominic Rout, Kalina Bontcheva, Daniel Preotiuc-Pietro, and Trevor Cohn. Where's @wally?: a classification approach to geolocating users based on their social ties. In *HyperText and Social Media 2013*, pages 11–20, 2013. DOI: 10.1145/2481492.2481494. 45

Matthew Rowe and Hassan Saif. Mining pro-isis radicalisation signals from social media users. In *Proceedings of the Tenth International AAAI Conference on Web and Social Media (ICWSM 2016)*, pages 329–338, 2016. URL http://www.aaai.org/ocs/index.php/ICWSM/ICWSM16/paper/download/13023/12752. 105

Victoria Rubin, Jeffrey Stanton, and Elizabeth Liddy. Discerning emotions in texts. In *The AAAI Symposium on Exploring Attitude and Affect in Text (AAAI-EAAT)*, 2004. 58

Victor Ruiz, Lingyun Shi, Wei Quan, Neal Ryan, Candice Biernesser, David Brent, and Rich Tsui. CLPsych2019 shared task: Predicting suicide risk level from Reddit posts on multiple forums. In *Proceedings of the Sixth Workshop on Computational Linguistics and Clinical Psychology*, pages 162–166, Minneapolis, Minnesota, June 2019. Association for Computational Linguistics. https://www.aclweb.org/anthology/W19-3020. 95

Fatiha Sadat, Farnazeh Kazemi, and Atefeh Farzindar. Automatic identification of Arabic dialects in social media. In *SoMeRA 2014: International Workshop on Social Media Retrieval and Analysis*, 2014a. DOI: 10.1145/2632188.2632207. xvii, 36, 38, 39, 40, 41, 85

Fatiha Sadat, Farnazeh Kazemi, and Atefeh Farzindar. Automatic identification of Arabic language varieties and dialects in social media. In *COLING 2014: Workshop on Natural Language Processing for Social Media (SocialNLP)*, 2014b. DOI: 10.3115/v1/w14-5904 85, 133

Fatiha Sadat, Fatma Mallek, Rahma Sellami, Mohamed Mahdi Boudabous, and Atefeh Farzindar. Collaboratively constructed linguistic resources for language variants and their exploitation in NLP application – the case of Tunisian Arabic and the social media. In *LG-LP 2014: Workshop on Lexical and Grammatical Resources for Language Processing*, 2014c. http://aclweb.org/anthology/W14-5813. DOI: 10.3115/v1/w14-5813 37, 38, 85

Adam Sadilek and Henry Kautz. Modeling the impact of lifestyle on health at scale. In *Proceedings of the Sixth ACM International Conference on Web Search and Data Mining*, WSDM

'13, pages 637–646, New York, NY, USA, 2013. ACM. DOI: 10.1145/2433396.2433476. 111

Takeshi Sakaki, Makoto Okazaki, and Yutaka Matsuo. Earthquake shakes Twitter users: Real-time event detection by social sensors. In *Proceedings of the 19th International Conference on World Wide Web*, WWW '10, pages 851–860, New York, NY, USA, 2010. ACM. DOI: 10.1145/1772690.1772777. 68, 70

Sushmitha Reddy Sane, Suraj Tripathi, Koushik Reddy Sane, and Radhika Mamidi. Deep learning techniques for humor detection in Hindi-English code-mixed tweets. In *Proceedings of the Tenth Workshop on Computational Approaches to Subjectivity, Sentiment and Social Media Analysis*, pages 57–61, Minneapolis, USA, June 2019. Association for Computational Linguistics. https://www.aclweb.org/anthology/W19-1307. DOI: 10.18653/v1/w19-1307 7

Baskaran Sankaran, Majid Razmara, Atefeh Farzindar, Wael Khreich, Fred Popowich, and Annop Sarkar. Domain adaptation techniques for machine translation and their evaluation in a real-world setting. In *Proceedings of the 25th Canadian Conference on Artificial Intelligence*, pages 158–169, Toronto, ON, Canada, May 2012. Springer. DOI: 10.1007/978-3-642-30353-1_14 80

Jagan Sankaranarayanan, Hanan Samet, Benjamin E Teitler, Michael D Lieberman, and Jon Sperling. Twitterstand: News in tweets. In *Proceedings of the 17th ACM SIGSPATIAL International Conference on Advances in Geographic Information Systems*, pages 42–51. ACM, 2009. DOI: 10.1145/1653771.1653781. 64

Hassan Sawaf. Arabic dialect handling in hybrid machine translation. In *Proceedings of the Conference of the Association for Machine Translation in the Americas (AMTA)*, Denver, Colorado, 2010. 84

Tatjana Scheffler, Berfin Aktaş, Debopam Das, and Manfred Stede. Annotating shallow discourse relations in twitter conversations. In *Proceedings of the Workshop on Discourse Relation Parsing and Treebanking 2019*, pages 50–55, Minneapolis, MN, June 2019. Association for Computational Linguistics. https://www.aclweb.org/anthology/W19-2707. DOI: 10.18653/v1/w19-2707 122

Jonathan Schler, Moshe Koppel, Shlomo Argamon, and James W Pennebaker. Effects of age and gender on blogging. In *AAAI Spring Symposium: Computational Approaches to Analyzing Weblogs*, volume 6, pages 199–205, 2006. 112

Dara Schniederjans, Edita S. Cao, and Marc Schniederjans. Enhancing financial performance with social media: An impression management perspective, 2013. URL http://www.sciencedirect.com/science/article/pii/S0167923612003934. DOI: 10.1016/j.dss.2012.12.027 xviii, 98, 99

H Andrew Schwartz, Johannes Eichstaedt, Margaret L Kern, Gregory Park, Maarten Sap, David Stillwell, Michal Kosinski, and Lyle Ungar. Towards assessing changes in degree of depression through Facebook. In *Proceedings of the Workshop on Computational Linguistics and Clinical Psychology: From Linguistic Signal to Clinical Reality*, pages 118–125, 2014. http://www.aclweb.org/anthology/W/W14/W14-3214. DOI: 10.3115/v1/w14-3214 92

Fabrizio Sebastiani. Machine learning in automated text categorization. *ACM Computing Surveys*, 34(1):1?47, 2002. DOI: 10.1145/505282.505283. 16

Djamé Seddah, Benoit Sagot, Marie Candito, Virginie Mouilleron, and Vanessa Combet. The French Social Media Bank: a treebank of noisy user generated content. In *Proceedings of the International Conference on Computational Linguistics COLING 2012*, pages 2441–2458, Mumbai, India, December 2012. http://www.aclweb.org/anthology/C12-1149. 32

Ivan Sekulic and Michael Strube. Adapting deep learning methods for mental health prediction on social media. In *Proceedings of the 5th Workshop on Noisy User-generated Text (W-NUT 2019)*, pages 322–327, Hong Kong, China, November 2019. Association for Computational Linguistics. https://www.aclweb.org/anthology/D19-5542. DOI: 10.18653/v1/D19-5542 94

Khaled Shaalan, Hitham M Abo Bakr, and Ibrahim Ziedan. Transferring Egyptian colloquial dialect into Modern Standard Arabic. In *Proceedings of the International Conference on Recent Advances in Natural Language Processing*, Borovets, Bulgaria, 27-29 September 2007, pages 525–529, 2007. 84

Cyrus Shahabi, Farnoush Banaei Kashani, Ali Khoshgozaran, Luciano Nocera, and Songhua Xing. Geodec: A framework to visualize and query geospatial data for decision-making. *IEEE MultiMedia*, 17(3):14–23, 2010. DOI: 10.1109/MMUL.2010.5692179. 117

D.A. Shamma, L. Kennedy, and E.F. Churchill. Tweetgeist: Can the Twitter timeline reveal the structure of broadcast events?. In *CSCW 2010.*, 2010. http://research.yahoo.com/pub/3041. 102

Beaux Sharifi, M-A Hutton, and Jugal K Kalita. Experiments in microblog summarization. In *Social Computing (SocialCom), 2010 IEEE Second International Conference on*, pages 49–56. IEEE, 2010. DOI: 10.1109/socialcom.2010.17 10, 72

Benjamin Shickel and Parisa Rashidi. Automatic triage of mental health forum posts. In *Proceedings of the Third Workshop on Computational Linguistics and Clinical Psychology*, pages 188–192, San Diego, CA, USA, June 2016. Association for Computational Linguistics. http://www.aclweb.org/anthology/W16-0326. DOI: 10.18653/v1/w16-0326 95

Benjamin Shickel, Martin Heesacker, Sherry Benton, Ashkan Ebadi, Paul Nickerson, and Parisa Rashidi. Self-reflective sentiment analysis. In *Computational Linguistics and Clinical*

Psychology, pages 23–32, San Diego, CA, USA, 2016. Association for Computational Linguistics. http://www.aclweb.org/anthology/W16-0303. DOI: 10.18653/v1/w16-0303 91

Han-Chin Shing, Suraj Nair, Ayah Zirikly, Meir Friedenberg, Hal Daumé III, and Philip Resnik. Expert, crowdsourced, and machine assessment of suicide risk via online postings. In *Proceedings of the Fifth Workshop on Computational Linguistics and Clinical Psychology: From Keyboard to Clinic*, pages 25–36, 2018. DOI: 10.18653/v1/w18-0603 95

Philippa Shoemark, Debnil Sur, Luke Shrimpton, Iain Murray, and Sharon Goldwater. Aye or naw, whit dae ye hink? Scottish independence and linguistic identity on social media. In *Proceedings of the 15th Conference of the European Chapter of the Association for Computational Linguistics: Volume 1, Long Papers*, pages 1239–1248, Valencia, Spain, April 2017. Association for Computational Linguistics. http://www.aclweb.org/anthology/E17-1116. DOI: 10.18653/v1/e17-1116 114

Tomer Simon, Avishay Goldberg, Limor Aharonson-Daniel, Dmitry Leykin, and Bruria Adini. Twitter in the cross fire: The use of social media in the Westgate Mall terror attack in Kenya. *PLOS ONE*. DOI: 10.1371/journal.pone.0104136 107

M.U. Simsek and Suat Ozdemir. Analysis of the relation between Turkish Twitter messages and stock market index. In *Application of Information and Communication Technologies (AICT), 2012 6th International Conference on*, pages 1–4, Oct 2012. DOI: 10.1109/ICAICT.2012.6398520 98

Priyanka Sinha, Anirban Dutta Choudhury, and Amit Kumar Agrawal. Sentiment analysis of Wimbledon tweets. In *4th Workshop on Making Sense of Microposts (#Microposts2014)*, pages 51–52, 2014. http://ceur-ws.org/Vol-1141/paper_10.pdf. 116

Marina Sokolova, Khaled El Emam, Sean Rose, Sadrul Chowdhury, Emilio Neri, Elizabeth Jonker, and Liam Peyton. Personal health information leak prevention in heterogeneous texts. In *Proceedings of the Workshop on Adaptation of Language Resources and Technology to New Domains*, pages 58–69. ACL, 2009. http://dl.acm.org/citation.cfm?id=1859148.1859157. 88

Gil-Young Song, Youngjoon Cheon, Kihwang Lee, Heuiseok Lim, Kyung-Yong Chung, and Hae-Chang Rim. Multiple categorizations of products: cognitive modeling of customers through social media data mining. *Personal and Ubiquitous Computing*. DOI: 10.1007/s00779-013-0740-5 102

Gabriel Stanovsky, Daniel Gruhl, and Pablo Mendes. Recognizing mentions of adverse drug reaction in social media using knowledge-infused recurrent models. In *Proceedings of the 15th Conference of the European Chapter of the Association for Computational Linguistics: Volume 1, Long Papers*, pages 142–151, Valencia, Spain, April 2017. Association for Computational Linguistics. http://www.aclweb.org/anthology/E17-1014. DOI: 10.18653/v1/e17-1014 89

Anthony Stefanidis, Andrew Crooks, and Jacek Radzikowski. Harvesting ambient geospatial information from social media feeds. *GeoJournal*, 78(2):319–338, 2013. DOI: 10.1007/s10708-011-9438-2 44

Dario Stojanovski, Gjorgji Strezoski, Gjorgji Madjarov, and Ivica Dimitrovski. Finki at SemEval-2016 task 4: Deep learning architecture for Twitter sentiment analysis. In *Proceedings of the 10th International Workshop on Semantic Evaluation (SemEval-2016)*, pages 149–154, San Diego, California, June 2016. Association for Computational Linguistics. http://www.aclweb.org/anthology/S16-1022. DOI: 10.18653/v1/s16-1022 60

Philip J Stone, Robert F Bales, J Zvi Namenwirth, and Daniel M Ogilvie. The General Inquirer: A computer system for content analysis and retrieval based on the sentence as a unit of information. *Behavioral Science*, 7(4):484–498, 1962. DOI: 10.1002/bs.3830070412 57

Carlo Strapparava and Rada Mihalcea. Semeval-2007 task 14: Affective text. In *Proceedings of the 4th International Workshop on Semantic Evaluations*, pages 70–74, 2007. http://dl.acm.org/citation.cfm?id=1621474.1621487. DOI: 10.3115/1621474.1621487 58

Carlo Strapparava and Alessandro Valitutti. WordNet Affect: an affective extension of WordNet. In *Proceedings of LREC*, volume 4, pages 1083–1086, 2004. 59

Frederic Stutzman, Robert Capra, and Jamila Thompson. Factors mediating disclosure in social network sites. *Computers in Human Behavior*, 27(1):590–598, 2011. URL http://fredstutzman.com.s3.amazonaws.com/papers/CHB2011_Stutzman.pdf. DOI: 10.1016/j.chb.2010.10.017 125

Hong Keel Sul, Allan R. Dennis, and Lingyao Yuan. Trading on Twitter: The financial information content of emotion in social media. In *System Sciences (HICSS), 2014 47th Hawaii International Conference on*, pages 806–815, Jan 2014. DOI: 10.1109/HICSS.2014.107 97

Amirhossein Tebbifakhr, Luisa Bentivogli, Matteo Negri, and Marco Turchi. Machine translation for machines: the sentiment classification use case. In *Proceedings of the 2019 Conference on Empirical Methods in Natural Language Processing and the 9th International Joint Conference on Natural Language Processing (EMNLP-IJCNLP)*, pages 1368–1374, Hong Kong, China, November 2019. Association for Computational Linguistics. https://www.aclweb.org/anthology/D19-1140. DOI: 10.18653/v1/D19-1140 79

Mike Thelwall, Kevan Buckley, and Georgios Paltoglou. Sentiment in Twitter events. *Journal of the American Society for Information Science and Technology*, 62(2):406–418, 2011. DOI: 10.1002/asi.21462 56, 62

Dirk Thorleuchter and Dirk Van Den Poel. Protecting research and technology from espionage. *Expert Systems Application*, 40(9):3432–3440, July 2013. DOI: 10.1016/j.eswa.2012.12.051 106

Christoph Tillmann, Saab Mansour, and Yaser Al-Onaizan. Improved sentence-level Arabic dialect classification. In *Proceedings of the First Workshop on Applying NLP Tools to Similar Languages, Varieties and Dialects*, pages 110–119, Dublin, Ireland, August 2014. Association for Computational Linguistics and Dublin City University. http://www.aclweb.org/anthology/W14-5313. DOI: 10.3115/v1/w14-5313 41

Ivan Titov and Ryan T. McDonald. A joint model of text and aspect ratings for sentiment summarization. In *Proceedings of ACL-HLT 2008*, volume 8, pages 308–316. ACL, 2008. http://www.aclweb.org/anthology/P08-1036. 75

Erik Tjong Kim Sang and Johan Bos. Predicting the 2011 Dutch senate election results with Twitter. In *Proceedings of the Workshop on Semantic Analysis in Social Media*, pages 53–60, Avignon, France, April 2012. Association for Computational Linguistics. http://www.aclweb.org/anthology/W12-0607. 100

Erik F. Tjong Kim Sang and Sabine Buchholz. Introduction to the CoNLL-2000 shared task: Chunking. In *Proceedings of the 2nd workshop on Learning language in logic and the 4th conference on Computational natural language learning*, pages 127–132. Lisbon, Portugal, 2000. DOI: 10.3115/1117601.1117631 27

Erik F. Tjong Kim Sang and Fien De Meulder. Introduction to the CoNLL-2003 shared task: Language-independent named entity recognition. In Walter Daelemans and Miles Osborne, editors, *Proceedings of the seventh conference on Natural language learning at HLT-NAACL*, volume 4, pages 142–147. Edmonton, Canada, 2003. DOI: 10.3115/1119176.1119195 29, 30

Alexander Tkachenko, Timo Petmanson, and Sven Laur. Named entity recognition in Estonian. In *Proceedings of the 4th Biennial International Workshop on Balto-Slavic Natural Language Processing*, pages 78–83, Sofia, Bulgaria, August 2013. Association for Computational Linguistics. http://www.aclweb.org/anthology/W13-2412. 29

Radhia Toujani and Jalel Akaichi. Event news detection and citizens community structure for disaster management in social networks. In *Online Information Review*, pages 113–132. Emerald Publishing Limited, January 2019. 108

Kristina Toutanova, Dan Klein, Christopher D Manning, and Yoram Singer. Feature-rich part-of-speech tagging with a cyclic dependency network. In *Proceedings of the 2003 Conference of the North American Chapter of the Association for Computational Linguistics on Human Language Technology-Volume 1*, pages 173–180. ACL, 2003. DOI: 10.3115/1073445.1073478 24

Erik Tromp and Mikola Pechenizkiy. Graph-based n-gram language identification on short texts. In *Proceedings of Benelearn 2011*, pages 27–34, 2011. URL http://www.liacs.nl/~putten/benelearn2011/Benelearn2011_Proceedings.pdf. 33, 34

Sho Tsugawa, Yusuke Kikuchi, Fumio Kishino, Kosuke Nakajima, Yuichi Itoh, and Hiroyuki Ohsaki. Recognizing depression from Twitter activity. In *Proceedings of the 33rd Annual ACM Conference on Human Factors in Computing Systems - CHI '15*, pages 3187–3196, 2015. ISBN 9781450331456. DOI: 10.1145/2702123.2702280 91

Elsbeth Turcan and Kathleen McKeown. Dreaddit: A reddit dataset for stress analysis in social media, 2019. DOI: 10.18653/v1/d19-6213 91

Özlem Uzuner, Yuan Luo, and Peter Szolovits. Evaluating the state-of-the-art in automatic de-identification. *Journal of the American Medical Informatics Association*, 14(5):550–563, 2007. DOI: 10.1197/jamia.m2444 88

Shannon Vallor. Social networking and ethics. In Edward N. Zalta, editor, *The Stanford Encyclopedia of Philosophy*. Stanford University, winter 2012 edition, 2012. 125

Esther van den Berg, Katharina Korfhage, Josef Ruppenhofer, Michael Wiegand, and Katja Markert. Not my president: How names and titles frame political figures. In *Proceedings of the Third Workshop on Natural Language Processing and Computational Social Science*, pages 1–6, Minneapolis, Minnesota, June 2019. Association for Computational Linguistics. https://www.aclweb.org/anthology/W19-2101. DOI: 10.18653/v1/w19-2101 101

Rob van der Goot. An in-depth analysis of the effect of lexical normalization on the dependency parsing of social media. In *Proceedings of the 5th Workshop on Noisy User-generated Text (W-NUT 2019)*, pages 115–120, Hong Kong, China, November 2019. Association for Computational Linguistics. https://www.aclweb.org/anthology/D19-5515. DOI: 10.18653/v1/D19-5515 20

Ashish Vaswani, Noam Shazeer, Niki Parmar, Jakob Uszkoreit, Llion Jones, Aidan N Gomez, Łukasz Kaiser, and Illia Polosukhin. Attention is all you need. In I. Guyon, U. V. Luxburg, S. Bengio, H. Wallach, R. Fergus, S. Vishwanathan, and R. Garnett, editors, *Advances in Neural Information Processing Systems 30*, pages 5998–6008. Curran Associates, Inc., 2017. URL http://papers.nips.cc/paper/7181-attention-is-all-you-need.pdf. 78, 104

Sudha Verma, Sarah Vieweg, William J Corvey, Leysia Palen, James H Martin, Martha Palmer, Aaron Schram, and Kenneth Mark Anderson. Natural language processing to the rescue? extracting "situational awareness" tweets during mass emergency. In *ICWSM*, pages 385–392, 2011. URL http://www.aaai.org/ocs/index.php/ICWSM/ICWSM11/paper/download/2834/3282. 108

Svitlana Volkova, Glen Coppersmith, and Benjamin Van Durme. Inferring user political preferences from streaming communications. In *Proceedings of the 52nd Annual Meeting of the Association for Computational Linguistics (Volume 1: Long Papers)*, pages 186–196, Baltimore, Maryland, June 2014. Association for Computational Linguistics. http://www.aclweb.org/anthology/P/P14/P14-1018. DOI: 10.3115/v1/p14-1018 114

Stephen Wan, Cecile Paris, and Dimitrios Georgakopoulos. Social media data aggregation and mining for Internet-scale customer relationship management. In *The 2015 IEEE International Conference on Information Reuse and Integration (IRI)*, 2015. http://ieeexplore.ieee.org/abstract/document/7300953/. DOI: 10.1109/iri.2015.17 118

Na Wang, Jens Grossklags, and Heng Xu.   An online experiment of privacy authorization dialogues for social applications.   In *Computer Supported Cooperative Work, CSCW 2013*, San Antonio, TX, USA, February 23-27, 2013, pages 261–272, 2013.   URL http://people.ischool.berkeley.edu/~jensg/research/paper/Grossklags-CSCW2013.pdf. DOI: 10.1145/2441776.2441807 125

Pidong Wang and Hwee Tou Ng. A beam-search decoder for normalization of social media text with application to machine translation. In *Proceedings of the 2013 Conference of the North American Chapter of the Association for Computational Linguistics: Human Language Technologies*, pages 471–481, Atlanta, Georgia, June 2013. Association for Computational Linguistics. http://www.aclweb.org/anthology/N13-1050. 78

Yue Wang, Jing Li, Hou Pong Chan, Irwin King, Michael R. Lyu, and Shuming Shi. Topic-aware neural keyphrase generation for social media language. In *Proceedings of the 57th Annual Meeting of the Association for Computational Linguistics*, pages 2516–2526, Florence, Italy, July 2019. Association for Computational Linguistics. https://www.aclweb.org/anthology/P19-1240. DOI: 10.18653/v1/P19-1240 76

Wouter Weerkamp and Maarten De Rijke. Credibility improves topical blog post retrieval. In *HLT-NAACL*, pages 923–931. Association for Computational Linguistics (ACL), 2008. 68

Jianshu Weng and Bu-Sung Lee. Event detection in Twitter. In *ICWSM*, 2011. 66

Janyce Wiebe, Theresa Wilson, and Claire Cardie. Annotating expressions of opinions and emotions in language. *Language Resources and Evaluation*, 39(2-3):165–210, 2005. DOI: 10.1007/s10579-005-7880-9 57

Theresa Wilson, Janyce Wiebe, and Paul Hoffmann. Recognizing contextual polarity: An exploration of features for phrase-level sentiment analysis. *Computational Linguistics*, pages 399–433, 2009. DOI: 10.1162/coli.08-012-R1-06-90 57

Benjamin Wing and Jason Baldridge. Hierarchical discriminative classification for text-based geolocation. In *Proceedings of the 2014 Conference on Empirical Methods in Natural Language Processing (EMNLP)*, pages 336–348. Association for Computational Linguistics, 2014. http://aclweb.org/anthology/D14-1039. DOI: 10.3115/v1/d14-1039 47

Ian Witten and Eibe Frank. *Data Mining: Practical Machine Learning Tools and Techniques*. 2nd Edition, Morgan Kaufmann, San Francisco, San Francisco, CA, USA, 2005. DOI: 10.1145/507338.507355 15

Wei Wu, Bin Zhang, and Mari Ostendorf. Automatic generation of personalized annotation tags for Twitter users. In *Human Language Technologies: The 2010 Annual Conference of the North American Chapter of the Association for Computational Linguistics*, pages 689–692. Association for Computational Linguistics, 2010. http://aclweb.org/anthology/N10-1101. 122

Wei Xie, Feida Zhu, Jing Jiang, Ee-Peng Lim, and Ke Wang. TopicSketch: Real-time bursty topic detection from Twitter. *IEEE Transactions on Knowledge and Data Engineering*. DOI: 10.1109/icdm.2013.86 65

Rui Yan, Mirella Lapata, and Xiaoming Li. Tweet recommendation with graph co-ranking. In *Proceedings of the 50th Annual Meeting of the Association for Computational Linguistics: Long Papers-Volume 1*, pages 516–525. Association for Computational Linguistics, 2012. http://www.aclweb.org/anthology/P12-1054. 74

Ruoyao Yang, Wanying Xie, Chunhua Liu, and Dong Yu. BLCU_NLP at SemEval-2019 task 7: An inference chain-based GPT model for rumour evaluation. In *Proceedings of the 13th International Workshop on Semantic Evaluation*, pages 1090–1096, Minneapolis, Minnesota, USA, June 2019. Association for Computational Linguistics. https://www.aclweb.org/anthology/S19-2191. DOI: 10.18653/v1/s19-2191 118

SteveY. Yang, Sheung Yin K. Mo, and Xiaodi Zhu. An empirical study of the financial community network on Twitter. In *Computational Intelligence for Financial Engineering Economics (CIFEr), 2104 IEEE Conference on*, pages 55–62, March 2014. DOI: 10.1109/CIFEr.2014.6924054 98

Yiming Yang, Tom Pierce, and Jaime Carbonell. A study of retrospective and on-line event detection. In *Proceedings of the 21st annual international ACM SIGIR conference on Research and development in information retrieval*, pages 28–36, New York, NY, USA, 1998. ACM. DOI: 10.1145/290941.290953. 69

Yiming Yang, Jian Zhang, Jaime Carbonell, and Chun Jin. Topic-conditioned novelty detection. In *Proceedings of the 8th ACM SIGKDD Conference on Knowledge Discovery and Data Mining*, Edmonton, Alberta, Canada, 23-26 July 2002, pages 688–693. ACM, 2002. DOI: 10.1145/775047.775150. 69

Reyyan Yeniterzi, John Aberdeen, Samuel Bayer, Ben Wellner, Lynette Hirschman, and Bradley Malin. Effects of personal identifier resynthesis on clinical text de-identification. *Journal of the American Medical Informatics Association*, 17(2):159–168, 2010. DOI: 10.1136/jamia.2009.002212 88

Jie Yin, Andrew Lampert, Mark Cameron, Bella Robinson, and Robert Power. Using social media to enhance emergency situation awareness. *IEEE Intelligent Systems*, 27(6):52–59, 2012. http://www.ict.csiro.au/staff/jie.yin/files/YIN-IS2012.pdf. DOI: 10.1109/mis.2012.6 70, 108

T. Young, D. Hazarika, S. Poria, and E. Cambria. Recent trends in deep learning based natural language processing [review article]. *IEEE Computational Intelligence Magazine*, 13(3):55–75, August 2018. ISSN 1556-603X. DOI: 10.1109/MCI.2018.2840738 7

Omar F. Zaidan and Chris Callison-Burch. Arabic dialect identification. *Computational Linguistics*, 40(1):171–202, March 2014. DOI: 10.1162/COLI_a_00169. 40

Marcos Zampieri, Shervin Malmasi, Preslav Nakov, Sara Rosenthal, Noura Farra, and Ritesh Kumar. Predicting the type and target of offensive posts in social media. *CoRR*, abs/1902.09666, 2019a. http://arxiv.org/abs/1902.09666. DOI: 10.18653/v1/n19-1144 103

Marcos Zampieri, Shervin Malmasi, Preslav Nakov, Sara Rosenthal, Noura Farra, and Ritesh Kumar. Semeval-2019 task 6: Identifying and categorizing offensive language in social media (offenseval). *CoRR*, abs/1903.08983, 2019b. http://arxiv.org/abs/1903.08983. DOI: 10.18653/v1/s19-2010 103

Rabih Zbib, Erika Malchiodi, Jacob Devlin, David Stallard, Spyros Matsoukas, Richard Schwartz, John Makhoul, Omar F Zaidan, and Chris Callison-Burch. Machine translation of Arabic dialects. In *Proceedings of Human Language Technologies 2012: The Conference of the North American Chapter of the Association for Computational Linguistics*, Montreal, Canada, 3-8 June 2012, pages 49–59. Association for Computational Linguistics, 2012. http://dl.acm.org/citation.cfm?id=2382029.2382037. 84

Torsten Zesch and Tobias Horsmann. FlexTag: A highly flexible PoS tagging framework. In *Proceedings of the Tenth International Conference on Language Resources and Evaluation (LREC 2016)*, pages 4259–4263, Portoroz, Slovenia, May 2016. 24

Yingyi Zhang, Jing Li, Yan Song, and Chengzhi Zhang. Encoding conversation context for neural keyphrase extraction from microblog posts. In *Proceedings of the 2018 Conference of the North American Chapter of the Association for Computational Linguistics: Human Language Technologies, Volume 1 (Long Papers)*, pages 1676–1686, New Orleans, Louisiana, June 2018. Association for Computational Linguistics. https://www.aclweb.org/anthology/N18-1151. DOI: 10.18653/v1/N18-1151 76

Bing Zhao, Matthias Eck, and Stephan Vogel. Language model adaptation for statistical machine translation with structured query models. In *Proceedings of the 20th International Conference on Computational Linguistics*, COLING 2004, Stroudsburg, PA, USA, 2004. Association for Computational Linguistics. DOI: 10.3115/1220355.1220414 80

Wayne Xin Zhao, Jing Jiang, Jing He, Yang Song, Palakorn Achananuparp, Ee-Peng Lim, and Xiaoming Li. Topical keyphrase extraction from Twitter. In *Proceedings of the 49th Annual Meeting of the Association for Computational Linguistics: Human Language Technologies-Volume 1*, pages 379–388. Association for Computational Linguistics, 2011. http://dl.acm.org/citation.cfm?id=2002472.2002521. 72

Kaimin Zhou, Chang Shu, Binyang Li, and Jey Han Lau. Early rumour detection. In *Proceedings of the 2019 Conference of the North American Chapter of the Association for Computational Linguistics: Human Language Technologies, Volume 1 (Long and Short Papers)*, pages 1614–1623, Minneapolis, Minnesota, June 2019. Association for Computational Linguistics. https://www.aclweb.org/anthology/N19-1163. DOI: 10.18653/v1/n19-1163 124

Liang Zhou and Eduard H. Hovy. On the summarization of dynamically introduced information: Online discussions and blogs. In *AAAI Spring Symposium: Computational Approaches to Analyzing Weblogs*, page 237, 2006. 9

Ning Zhou, W.K. Cheung, Guoping Qiu, and Xiangyang Xue. A hybrid probabilistic model for unified collaborative and content-based image tagging. *Pattern Analysis and Machine Intelligence, IEEE Transactions on*, 33(7):1281–1294, July 2011. DOI: 10.1109/tpami.2010.204 107

Yukun Zhu, Ryan Kiros, Rich Zemel, Ruslan Salakhutdinov, Raquel Urtasun, Antonio Torralba, and Sanja Fidler. Aligning books and movies: Towards story-like visual explanations by watching movies and reading books. In *Proceedings of the IEEE international conference on computer vision*, pages 19–27, 2015. DOI: 10.1109/iccv.2015.11 118

Ayah Zirikly, Philip Resnik, Özlem Uzuner, and Kristy Hollingshead. CLPsych 2019 shared task: Predicting the degree of suicide risk in Reddit posts. In *Proceedings of the Sixth Workshop on Computational Linguistics and Clinical Psychology*, June 2019. 95

Jonathan Zomick, Sarah Ita Levitan, and Mark Serper. Linguistic analysis of schizophrenia in Reddit posts. In *Proceedings of the Sixth Workshop on Computational Linguistics and Clinical Psychology*, pages 74–83, Minneapolis, Minnesota, June 2019. Association for Computational Linguistics. https://www.aclweb.org/anthology/W19-3009. DOI: 10.18653/v1/w19-3009 92

Arkaitz Zubiaga, Damiano Spina, Enrique Amigó, and Julio Gonzalo. Towards real-time summarization of scheduled events from Twitter streams. In *Proceedings of the 23rd ACM conference on Hypertext and social media*, pages 319–320. ACM, 2012. DOI: 10.1145/2309996.2310053 74

Authors' Biographies

ANNA ATEFEH FARZINDAR

Dr. Anna Atefeh Farzindar is a faculty member of the Department of Computer Science at University of Southern California (USC) in Los Angeles. She was the CEO and co-founder of NLP Technologies Inc., a company specializing in Natural Language Processing (NLP), established in Montreal, Canada (2005–2016) and was the Adjunct Professor at University of Montreal (2009–2015). She received her Ph.D. in Computer Science from the University of Montreal and her Doctorate in automatic summarization of legal documents from Paris-Sorbonne University. She is the co-author of several books on NLP and Data Science, including Natural Language Processing for Social Media and Transforming Healthcare with Data and has more than 40 refereed publications.

She has served as Industry Chair of Canadian Artificial Intelligence Association (2013–2015), Chair of the technology sector of the Language Industry Association Canada (AILIA) (2009–2013), vice president of The Language Technologies Research Centre (LTRC) of Canada (2012–2014), a member of the Natural Sciences and Engineering Research Council of Canada (NSERC) Computer Science Liaison Committee (since 2014) and Member of the Canadian Advisory Committee of International Organization for Standardization (ISO). She was Honorary Research Fellowship at the Research Group in Computational Linguistics at the University of Wolverhampton, UK (2010–2012) and Lecturer at Polytechnique Montreal, engineering school (2012–2014).

She received Femmessor-Montreal awards 2015, Succeeding with a balanced lifestyle, in the Innovative Technology and Information and Communications Technology category because of her involvement in the arts. Her paintings have been published in a book titled One Thousand and One Nights, in which the palette of vivid colors and her unique contemporary style revolved around on the place of women in modern society. www.farzindar.com

DIANA INKPEN

Dr. Diana Inkpen is a Professor at the School of Electrical Engineering and Computer Science at the University of Ottawa, ON, Canada. She obtained her PhD in 2003 from the University of Toronto, Department of Computer Science. She obtained her M.Sc. from the Department of Computer Science, Technical University of Cluj-Napoca, Romania, in 1995, and a B.Eng. from the same university, in 1994. Her research interests and expertise are in natural language processing and artificial intelligence, in particular lexical semantics as applied to near synonyms and nuances of meaning, word and text similarity, classification of texts by emotion and mood, information retrieval from spontaneous speech, information extraction, and detecting signs of mental health problem from social media.

Dr. Inkpen was an invited speaker for the KDD 2018 Workshop on Issues of Sentiment Discovery and Opinion Mining (WISDOM 2018, London, UK, Aug 2018), for the International Conference on Pattern Recognition and Artificial Intelligence (ICPRAI 2018, Montreal, QC, Canada, May 2018), for the Applied NLP track at the 29th Florida Artificial Intelligence Research Society Conference (FLAIRS 2016, Key Largo, FL, May 2016), for the 28th Canadian Conference on Artificial Intelligence (AI 2015, Halifax, NS, June 2015) and International Symposium on Information Management and Big Data (SimBig 2015, Cuzco, Peru, September 2015). She was Program Committee co-chair for the 25th Canadian Conference on Artificial Intelligence (AI 2012), Toronto, Canada, May 2012, for the 7th IEEE International Conference on Natural Language Processing and Knowledge Engineering (IEEE NLP-KE'11), Tokushima, Japan, November 2011 and for the 6th IEEE International Conference on Natural Language Processing and Knowledge Engineering (IEEE NLP-KE'10), Beijing, China, August 2010. She was named Visiting Professor at Guangdong University of Foreign Studies, China, in June and July 2017, and Visiting Professor of Computational Linguistics at the University of Wolverhampton, UK, from September 2010 to August 2013.

She led and continues to lead many research projects with funding from Natural Sciences and Engineering Research Council of Canada (NSERC), Social Sciences and Humanities Research Council of Canada (SSHRC), and Ontario Centres of Excellence (OCE). The projects include industrial collaborations with companies from Ottawa, Toronto and Montreal. She published more than 30 journal papers, 100 conference papers, and 9 book chapters. She was in the Program Committees of many conferences in her field, a reviewer for many journals. She is the editor-in-chief of the *Computational Intelligence Journal* (Wiley) and an associate editor for the *Natural Language Engineering Journal* (Cambridge University Press).

Index

Printed in the United States
by Baker & Taylor Publisher Services